What people

The Way of the

I was up until 1am last night reading P.T. Mistlberger's book which impressed the hell out of me. All the questions I had about the men's movement were answered clearly. He has presented us with an excellent exposition of the men's movement. Once the book is started it is difficult to put down. You will enjoy the clarity of thought presented and come away with considerable understanding of the problems facing men in the 21st century.
Myron MacDonald, M.D., co-founder of Greenpeace

I believe that we are currently in the most difficult time in history for men. Many men are lost, confused, and alone and for the most part have few, if any, good men in their lives. *The Way of the Conscious Warrior* is a must-read for all men. It is a very well-researched history of men and masculinity and will help the reader understand the nature of masculinity and how the unique challenges of the modern-day man came to be. Cultivation of the conscious, courageous warrior offers one of the best hopes for returning balance to our Western culture.
Bob Munro, founder and CEO of The Art of Masculinity (www.artofmasculinity.com)

I have often thought that the men's movement lost its way after its heyday in the early nineties. I hope that this intelligent, insightful, and wide-ranging book will help get it back on track.
Richard Smoley, author of *Inner Christianity: A Guide to the Esoteric Tradition*

The fact is this: courageous, self-aware, integrated men get more out of life. If you are a man who wants to become more confident, accomplished, and whole, this book will help you put your wounding to bed, and help you move forward in life. With chapters regarding shadow figures, maturation, and practical steps for deepening your relationships, it is a potent balm for the modern man. The most balanced, eloquent, and deeply practical book I have read regarding men's work and masculine development. *The Way of the Conscious Warrior* is the ultimate resource for any man who wants to engage life fully. Highly recommended.

Jordan Gray, author and relationship coach at JordanGrayConsulting.com

The Way of the Conscious Warrior

A Handbook for 21st Century Men

The Way of the Conscious Warrior

A Handbook for 21st Century Men

P.T. Mistlberger

CHANGEMAKERS
BOOKS

Winchester, UK
Washington, USA

JOHN HUNT PUBLISHING

First published by Changemakers Books, 2019
Changemakers Books is an imprint of John Hunt Publishing Ltd., No. 3 East Street,
Alresford, Hampshire SO24 9EE, UK
office@jhpbooks.net
www.johnhuntpublishing.com
www.changemakers-books.com

For distributor details and how to order please visit the 'Ordering' section on our website.

Text copyright: P.T. Mistlberger 2018

ISBN: 978 1 78535 874 6
978 1 78535 875 3 (ebook)
Library of Congress Control Number: 2018948887

A CIP catalogue record for this book is available from the British Library.

Design: Stuart Davies

The quotation marked NLT is taken from the Holy Bible, New Living Translation, © 1996, 2004,
2015 by Tyndale House Foundation. Used by permission of Tyndale House Publishers, Inc., Carol
Stream, Illinois 60188. All rights reserved.

UK: Printed and bound by CPI Group (UK) Ltd, Croydon, CR0 4YY
US: Printed and bound by Thomson-Shore, 7300 West Joy Road, Dexter, MI 48130

We operate a distinctive and ethical publishing philosophy in
all areas of our business, from our global network of authors to
production and worldwide distribution.

Contents

The real accomplishment in life is the art of being a warrior, which is the only way to balance the terror of being a man with the wonder of being a man.
—Carlos Castaneda's Juan Matus

He who conquers others is strong;
He who masters himself is mighty
—Tao Te Ching

Preface

In April of 1992 I found myself in a school gymnasium, somewhere in the northwest corner of Washington state. Crammed in with me were over 200 men. We were partaking in a 'men's weekend workshop' led by a dynamic, overbearing, and street-smart middle-aged facilitator. The workshop was a 48-hour intensive, called simply 'The Weekend,' and was designed to accomplish many things, all of which could be reduced to 'realizing what it means to be a man.' The entire workshop, full of emotional drama, loud arguments, painful confessions, passionate and wildly humorous sharing, and insightful commentaries, was an effective way of encountering parts of one's mind. However, the part I recall mostly vividly was the end, where something especially memorable happened. All the men, by then covered in war-paint, half-naked, and exhausted after two days of limited sleep and ongoing processing, stood in a large circle and were encouraged, one at a time, to circle the pack and extract one 'weak warrior,' a man they didn't think could have the backs of other men, and take him out of the circle. These were to be the banished warriors.

At one point a guy was scanning the circle of men for the next to be removed, when his eyes fell briefly on me. I instantly felt a deep anger well up inside, the certainty that if he tried to extract me I would punch him in the face. The moment I summoned that anger he backed away from me and went after someone else. If there was a lesson in there it was clearly related to force of presence. A man who carries this is to be reckoned with. A man who falls asleep in that regard will be picked off by the forces of life. Or something like that.

The extracted men—there turned out to be a dozen or so of these unfortunate souls—were then banished to a basement room where they were required to sit in darkness with glowing

1

green rings around their necks. Overhead, they could hear the thunderous sounds of the 200 warriors who had just banished them to the basement, leaving them to contemplate their lack of masculine grit and firepower.

It seemed a cruel fate for the dozen banished guys who had paid hundreds of bucks to participate in a workshop to help them grow as men. And just when I found myself seriously doubting the value of the process, the facilitator called for the exiled men to be retrieved by the greater band of warriors. They were brought up from the basement, visible only as floating, glowing green rings in the darkened gymnasium, and welcomed warmly and strongly back into the tribe. They were not shamed. They were embraced. Some wept openly. It was all powerful and moving.

Such workshop practices are, in a sense, easy fodder for criticism. And to be sure, the 'jury being out' on the efficacy of such processes is not limited to critical analysis. Not all who participate in the inner work of the so-called men's movement benefit equally, or at all for that matter. Speaking personally, I can vouch for the potency and effectiveness of men's groups, as both a participant and a facilitator over the past 30 years. I got involved for personal reasons, as all do, but over time I began to see more clearly the deeper and larger issues at play in the need for men to learn to reconcile the courage of the warrior with the clarity of the conscious man. It is to that theme that the present book is dedicated.

Introduction: The Men's Movement Revisited

This is a book for men, especially early twenty-first-century Western men who are grappling with unique early twenty-first-century issues.

In a book such as this, generalizations—some of which may be of a sweeping nature—do occur. The usage of such generalizations is usually the most common criticism of gender studies works, but the generalizations are necessary to coherently present the key ideas. The most common generalizations involve references to the terms 'masculine' and 'feminine' and all that these words imply. It should be understood these terms point toward qualities and tendencies that exist inside of us, regardless of our gender or sexual orientation. That said, an assumption in effect here is that if we are male then we have very specific lessons around masculinity to address.

'Gender essentialism' is a term that refers to the idea that men and women have inherent qualities that are distinct and unique to their gender. I am aware of the various sociological critiques that gender essentialism has met with over the past few decades (from both feminist women and pro-feminist men), some of whom go so far as to argue that there *are* no such intrinsic things as 'masculinity' and 'femininity' beyond arbitrary social constructs.

My own interest in these matters is more practical. Although I've studied the literature on all sides of the debate, I've also been involved directly in field work both as a student and as a facilitator of men's transformational work since the early 1990s. As the wily Greek-Armenian spiritual teacher G.I. Gurdjieff once said, 'To be an awakened man, you must first *be* a man.' I can think of no clearer expression of the matter at hand. For me the issue does not lie in academic debate, but rather in practical work on self. For many modern men that necessitates looking more deeply into the nature of male identity and all that that involves.

The Way of the Conscious Warrior

The title of this book, *The Way of the Conscious Warrior*, presents a set of ideas that are aimed mainly at three specific categories of modern men. These categories are 1) men who have emphasized the warrior aspect of masculinity but have lacked self-observation; 2) men who have sought to develop the conscious aspect of their nature but not the warrior part; and 3) men who are experiencing a general alienation from their masculine identity, whether played out internally via all the faces of self-doubt, or externally via weak relations with, and a low level of trust for, the fellow men in their lives. (The terms 'warrior' and 'conscious' are examples of those generalized categories that are potentially meaningless if overused; their meaning in the context meant here will be expanded on throughout the book.)

The idea of this book is to present a teaching that offers a balance point between the extremes of passive introspection and hard-edged aggressiveness, as well as a general commentary on examples of men, historical and current, who have either embodied this balance or clearly failed to. Men who work on themselves via conscious efforts that may include meditation, psychotherapy, personal development seminars, or any of the widely available forms of personal growth, but who lack any sense of, or relationship with, warrior qualities, may be said to be not fully formed in their masculinity. Conversely, men who are rough, tough, and who seem to confidently express stereotypical warrior qualities, but who lack any sort of bona fide introspective side and have done little to no actual work on themselves (on psychological and spiritual levels), may be said to be not fully formed in their masculine either.

From the psychological standpoint, the essence of 'conscious warriorhood' is best described as 'divided attention'. This term does not refer to the scattered attention (and its various deficit forms) so common in twenty-first-century Western high-tech life. It rather refers to the importance of living a life in which awareness of self (subject) is integrated into a life of awareness of all that is around us (object). In this view the 'arrow' of consciousness is directed outwardly toward others and our environment, while at the same time being directed inwardly into awareness of self. Awareness of self may be said to be the 'conscious' part, with awareness of what is outside of us relating to the 'warrior' part.

A warrior who operates mechanically, unaware of large parts of himself, is not a conscious warrior. Conversely a man who is aware of himself but oblivious to his environment, not to mention the reality of others around him, is passively self-absorbed. The conscious warrior, as meant here, is one who combines the self-awareness of the mystic or monk with the alert awareness of the outer world of the warrior.

Of course, not all monks or mystics are merely passively self-absorbed. Some embody the alert outward sensitivity of the warrior. But many modern Western men incline toward passivity whether they embrace an inner discipline or not. 'Passive self-absorption' is meant here as indicative of modern tendencies toward avoidance of life and over-indulgence in introversion (via absorption in online life, for example).

The other side of the pole, the extroverted man who is aggressively involved (in whatever fashion) with the world around him and generally lacks self-awareness, is a figure of concern, but such men rarely read books like this or participate in the inner work of the modern so-called men's movement. Those that do are usually following on the heels of some sort of psychological crisis which involves a direct experience of being humbled or otherwise exposed to elements of life that proved harsher than anticipated. The warrior who lacks consciousness sooner or later finds out that he cannot control life. This discovery can be a positive crisis in that he can use it for developing himself. The present book is also intended for men who find themselves at such a crossroads.

Warrior Qualities

There is no complicated or mysterious (or especially ancient) history behind the English word 'warrior'. It derives from a fourteenth-century Old French term (*werreier*) which simply meant 'one who wages war'. The word has in recent decades come to be associated with something more than mere warfare, however. And it must be said that this is not because humanity has somehow left warfare behind. On the contrary, the facts are not encouraging on that front. It appears that we humans have been consistently given to warfare throughout recorded history and far beyond; and that tendency shows no sign of letting up in current times, despite all our advances on other fronts.

Archaeology has uncovered evidence of primitive warfare as far back as 14,000 years ago, at a dig in northern Sudan, where half of the discovered skeletons show signs of violent death caused by pointed objects consistent with battle weapons.[1] Digs in Kenya have also uncovered clear evidence of warfare, with 10,000-year-old skeletons displaying wounds consistent with attacks from battle weapons, alongside artifacts of weapon remains.[2]

Very old and revered religious scriptures such as the Judeo-Christian Bible, or the Hindu *Bhagavad Gita*, are full of depictions of warfare, be they terrestrial or not, and others, such as Islam's Quran, contain aggressive exhortations to battle. There is little evidence for cultures of 'peaceful savages' in the past, and not much evidence that we are less savage in the domain of warfare than we have always been. There have been thousands of wars in recorded history. The most recently completed century (the twentieth) was by far the most brutal in terms of casualty numbers—over 100 million (most of these civilians) were killed in warfare alone.

War and the cultures that support it have, of course, been integral parts of the fabric of human civilization. There is even a sound historical argument that war has been the prime causal factor behind many of the most significant advances in human culture—people do, after all, band together in the face of a serious adversary, be that adversary the elements of Nature, or the arrows of a rival tribe or the bombs of a rival nation. And when people band together, they accomplish things. That said, war as conducted throughout history by leaders and their soldiers has only rarely been just (obvious exceptions such as the war fought by the Allies in World War II notwithstanding), let alone noble.

So much for war. As for the idea of 'warriorhood', wars are of course fought by warriors—or more accurately, by soldiers— and these are almost always younger men who are commonly under the command of older men. Most of these older men are former soldiers themselves, but in many cases are commanded by popularly elected officials who lack direct military experience and carry no qualifications for battle leadership. This has been true for much of the history of civilization, because even in the case of dictatorships or monarchies, the ruling figure (be it dictator, king, queen, or regent) commonly had no more military experience than a modern democratically elected politician. And yet despite this he or she commanded armies all the same.

When the warrior (in his ideal form) is removed from the battlefield, his qualities can be seen independent of a purpose to defeat the enemy. Many of these qualities are obviously admirable: courage, tenacity, endurance, determination, the commitment and humility to serve a greater cause, and a selflessness in its ideal form that is perhaps the masculine equivalent of a mother's selflessness in giving birth to and raising a child. Alongside all this the ideal warrior also carries

7

the common-sense discipline necessary to get on with the matter at hand, to not become bogged down in trivial matters, and to be relatively indifferent to the judgments of others about who he is. His direction in life is *forward*. He is not insensitive—on the contrary, the ideal warrior is highly sensitized to his environment and to the characters of the people around him—but he does not let the opinions of others immobilize him. His skin is not thin.

The ideal warrior is loyal, but in a way that needs to be explained carefully. The old code was more to do with an unquestioning obedience and loyalty to one's commander, leader, or overlord. This approach certainly took care of the more immature, rebellious, undisciplined part of a man's character. The idea of 'I want to do things my way only' can be a sign of one of three things: a very advanced wise man, a bitter and jaded man, or a resentful, immature boy. The latter two are far more often the case. In this sense, membership in a military force can be a good training for young men, teaching them some measure of humility, cooperation, and recognition of the importance of discipline and structure in life, along with respect for elders.

However, there is a dark side here as well, obviously, and that relates mostly to *blind* trust. A good trainer of warriors is not one who seeks to turn them all into unquestioning robots. Too often throughout history massively destructive wars were carried out by young soldiers who lacked the ability to question their orders (and for understandable reasons, as this could easily result in severe punishment or even death). In seeking to capture the best qualities of warriorhood it's necessary to develop the ability to discern, doubt, and question things. This is of course a balancing act, and something of a Catch 22. To have the discernment to detect when it's appropriate to trust, and when to doubt and question, requires some life experience, but one cannot acquire that life experience without first going through certain things. One cannot really tell a good leader or teacher from a mediocre leader or teacher (let alone a bad one) without first having had at least some experience as a follower or student.

To be a 'conscious warrior' is no small thing, and not something learned overnight. In many ways the two words may seem a bad match. Consciousness as a developed quality is usually associated with thinkers, contemplatives, meditators. Warriorhood is usually associated with more primordial qualities such as fierceness, strength, tenacity, courage, combativeness. Monks throughout history have typically rejected aggression and certainly violence, and fighting men have rarely embraced spiritual disciplines. There have been, however, standout exceptions, such as some of the Japanese samurai, the Chinese Shaolin Buddhist warrior-monks, the Christian Knights Templar, or certain of the shaman-warriors of the American Plains Indians. Many warriors from these traditions—while not exactly monks—had some sort of legitimate spiritual practice, and most were qualified fighters.

Modern Western men dwell, for the greater part, in a softer time where harder masculine traits have been thoroughly de-emphasized and a general prevalent atmosphere of feminine sensitivity has grown and become widespread. 'Feminine sensitivity' in and of itself is obviously not a bad thing, and indeed has been a necessary countermeasure to centuries of desensitized brutality. However, men who lose their harder masculine qualities in the service of supporting a culture preoccupied with sensitivity and political correctness tend toward ineffectiveness in both their work and their love lives. The secret alchemy needed to address this issue is, above all, concerned with *balance*.

Changing Times

Early twenty-first-century Western men inhabit a very complex and challenging time in history. After centuries of social and political marginalization Western women achieved a measure of status in the early twentieth century, particularly when they obtained, in some nations, the right to vote and eventually the right to run for political office as well. There has been an ongoing debate among historians as to what degree the vast carnage of World War I (1914–18), in which approximately ten million mostly young men were wiped out via the horrors of trench warfare, led to the empowerment of women (as many of them began filling roles in society that the suddenly missing men could no longer do). The argument against this is the fact that women were given the vote in several countries prior to World War I, such as in New Zealand (1893), Australia (1901), and parts of Scandinavia (1906–13). Other nations, though not directly involved in the war, also gave women the vote (Denmark in 1915 and Holland in 1917).

Either way, it's clear that a movement toward the empowerment of women was occurring prior to World War I, although doubtless the effects of the war encouraged more of it. During and shortly after that war, the vote was given to women in Russia (1917), Germany and Austria (1918), Canada (1918), the USA (1919), Czechoslovakia (1920), and the UK (1928). But these were, overall, the few. Most countries in the world lagged, even developed nations such as France (1944) and Italy (1945). Some have only just in the twenty-first century granted women the right to vote, such as Bahrain (2002), Oman (2003), the United Arab Emirates (2006), and late to the party, Saudi Arabia (2015) — a full century after the suffrage pioneers.

In North America and other parts of the 'First World' all this has been gradually accompanied by the idea of women's liberation, a notion that involves many elements but has had the overall effect of making women much more aware of social inequality and the consequences connected to it. The first wave feminism movement — though having its roots in eighteenth-century France and gaining traction in parts of late nineteenth-century North America and Western Europe — really came into its own in the 1920s, a decade of significant social changes following the economic upturn in the aftermath of World War I. For the next three decades, with the coming of the Great Depression of the 1930s, World War II (1939–45), and the Cold War era of the 1950s, the idea of women's liberation was, in general, put on the back burner. However, by the 1960s it had re-emerged in a more potent second wave. A key element of this second wave was the wide availability by the early 1960s of the oral contraceptive pill, which created the possibility of women forgoing motherhood in favor of developing a career. This second wave is generally recognized by historians as having ended in the late 1980s, to be supplanted by a so-called third wave feminism birthed roughly in the early 1990s. The third wave differs from the second in its sharper awareness of issues related to anti-racism, lesbianism, the 'queer culture', and a general interest in the breaking down of language and media stereotypes.

The overarching reasons and motives behind feminism and the necessity of women's liberation of some sort is largely beyond reproach. Throughout history in most cultures on earth, once married, a woman was legally subordinate to her husband in many ways. She essentially had to conform to his will in most matters; her very individuality was facelessly blended into his, her legal rights minimal, or, as the more technical term had it, 'suspended'. The reality was that the woman in many ways lost considerable individuality once joined matrimonially with her man. Legally she was little more than a nullity whose main function was to tend to her husband and give birth to his children. That a movement for 'women's liberation', at least in the West, arose is surprising only from the standpoint of how long it took for it to happen.

However, the psychological effect *on men* of women's liberation has been less clearly looked at or understood. The Industrial Revolution, and particularly its effects from the late nineteenth century on, unquestionably changed the ways in which families operated—fathers were in general less present, being off in factories and offices, coming home late and tired, with little energy left over for socializing with their children. The decades following the Second World War saw generations of men being raised largely by their mothers, as the fathers were off rebuilding the world or in some fashion involved in the booming post-war economy. Of course, there were exceptions to this trend—men who were productive and responsible providers as well as psychologically competent parents. However, most men born after the mid-1940s (the Baby Boomer generation and beyond) can relate to the idea of being raised in a family where the father was minimally present. He was usually the breadwinner, the main provider, and he may even have been respected (or feared), but he was typically not very involved in the emotional lives of his children. He was important via his absence, material support, and even his reputation, but less so by his interactive presence. This latter was the domain of the mother.

The consequences of this have been well described in the literature of the so-called modern men's movement, perhaps most effectively and eloquently by Robert Bly in his 1990 landmark work *Iron John*. The main point (drawing from both psychoanalytic theory and common sense) is that young boys, when growing up, typically encounter a time—somewhere between the ages of 6 and 10—when they begin to truly understand that they are of a different gender than their mother. It's at this point that they are supposed to bond more deeply with the father, and eventually be initiated into the world of young manhood. However, since the advent of the Industrial Revolution and especially the aftermath of the great world wars of the twentieth century, this mentoring or initiation by the father (or male 'tribal elders') was either of diminished quality or absent altogether. Consequently, most young men (especially those born after the mid 1940s) were raised largely by their mothers with marginal contact with their tired fathers in the evenings or on weekends. A consequence of that is how such boys come to regard masculinity—and most particularly, their own masculinity—and older male figures in general. Overall, it has not been positive.

Bly, for one, characterized the youthful male of the 1950s (that is, men born roughly between 1925 and 1940) as 'boyishly optimistic' with a tendency to see women as bodies first and souls second. The 1950s man was disciplined, hardworking, traditional, and given to the 'us vs. them' mentality, a product of the world war he grew up in the shadow of. However, the young man of the 1960s (born typically in the latter half of the 1940s, the early wave Baby Boomers, some of whom became the first hippies) was something markedly different. Anti-establishment, in many cases anti-war in reaction to the very unpopular Vietnam War, and influenced by burgeoning feminist values along with spiritual ideas imported from the East, he demonstrated a softer nature. This was carried on and, in many ways, accentuated in the 1970s young man (born mostly in the 1950s), the late wave Boomers and marginal hippies who by now had become in some ways shaped by feminist ideals and the beginnings of ongoing awareness of civil rights and heightened sensitivity toward political correctness.

The trend toward softness and rejection of traditional masculine virtues continued with the 1980s–90s young male (the first Gen-Xers, born mostly in the 1960s and early 70s), with the added element of increasing technological complexity in communications, and the effect this had. Most of the significant works written on the modern men's movement were published in the 1990s (Bly's *Iron John* in 1990, Keen's *Fire in the Belly* in 1991, Moore and Gillette's *King, Warrior, Magician, Lover* in 1992, and Deida's *The Way of the Superior Man* in 1997), so none of these authors could fully see what was coming next. The era from 2000 on—punctuated by such watershed events as the terrorist mega-attacks of September 11, 2001 and the inauguration of the 'Facebook age' in 2004, alongside great advances in computer, smart phone, and home entertainment technology—has resulted in whole new challenges in early life masculine development.

The late 'Gen-Xers and 'Millennials'—those born mainly in the 1980s and early 1990s—are now dealing with entirely new paradigms that have no precedence. In past times, the social nature of a given community would change very little over many generations. Rapid social changes did indeed occur in early modern Europe (from the seventeenth century on) with such momentous events as the Scientific Revolution, the French Revolution (which toppled much of the aristocracy), and the Industrial Revolution, but even in these cases such change tended to have slow grassroot effects, with results showing only gradually over several generations. In current times, our communication technology has been advancing so rapidly that it is not easy to understand the full psychological impact it is having on younger men. But in general, the effect is working to blunt the sharper qualities of masculinity—directness, emphasis on purpose and accomplishment, and the confidence that arises from success in those areas. In short, many modern men are struggling to retain the better qualities of the warrior.

Part One

The Dilemma of the Twenty-First-Century Western Man

Chapter 1

A Brief History of the Men's Movement

The modern men's movement is not, and has never been, anything unified or consistent in doctrine or tone. Birthed in the late 1960s and 1970s mainly in the UK and the USA, there have been, essentially, three elements within it. One has consisted of a pro-feminist men's movement, which has typically involved men gathering to look at the ways in which traditional masculine values have been inappropriately used to the detriment of women (and men). This group in general supports feminism both ideologically and, at times, practically (by, for example, participating in feminist activism). It has been involved in the attempt to deconstruct patriarchy in its more negative sense, and as such has been geared toward the overall support and empowerment of women. The anti-sexist men's movement began in the early 1970s in the USA, but it was not until the early 1980s that it became organized, taking the name National Organization for Changing Men in 1983. This name was changed to the National Organization for Men against Sexism (NOMAS) in 1990. They promote anti-racism, pro-feminism, gay-affirmation, and enhancing men's lives, and are still active as of 2018.

The second strand within the men's movement began in the mid-1970s with an anti-feminist approach—that is, it was largely reactionary—and holds as its position the consolidation of traditional masculine qualities and a vigilance against aggressive feminism. This second element of the men's movement has something of a connection with the so-called seduction community, although probably most men who participate in 'art of pick-up' seminars and teachings are not especially concerned with the sociology of gender issues. Nevertheless, some elements of the seduction community do teach, however crudely, methods that are not concerned simply with manipulation but also with the enhancement of certain masculine qualities.

The third element within the men's movement is usually referred to as the 'mythopoetic' men's movement, mainly because it has an intellectual and literary aspect as well as an interest in the growth of men as masculine individuals. The mythopoetic men's movement is concerned not just with the safeguarding of masculinity, but with the overall growth of men as human beings as well. It had its genesis mainly in the early 1980s. The term 'mythopoetic' was coined by the psychologist Shepherd Bliss in 1986; it derives from *mythopoesis*, which means 're-mythologizing', and in this context, 'revisioning masculinity for our time', utilizing myth, poetry, and ritual in its workshops for the general public.[1]

The mythopoetic branch holds in common with the anti-feminist men's movement the fact that it began largely in reaction to the second-wave feminism of the 1970s. Early pioneers and champions of the mythopoetic men's movement have been figures such as author and mythologist Michael Meade, poet Robert Bly, psychologist Shepherd Bliss, psychoanalyst Robert Moore, and mythologist Douglas Gillette. These men in turn drew inspiration from earlier well-known figures such as Jungian psychotherapists James Hillman, James Hollis, and Robert Johnson, from C.G. Jung himself (for psychoanalytic insights), and Joseph Campbell (for mythology). Bly's work (*Iron John*, 1990) put the men's movement on the map, bringing on both admiration and ridicule from the public, and remaining for over a year on the *New York Times* bestseller list (it eventually sold hundreds of thousands of copies). This book used the 1820 German Grimm brothers' myth of *Iron Hans* as a vehicle to comment on masculinity, although to be fair the method had been used two decades earlier by Robert Johnson, whose book *He* (1974) used the twelfth-century Grail mythology of Chretien de Troyes for the same purpose. Johnson's book was much shorter and he did not write with the flair of Bly.

The differences between the pro-feminist and the mythopoetic men's movements has been defined as follows: pro-feminist groups have been more concerned with social and political change and activism, whereas mythopoetic groups have been focused mainly on personal growth; or, pro-feminist men are concerned mainly with the damage wrought by patriarchy on women, whereas mythopoetic men are focused more on the damage caused by patriarchy (and to a lesser extent, feminism) on men. These are rough generalizations of course, and don't apply in many individual cases, but they give a good general overview of what the respective movements tend to focus on.[2]

A great number of communities based on the men's movement have appeared, flourished, and faded (with some surviving) since the 1970s. The 1990s was perhaps the peak period for men's movement workshops and trainings, with popular events going by such names as 'Wild Man Weekend', 'Inner King Training', 'Warrior-Monk', 'Gathering of Men', 'Woodland Passage', 'Spirit Journeys', and (emphasizing initiation) 'Metamorphosis'.[3] Two of the more successful and widespread men's movement communities were the ManKind Project and the Sterling Men's Division. The former, founded in 1985 by Rich Tosi, Bill Kauth, and Ron Hering, was initially called the New Warrior Network and based its ideas mainly on the writings of Bly, Moore, and Gillette. Its motto is 'Changing the World One Man at a Time'. The latter was founded in 1979 by A. Justin Sterling (b. 1944), a maverick sociologist who had originally trained under Werner Erhard in the 1970s.

All these more or less fell under the mythopoetic branch. As for what exactly is done in mythopoetic men's workshops—cynically lampooned by some as gatherings of 'weekend warriors'—these are mostly variations of experiential processes such as circle-sharing (where participants are encouraged to be honest, non-defensive, and non-boasting), ritual initiations, drumming, some emotional-expression exercises (including shadow-work), empowerment exercises, vigorous physical activities, and so on. Theory is usually kept to a minimum; the emphasis is largely on authentic, direct experience and honest communication. Naturally, the skill and experience level of the workshop facilitators influences the quality of the gathering.

In passing it can be noted that the men's movement has also entered the mainstream religious domain. A Christian organization, founded in 1990 by the former American college football coach Bill McCartney (b. 1940), called the Promise Keepers, originated in part as a massive men's support group. Although most of their core principles are religious in tone (obedience to God's word via the Holy Spirit, etc.), of note is their Principle 2: *A Promise Keeper is committed to pursuing vital relationships with a few other men, understanding that he needs brothers to help him keep his promises.* It would seem God alone is no longer enough. Religious men also need other men.

Essentialism and Feminist Concerns about the Men's Movement

As mentioned in the Introduction, a main argument historically put forth by some male pro-feminist academics against elements of the men's movement is that the whole thing is based too much on *essentialism*, which in this context is the idea that men and women have essential differences that result in them being so far apart psychologically that separation and 'movements' (for men or women) are not just justified but necessary. The main criticism is that these differences—'masculinity vs. femininity' being the prime example—are more the product of social constructions, and less of intrinsic differences. Those following the mythopoetic paths are regarded as 'loose essentialists', meaning, they can celebrate their differences with women while at the same time working toward a more integrated and developed sense of what it really means to be a man. The criticism of this is that it allows men to 'have it both ways', to retain the 'moral license' to maintain their character as it is, while at the same time growing in any direction they wish.[4] This idea has been rebutted by leaders within the mythopoetic movement, such as Shepherd Bliss, who in *The Politics of Manhood* (an anthology of essays mostly critical of the men's movement) responded:

> I am not that straw man that some ultra-feminists describe as an 'essentialist'. I do believe that archetypes influence our behavior, but I also believe in the social construction of reality…it is not either-or, that you either believe in archetypes or the social construction of reality; you can have both-and, unless you are a fundamentalist.[5]

The darker face of essentialism, and the one of most concern to some feminist writers, is the idea that men involved in the men's movement will simply use essentialist ideas to reinforce the very qualities that feminists rail against. The Pagan leader and author Starhawk once put it succinctly: 'Our fear is that the men's movement will do what men have always done, at least since the advent of patriarchy: blame women for their problems and defend their own privileges.'[6]

Speaking personally, based on three decades of involvement in men's work, I can suggest that Starhawk can rest easy. Men's work—certainly the elements of it that I've witnessed—is not party to any effort, however covert, to blame women, much less defend men's privileges. The clear majority of men involved in the men's movement, certainly the mythopoetic branches of it, are there to work on themselves, to improve their lot in life, and to connect with other men. If there are any nefarious plots being hatched in men's groups and inner-work communities against women (much less against feminism), I have yet to see it. Yes, sometimes pain or anger is released, and sometimes this pain or anger is related to a man's relationship with women. But if the group of men at issue is led by any leader or leaders of worthy caliber, wounds are always worked with in the direction of healing, not aggravating or merely assigning blame. It is vital that a man deal with his personal accountability in life; this and related issues are, above all, emphasized in men's meetings, and certainly in the larger, more established mythopoetic groups.

The Patriarchy

To grasp the men's movement, feminism, and related issues, it's useful to have some understanding of the term 'patriarchy'. The word literally means 'rule of the father' (from the Latin words *patria*, 'lineage'; *pater*, 'father'; and Greek *arkho*, 'I rule'). Since the 1970s the idea of patriarchy has taken on connotations beyond its original literal meaning (and came, in many respects, to replace the term 'male chauvinism'). A patriarchal culture is now implied to be a culture where men carry greater significance than women in the domain of politics and the power structures that run things and do so to the limitation and unfair detriment of women. Sociologist Sylvia Walby proposed the following general outline to define patriarchy:

1. The state: women are unlikely to have formal power and representation
2. The household: women are more likely to do the housework and raise the children
3. Violence: women are more prone to being abused
4. Paid work: women are likely to be paid less
5. Sexuality: women's sexuality is more likely to be treated negatively
6. Culture: women are more misrepresented in media and popular culture[7]

Evidence for patriarchal culture is found stretching back to the beginnings of recorded history (over 5,000 years ago), although the evidence is not consistent. For example, some women in ancient Egypt appeared to have a measure of freedom and autonomy unknown to women in ancient Greece. Greek and Hebrew cultures of antiquity were, in general, heavily patriarchal. Aristotle was noted for his views on the superiority of men over women in the intellectual, moral, and physical domains. He regarded women as inhabiting a level between that of child and adult and proclaimed that it was natural for men to rule women mainly because (according to him) men can balance their passions with reason, whereas a woman is dominated by passions. (Aristotle's views influenced the Catholic Church to some extent and its resultant tradition of excluding women from the priesthood. He was also a key mentor of Alexander the Great, whose policies impacted much of the civilized world during his brief but spectacular rule.)

Different theories abound as to the history of patriarchy. The popular New Age view that a matriarchy was dominant on the planet prior to the age of the patriarchy is not supported by anthropologists; most rather find evidence for a rough egalitarianism prior to the advent of obvious patriarchy some 5,000–6,000 years ago. One theory that has some credibility is that significant climate changes — leading to widespread famine — of 6,000 years ago resulted in the appearance of vast tracts of desert and wastelands that required men to take the lead in exploration, hunting, and warfare to safeguard and feed villages and communities, thus giving men political and social power as well.

However it came about, patriarchy in the classical sense of 'rule of the father' has dominated most of civilization (East, Central, and West) for the past few thousand years. Isolated cases of political rule by females have certainly existed, but even in these cases such women commonly presided over male militaries and courts while being advised by male courtiers or commanders.

Patriarchy has, to a large extent, been propagated and

maintained by the culture of war, and the need to train soldiers to enforce the rule of leaders. This culture of violence has arguably changed little throughout recorded history. As Starhawk put it:

> The problem with men is not, as Robert Bly suggests, that male initiatory process has broken down. The problem is that it's working all too well to shape young boys and girls into the type of men and women required by a society dominated by war...war requires soldiers...not inner warriors or archetypal warriors or spiritual warriors, but soldiers: weapon-like, obedient to their handlers, and unthinkingly, unfeelingly brutal to their victims.[8]

The difficulty with sweeping critiques of the culture of warfare is that it too easily slips into a general condemnation of masculine aggression and facility with violence in general. And yet, righteous warriors—many of whom were brutally fierce fighters who were, yes, involved in violent scenarios—have been as common in history as have marauding tyrants. If the Allies of World War II had not pushed back and ultimately defeated the aggression of the Axis powers, the world would be a very different one today. Were the fire-bombings of German cities late in the war, or the nuclear destruction of Japanese cities in 1945, truly necessary for the victory of the Allies? Perhaps not, but then again, perhaps they were. Hindsight may be 20-20 but it is also frequently pointless. All that is known for sure is that life on this planet, and the history of civilization, has been darkened by the specter of mortality and the primitive requirements of survival—a survival that has not been possible without the application, from time to time, of force.

A significant critique lodged by pro-feminist writers against the modern men's movement, including the mythopoetic branch, is that it fails to identify the patriarchy hidden within the glorification of admirable masculine mythic figures and legends. From this perspective, the modern men's movement is seen as simply a rehash of patriarchy in a different form—an attempt to keep it alive, to maintain the status quo, in the face of the growing empowerment of women.

Many of these critiques suffer from a lack of direct experience of the inner workings of men's growth trainings, workshops, and groups. The critiques of male pro-feminist scholars tend to show this deficiency. While there is obviously a place for academic criticism, I do wish that some of the (male) critics would partake in a typical men's gathering themselves to see and experience first-hand what goes on. Some have, in fact, done this, but one usually gets the feeling that they participated more as a journalist to compile field notes in which to later marshal their observational critiques. One can indeed participate in a men's growth gathering and not really participate at the same time.

In many ways the history of the so-called men's movement is the history of the struggle of men to stay connected, to engage in legitimate relationship with each other. The irony of intellectual criticisms of men's movement gatherings is that they are formulated from a place of observation, not participation—and yet it has been this detached observational perspective that has been a problem behind the history of so many failed relationships: between individuals, yes, but also between organizations, nations, and religions. Modern science has its basis in objective observation, and in the realm of science this is essential. But observation without participation has been more problematic when it comes to one race, religion, culture, or nation attempting to understand another—or one man attempting to understand another man. The psychological and spiritual basis of the men's movement—at least the so-called mythopoetic branch, and related branches—has been the effort to help men be less isolated in their minds, their prejudices, and their egocentric views, and to truly come to understand one another. This is a noble and worthy project.

Chapter 2

Twenty-First-Century Challenges: The Feminized Man, the Distracted Man, and Related Issues

The patriarchy of feminist lore is in full retreat. Three decades of media male-bashing, father-averse family courts, and feminized classrooms have led millions of male hegemons to drop out—from education, marriage, fatherhood, and even the workplace.
Christina Hoff Sommers

Feminization

If you google 'feminized man' you may end up with a bunch of kinky sex sites crowded at the top of your search page. This is not the kind of 'feminized man' that we'll be looking at in this chapter (although arguably, the man who submits to extreme eroticized dominance from a woman is simply a sexualized version of what we'll be considering). It should also be clearly recognized that the term 'feminized' is not meant as a pejorative knock against women or gay men, but rather to highlight a condition *in men* wherein a man, straight or gay, lacks a healthy and vital sense of his own masculinity. (The rough equivalent for women would be a 'masculinized woman'; such a term would not be a knock on men or on lesbian culture, but rather a comment on a woman's disconnection from her natural femininity, regardless of sexual orientation.)

On a sociological level 'feminization' refers to the emphasis and focus in society on feminine values and qualities (such as, for example, in education, where a majority of early grade school teachers are female, and via the entertainment industry, with its emphasis on appearance and style). The underside of feminization is what is sometimes called the 'feminization of poverty' (a term coined by the sociologist Diana Pearce in the late 1970s) which refers to the fact that a majority of those in poverty tend to be female, much of that (in First World nations) stemming from the greater than ever number of single mother households. That women have suffered from (and continue to do so) the effects of a gender bias in the workforce that tends to reward males with higher-paying jobs, and therefore reinforces the 'feminization of poverty', is not in question. The problem that more interests us is what factors are behind these greater numbers of single mother households? Why do so many marriages and relationships between parents fail?

There are many factors behind this, obviously, but the one that mainly concerns us here is some of the imbalance resulting from cultural feminization and, particularly, the way in which modern men have themselves become feminized. A premise maintained here is that most feminized men do not tend to do well in relationships with romantic partners, and commonly do not do well in their work life either. Let's look at some of the probable reasons behind this.

The Feminized Man

What is a 'feminized man'? This is a generalized term that is meant to point toward certain tendencies that commonly are encouraged or emphasized in modern Western men. There is a broad range of 'degree of feminization' in men. Some may be greatly feminized, others only marginally. Some may see themselves as 'balanced' between the male and female polarities, although this usually suggests a man who is in fact more feminized than he may realize.

It should also be understood that 'feminization' of a man as discussed here has nothing to do with male–female virtues or their value or merits. An assumption here is that every male has a female component (and vice versa), and if one objects to the usage of the term 'component', then 'tendency' is a good substitute. 'Feminization' of the male here refers to the idea of how a man loses touch with his natural masculine core and instead takes on feminine values or qualities, in a way that in the long run is usually not good for him, although this is often not easy for him to see (and may even result in him becoming defensively reactive if it is pointed out to him).

A 'feminized man', as meant here, generally exhibits at least some of the following characteristics:

- he has an underlying (though not always consciously recognized) mistrust of masculine nature;
- he is not especially close to his father (either very unhealed with him, greatly or somewhat contemptuous of what he represents, or generally unsympathetic toward him);
- he carries a consistently hostile tone (or undertone) toward older, successful men (and the 'establishment');
- he is concerned with gaining the approval of women and may be given to vanity;
- he finds it difficult to stand up to women and struggles with finding his place in the world;
- he fears competition with men;
- he is given to being easily upset or offended by men or women — and by extension, easily pushed around (or, on occasion, volatile);
- he fears stepping boldly into his life in a way that manifests his masculine assertiveness and sense of direction and purpose, mostly because he lacks the confidence that he actually has any real masculinity.

It's helpful at this point to break down some of these issues related to feminization to look more closely at them.

The Father Link

An outstanding feature of the feminized man — and arguably,

the main cause behind it—is his distant (and in some cases, non-existent) relationship with his father. As mentioned above, many fathers of recent decades have been marginal parents, beyond providing material support toward the raising of their children. A man needs to 'show up' in life to live his masculinity fully, and this obviously applies to parenting in the case of fathers. But such a father cannot do much 'showing up' if he himself is exhausted at the end of a day of work, or, more to the point, lacks the motivation or desire to do so (for endless possible reasons).

We are not here so concerned with the psychological causes behind low-quality fathering, but more with the consequences for a man who grew up with the experience of having a father who did not seem that interested in him. The point here is not to simply blame the father and leave it at that. To do so is to remain stuck at an immature level of self-exploration. It is one thing to stop denying and admit that you have anger and hurt around a parent (or to wallow in the victim-position) and another entirely to get on with the process of healing the wound.

How does a young man (or man of any age) heal the father-wound? While some psychotherapy is usually useful—in the sense of exploring older memories, and the often-repressed thoughts and feelings that accompany them—it's been my experience, based on four decades of 'field work', that men need to go beyond the mere processing of feelings and memories to achieve some sort of satisfaction and confidence in how they regard their father (and in how their lives work overall). A man needs to avoid the trap of endlessly talking about his feelings at the expense of avoiding action in his life. While some depth therapy is usually important for most men who are interested in growing and waking up in general, it needs to be balanced with the understanding that it is in the realm of taking action that he's going to experience real healing of old issues.

The words 'taking action' obviously must be clarified. Too many men have acted in ugly, unconsciously driven ways that were motivated merely by the need for vengeance or to uphold egotistical pride or other dubious agendas. 'Taking action' here refers to getting on with moving forward in life. When a man avoids moving forward in life he is often acting out a desire to blame or punish his father by holding him accountable for why his life is not what it could be. Deep down he's angry at his father, and so proves his point that his father was incompetent by failing in his own life. (Of course, it's a given that sometimes he is punishing the mother by such actions, or both of his parents, or some other significant mentor figure from his formative years, but we are here focusing on the father.)

A common scenario is that of the young man who ends up crusading against the 'powers that be' — which could range anywhere from resenting powerful older men, to mistrusting his boss at work and thereby compromising his own performance, to getting caught up in conspiracy theories that have as their basis the corruption, lies, and inevitable evil agenda of complicit older men who rule the world — all the while using his crusade as a way to avoid forward movement in his own life. 'Moving forward' can, of course, imply many things, so it's helpful to bring in some clarity here. It's not to suggest that no younger man can have a legitimate grievance about the existing power structures and belief systems of the world (the 'establishment'), or that younger men cannot make effective leaders or even formulate revolutionary ideas that change the world. (They certainly can, as men like James Clerk Maxwell, Thomas Edison, Albert Einstein, and Steve Jobs, to name but four men who revolutionized the world at a young age, amply proved.) But their ideas (or leadership) will likely not be effective if the underlying motive is based on a desire to punish the father or authority structures that embody (for him) the 'dark father' quality.

The Dark Father

The 'dark father' is the image a younger man carries in his mind that is based on his negative memories of his father. These negative memories can of course vary widely, depending on the character of the father and the disposition of the son.

Around 1820, when the famous Spanish artist Francisco Goya was an old man, he painted *Saturn Devouring His Son*, a work that was part of his 14 'Black Paintings' that he produced late in life. The imagery in the painting is powerful, dark, and macabre, featuring a wild-eyed Saturn in the act of eating his son. This well-known painting helped popularize the Roman myth of Saturn (deriving from the older Greek myth of Cronus) who eats his children as soon as they are born, so as to ensure that none will supplant him. His sixth son, Jupiter (Zeus to the Greeks), is hidden by his mother, and eventually overthrows his father. (In the Greek myth, Cronus overthrew his own father, Uranus, in a particularly gruesome fashion by castrating him. The goddess Aphrodite emerged, ironically, from the disembodied testicles of Cronus, reminiscent of Eve emerging from Adam's rib.)

These myths speak to the fundamental mistrust that often lies between father and son—based either on the father's fear of being overshadowed by the son and the need to keep him in line (or simply overpower him)—or the son's underlying resentment toward the father. Freud made much of this dynamic via his Oedipal theory, based on the idea that a young boy desires closeness with his mother (sex and love being indistinguishable for the very young) and sees his father as being in the way, thereby seeking to remove him, or just generally compete with him. The way the boy eventually overcomes this is by identifying with his father, ideally in healthy ways. Alas, the modern young man often fails to experience this healthy father-identification (or any significant identification at all), thus remaining overly attached to his mother and her view of reality. In his adult relationships with women he tends to be drawn to women who bear general pattern-matches with his mother. He is also prone to developing a kind of split between his heart and his sexuality, with the result being that he comes to view women in a dualistic fashion—she is either a goddess or mother-figure to be worshipped, fought for, and always to gain the approval of, or she is a whore to be sexually used. A common scenario for a modern man of this sort is to find himself in a long-term relationship in which he is gradually more and more domesticated—to use a strong metaphor, something like a dog trained to serve its master—all the while seeking much of his sexual outlet via online pornography.

A young man who never properly identifies or bonds with his father grows up with an equally ambivalent relationship with men in general. The 'dark father' gets projected onto powerful, successful, older men, who are viewed with inherent suspicion. If the man is conspiratorially minded, he may come to believe in vast and nefarious conspiracies, such as faked moon-landings, 'chemtrails' being sprayed over the Earth so as to control populations, evil governments and leaders in cahoots with each other for the sole purpose of subjugating the masses, and so forth. (This is not to suggest that no conspiracies or evil agendas by 'ruling masters' exist; the point here is to see to what extent a man can get caught up in such conspiratorial thinking, driven mainly by the unconscious motive of desiring to 'bring down the king', his father, and by extension, all older established men.)

Most commonly such a man struggles with his self-esteem and lacks material success in his life. Or, if he is uncommonly resourceful, he may achieve considerable outer success (motivated partly by his competitive desire to surpass his father), all the while struggling in his closer relationships. He may also find himself in a long-term relationship with a strong woman who controls him in many subtle (and not so subtle) ways, at the same time achieving only marginal or little success in his outer life.

There is a great deal of gradation and shading in all of this, but the main point being stressed here is that a man who seeks to actualize his best potential in life must examine his connection to his father. Most modern men, if honest, will find much inner and outer work waiting to be done in this area.

The Mother Link

Many younger men who have a weak sense of their own masculinity were negatively influenced by their mothers in ways that they cannot always spot, often for their whole lives. The influence we speak of here relates to all the ways the mother may have been involved in undermining the father, harmfully triangulating (speaking ill of the boy's father to the boy when the father is not present), or in general getting inside his head in such a fashion that it amounts to a kind of indoctrination. This 'indoctrination' may involve the mother transmitting her views of the masculine (including all her personal wounds originating with her father, her husband, the boy's father, male power structures in the world, and so on) to the boy, such that he becomes a full member in her feminized, largely negative view of masculinity. If such indoctrination is effective the boy becomes emotionally allegiant to his mother, a common consequence of which is to be alienated not just from his father, but from his own masculine core—all of which tends to make him suspicious of men in general and prone to conflicts with them. None of that has anything to do with the father's moral quality. He may have been a depraved criminal, and it may have been absolutely in his son's best interest to have nothing to do with him. But the boy will still face problems growing up if his view of masculinity is entirely shaped and influenced by his mother's perspective.

Few women, in my experience, 'indoctrinate' their sons with their view of reality with any malicious intent. Most mothers, whether single or forming part of a dysfunctional marriage, desire the best for their boys. The problem is rarely the intent of the mother. The dilemma is simply that she is female and by this fact alone cannot *comprehensively* impart to him the view of reality that he is going to need if he is to properly unfold his masculine wings in the world.

Psychoanalysis and the Pharmaceutical Industry

Psychoanalysis has its roots in Freud and his acolytes (Jung, Adler, Rank, Horney, and the later human potential therapists who sprang from them, such as Maslow, Rogers, Perls, Reich, et al.). Robert Bly in *Iron John* suggested that modern psychotherapy puts a great deal of emphasis on the mother in part because its founding figures (Freud and Jung) were themselves 'mother's men'.[1] This is probably a too loosely generalized assessment (Bly's generalizations are often poetic, and on the mark, but occasionally overlook too many details). However, unquestionably the entire approach of psychotherapy has a feminized element to it owing to the focus on the processing of feelings, often at the expense of action. A modern man who undergoes psychotherapy or some of the modern personal growth forms of interpersonal processing does run the risk of neglecting his masculine side—even though, paradoxically, he may enter such therapy in the first place because he's been told (usually by women) that there's something wrong with his masculine side. He's either too masculine or (more commonly) too feminine.

If he's too feminine the psychotherapy may help him understand parts of his dysfunction more clearly, but the understanding rarely translates to more than intellectual data. It's hard for him to do anything with the information because he's thinking about his feelings and justifying his wounds accordingly. He's not acting. If he's too masculine, he may feel threatened by psychotherapy because he instinctively mistrusts its emphasis on feelings. He doesn't want to just become like his woman. And so, he never fully engages the psychotherapy process anyway. He half-heartedly attends sessions to satisfy his woman, and secretly waits to get back to his high-definition TV.

The role of the pharmaceutical industry in the feminization of modern men is less clear and a full discussion of it is beyond the scope of this book, but it can be noted that a psychological issue such as ADHD (attention deficit hyperactivity disorder) is greatly on the rise in terms of diagnosed cases in the early decades of the twenty-first century (mostly in young people). Prior to the 1970s such matters were dealt with mainly via psychotherapy, but are now handled primarily via medication (Ritalin, etc.) to the great profit of the pharmaceutical industry (which is not to deny the efficacy and case-specific value of these drugs). The cause of all this 'attention deficit' is not well understood, though a prime culprit appears to be modern gaming technology and social networking, part of what I call the 'Twenty-First-Century Distracted Man'. It's very commonplace to hear of stories of adolescent boys who barely emerge from their bedrooms after school, so absorbed are they in their online life. Boys and young men have, throughout history, embraced games of all sorts, especially the competitive ones. But prior to the late twentieth century most of such gaming took place outdoors, or at the least, in direct *physical* interaction with other young men. A twenty-first-century boy is now presented with an almost infinite choice of virtual reality entertainment possibilities. He's been given the keys to a fantasy holodeck. It's little wonder he bores quickly and easily, so aware is he of other possibilities that await him around the corner on his browser.

A key element in the development of the masculine spirit (as it is with the feminine) is embodiment. Males have, in the main, been endowed with considerable physical power, and it is a given that such physicality is meant to be experienced and exercised in some fashion. Men of any age who overindulge in online life run the risk of neglecting their embodied life, and therefore become softer in general.

Declining Testosterone Levels

There is something of a mystery going on in the physiology of North American men over recent decades, and, according to a recent study in the *Journal of Clinical Endocrinology and Metabolism*, it has to do with declining testosterone levels.2 Some have speculated that the causes are in the water we drink, obesity, or an increasingly sedentary lifestyle. Others point toward simpler facts, namely that men in earlier times had higher testosterone levels in general, and that the decline was necessary and part of the overall 'civilizing' of the male gender required for developed societies that have some measure of order.

It's natural for testosterone levels in men to decline slightly with age, but in this case, we're talking about an overall decline across recent generations of men. While the long-range idea of men of thousands of years ago having higher levels of testosterone than contemporary men makes sense (and suggests how powerfully masculine some characters from ancient, technology-simpler times doubtless were), what is more troublesome is the fact that modern lifestyles are probably contributing to an acceleration toward softness at the expense of appropriate masculinity.

Depression and the Mother

Classical psychoanalysis bases one of its key insights on the idea that depression and depressive tendencies are related to the loss of a love-object, and the most basic and primal love-object is of course the mother. (It is in this regard that Bly's knock on Freud for being a 'mother's man' is of questionable relevance, as the universality of the connection between the mother and *the* original source of love is obvious. It also does not seem to be rocket science to draw a connection between deficiencies in the mother-connection and future psychological challenges.) In a paper written in 1917 called *Mourning and Melancholia* Freud had noted the striking commonalities between grieving and depression (back then it was called 'melancholia') — 'a profoundly painful dejection, abrogation of interest in the outside world, loss of capacity to love, inhibition of all activity'. What makes depression worse than grief, however, is that it is accompanied by self-rejection and declining self-esteem. The depressed man thinks lowly of himself, mainly because he believes himself to be the problem (he is guilty) since it is difficult for him (when young) to view his mother in a negative light. She cannot be the problem; it must be him. The American psychoanalyst Alexander Lowen (1910–2008), in *Depression and the Body*, made a startling observation: 'the child who is most rejected and abused in a family becomes the adult who is most devoted to the mother. This is the child who also feels the most unworthy, most guilty, and most filled with self-hate.'[3]

The mother is such a taboo to criticize for the boy or young man precisely because she is so essential not just for his survival and well-being, but also for his original feelings of pleasure. A man who is pleasure-deprived spends much of his life looking for pleasure but never quite getting his needs met, which fuels his resigned attitude and overall disposition. He literally never gets enough (of anything), and so is perpetually frustrated and, in more extreme cases, potentially dangerous. This is very relevant for modern men because of the over-reliance on the mother and the feminine in general. If a man can't face up to his deeper feelings toward the feminine, of which the mother is the root, then he never quite feels alive because he can't fully *feel*. He spends too much time in his head with a rigid, mechanical approach to life. Eventually, if this course direction is not corrected, he drifts into numbness and depression — or less commonly, he explodes outwardly in weirdly impulsive or destructive behavior.

The question of action is important, because processing feelings, while essential, is never solely sufficient. However, a man can't act vitally in life if his feelings are too cut off. He is literally not alive enough to act and accomplish significant things. Hence, he needs to realistically assess his feelings toward the mother and the feminine, so as to begin the process of freeing himself up. It's something of a balancing act. The man who feels too much, who doesn't act and can't think clearly, is not in his masculine core. He is feminized. However, the man who spends most of his time in his head, cut off from feelings, is not in his masculine core either. He is robotic.

The Naive Spiritual Man

Bly, in *Iron John*, offered excellent and penetrating insights into what he called the 'naive' or 'ascending man'. He characterized this man as 'New Age', a term that was doubtless more fitting for the time when he was writing the book (the late 1980s, which was probably the peak period of the twentieth-century New Age movement). The 'naive spiritual man' of the early twenty-first century is different in some ways from this type of man of the late twentieth century. It is arguable that the world is a darker place now in general—more dangerous than the relatively optimistic era that saw the Cold War ending, the Berlin Wall coming down, and the Soviet Union dissolving—mainly because of the growth of radical Islamic extremism and the shadowy, covert agencies created as countermeasures against it. There is also more general awareness now of environmental issues (mainly global warming). But these are large-scale concerns. The 'naive young man' is still alive and well, as he has been in all eras.

Probably the outstanding features of the naive spiritual man is a weak connection with his father, lack of trusting relationships with older, established men, and fear of embodying the earthier and more practical elements of his masculine power. Wedded to this is his 'magical' personality type, in which he seeks to express himself in the world via his passive (and occasionally active and artsy) rebelliousness, or perhaps his membership in some sort of alternative community based on lofty principles. In general, he seeks to rise above the problems of the world by establishing his identity as in some way special or different from mediocrity.

One can identify some of these, or related tendencies, in certain boys who grew into very powerful, effective, revolutionary men throughout history, to be sure. However, far more commonly such men disappear into the sands of time, their stay on planet Earth amounting to little, as their life force is squandered in fighting against the ghosts of older, powerful men whose clunky and rusty armor they wish to avoid wearing at all costs, but usually end up being buried under in their very effort to rise above them.

The Twenty-First-Century Distracted Man

Early twenty-first-century young men, raised on the glories of the Internet, are subject to almost as many temptations and distractions as a *Star Trek* crew member who had access to a virtual reality 'holodeck'.

Back around the year 1980 I had a spiritual mentor who instructed me in a guided meditation. The end of the meditation involved sitting at a desk in a secret house that had a 'magic screen' in front of me to which I could ask any question I wanted and from which I would receive a quality response. This screen (as visualized in 1980) strongly foreshadowed the modern flat-screen monitor. And the 'great source' that would provide a quality answer to my questions eerily anticipated the 'great eye' of Google (and, increasingly, YouTube). Google and YouTube are the modern-day equivalents of the esoteric idea of the 'akashic records', a kind of massive memory vault that can provide sought-for information at the drop of a hat. Of course, the akashic records were understood to be perfect memory banks in which all things of note that ever happened were recorded. Google and YouTube are (probably fortunately) not yet at that level. They are powerful repositories that contain vast amounts of information, or at least point toward such information. But they are far from perfect. Ironically, it's this very imperfection (and doubtless to future eyes, crudeness) that can make these things so addictive. Information is sought that yields only a partial answer, or a tantalizing clue, or worse, leads to a parallel interest or something entirely unrelated that sends one off on a virtual goose chase. Before one knows it, hours have passed and one has forgotten the original pursuit. (Or as the common YouTube refrain in the comments section has it, 'thumbs up if you know how you got here'.) To live a life bouncing from one link to another is a good metaphor for an unstructured, aimless life—the life of the sun-loving 'surfer'.

The Distracted Man always has a full schedule, or mostly full, but he rarely goes deeply into anything. He reads multiple books at once, not for any serious research reasons, and often doesn't finish them. He can't finish them in part because he needs to get back online. He cannot commit to anything because there's no room in his schedule (so he thinks). He is skittish, touchy, and prickly, always looking for something that isn't there. Above all he resists being a teammate. Because he tends not to trust older men (and certainly not 'established' men) he usually avoids getting involved in anything—and certainly anything run by older men—that suggests that he may lose some of his freedom. Of course, the freedom he may be losing is an immature form of freedom—'I can do whatever I want, when and where I want'— the refrain of the frustrated and angry adolescent whose life has been manipulated by forces around him. The freedom that can arise from real commitment in life is a deeper, riper freedom that can yield real and ripe fruit. But the Distracted Man has no experience of this and instinctively mistrusts anything that may take away his 'masturbatory freedom', that is, to be perpetually distracted on his own terms in his own way in his own private world.

Because the Distracted Man has great difficulty yielding to structure and discipline, especially the kind implemented by anything bearing the semblance of an established power structure (read: something created by older men), he accordingly never acquires the training he needs to progress in life. He's always jumping the gun, trying to get ahead before he's begun, trying to run the race before he remembered to put on his pants and his track shoes. He eats packaged meals because he's too distracted to cook anything. He cuts corners to save time, so he has more time for doing things strictly on his terms.

Pornography

It was once estimated in the early days of the mass usage of the Internet (mid-1990s) that 'one-third of the Internet was porn'. Perhaps that was true back then (trust porn to get the jump). It is probably not true now, given the behemoth that the Internet has grown into. But no doubt porn still comprises a respectable percentage of it. (For the record, a recent *Psychology Today* piece suggests, based on some statistical studies, that approximately 10 percent of Internet use involves porn.[4])

Back in the day (as in, before the 1980s), porn was limited to smutty magazines (or respectable ones like *Playboy* or the racier *Penthouse*) that a boy hid under his box spring. I still remember when the glossy sci-fi magazine *Omni* appeared in the 1970s. Because it was produced and edited by the same people who put out *Penthouse*, whenever I read *Omni* I was strangely reminded of naked women, even though the magazine was more about Captain Kirk and his kith and kin than it was about Bob Guccione and his.

Men in current times have vast pornographic resources they can tap. They can access tens of thousands of online pornography sites, featuring thousands of anonymous women engaged in sex acts with largely faceless men. It's one step short of *Star Trek* replicator-sex. The downside of all this is that many modern men expend much energy in sexual release while watching porn, and accordingly may be less inclined to even bother relating with flesh-and-blood people. The whole thing serves to make men more introverted, less willing to take risks (and on occasion, prone to more serious addictions). All that can, and often does, work counter to the warrior qualities of courage and the willingness to take appropriate risks. Worse, porn usage can and often does lead to serious addiction and that can have damaging consequences.

An obvious problematic issue is the pornographic emphasis on objectifying women; however, the deeper (and raw) truth is that many men already objectify women to varying degrees, seeing them primarily as bodies and secondarily as anything else. I'm reminded of a savage stand-up routine by Bill Maher. He was commenting on women's angst around how to present themselves to the world—all the paraphernalia around style and appearance. 'Ladies,' Maher announced with his patented bluntness, 'for men, only one thing matters: new vs. old.' And he wasn't referring to fashions.

This sort of stuff angers most self-respecting women, but for men it's important to look at it for another reason: postmodern feminized men (and certainly 'spiritual' men) tend to struggle with their baser instincts and many act affronted when presented with the idea that they are as crude as any other men. This invites all the problems that accompany denial, repression, and the inner split between instinct and cultivated persona. A 'spiritual man' who represses his baser nature is not really transcending it. He's merely becoming a spiritualized ego.

When I was a young man in Montreal in the late 1970s I worked for several years in my father's meat-packing plant. This was a rough place and it was manned by rough and tough guys, the classic 1960s–70s anti-hippie, blue collar, hard hat, lunch pail type. On one occasion one of my co-workers, a married guy in his early thirties, suggested I take one of the two female employees in the entire plant—the prettier one—into the back storage-room and 'bang her'. This sort of talk was always recognized as base and stupid, even by these kinds of guys, but there was something appealing about the lack of artifice. It was stupid but real. (And no, I didn't take her into the back room—not that she would have wanted to go with me anyway.)

A few years later I found myself living in a communal house in Toronto, one dedicated to the teachings of the radical Indian guru Rajneesh (in later years known as Osho). I was sitting in the living room one morning with a couple of fellow disciples, watching TV. At some point a buxom woman appeared on the screen. 'Man,' grunted the guy sitting beside me, 'check out those tits!' He was a meditator apparently committed to his spiritual enlightenment. But was he much different from the guy in the meat-packing plant who encouraged me to bang my co-worker in a storage room? In some ways, he was. The guy in the meat plant was hard-working, married, and raising a family. Despite his rough and crude ways, he must have attained some level of responsibility. The spiritual seeker in the Rajneesh communal house was an unmarried, childless, unemployed carpenter wearing beads, eating vegetarian food, and collecting unemployment insurance. But of course, he was more 'elevated' than the laborer. Or not.

I'm not suggesting here that all men are alike, regardless of their intent, level of education, refinement, or lack thereof. It is difficult to bridge the gap between Genghis Khan and Leonardo da Vinci. Nevertheless, there are what could be defined as universal masculine traits, one of which is to be drawn to, or mesmerized by, the form of the female. Genghis Khan probably had a healthy sex drive, at least as a young man (and he did have several wives). Leonardo may have been gay (the records indicate he was), but clearly, he was also taken in by the form of women. His most famous work, *Mona Lisa*, took him over a decade to finish. He carried it around with him for the last several years of his life and was constantly touching it up to perfect it.

The female form is like that to the male mind (straight or gay): a vast and endlessly fascinating universe of subtlety, never to be precisely captured, thereby allowing the masculine trait of adventurism and the desire for conquest (whether militarily, artistically, or intellectually) to be exercised. That is the way it is approached in the best sense. Pornography is a lower way, obviously, but no man who surreptitiously watches porn should get caught up in righteously condemning it, lest he wish to be a mere hypocrite.

Arguably, porn is not all bad. Perhaps there have been some would-be rapists who have had their libidinous urges and emotional needs to objectify women sufficiently reduced by pixilated images of nubile nudes enough to take them off the potential criminal map. Then again, the reverse may occur—a man so frustrated by two-dimensional sex that in desperation he seeks the real thing—but given that most rape is more about power than lust, all these considerations may be irrelevant. Probably most potential rapists are not particularly satisfied by what mere online porn has to offer.

Researching online for studies on pornography is interesting, because it highlights one of the problems with Google as a tool for research. For example, if you search for 'effect of porn on the brain' you may indeed find what seems to be scientifically sound studies railing against the dangers of porn as an addictive problem, but on closer inspection many of these sites are soon revealed to be agenda-driven (most commonly, they are religious and specifically, Christian). This is because Google algorithms are designed not to necessarily tell you what *you* are looking for, but rather, what *most people* are looking for.

A 2013 study cited in *Psychology Today* and published in the journal *Socioaffective Neuroscience of Psychology* examined 52 'sex addicts' and found that when presented with erotic imagery their brains showed no electrical evidence of the desensitization common to drug addicts. The upshot of the study was that the 'sex addicts' showed evidence of high libido common to people with high sex drives, rather than that the porn they watched was somehow damaging their brains or *causing* them to be sex addicts.[5] Sex addiction as a pathology is not found within the Diagnostic and Statistical Manual of Mental Disorders (this venerable tool—the most recent version is the DSM-V— is the acknowledged doctrinal 'authority' on the modern understandings of mental pathology). The matter, however, is far from decided, with vocal proponents on both sides arguing for sex addiction either as a real and specific pathology, or as an excuse for other, deeper issues related to will and the failure to be responsible for one's subjective states of mind. More to the point, compulsive acting out, such as in so-called sexual harassment, is—*at first glance*—more properly related to power and its usage. This idea is seemingly backed up by the reality that those men accused of sexual harassment are invariably in positions of power and fame (or they were—even George W. H. Bush, 93 at the time and in a wheelchair, was accused in 2017 by three women of improprieties).

Sexual Harassment and the Weinstein Effect

As of this writing in early 2018, North American men in positions of power, largely in politics and the entertainment industry, have been dropping like flies as one after another has accusations of sexual harassment or abuse leveled against them. The accusations alone have proved pretty much a death sentence for the careers of these men. In the more high-profile cases there has been no sanction or time-limited penalty, and redemption has been out of the question; their entire careers have just been waxed.

It all began when Harvey Weinstein, a powerful Hollywood producer and one of the founders of Miramax, which was the studio behind such famed movies as *Sex, Lies, and Videotape*, *Pulp Fiction*, and *Shakespeare in Love*, was accused by over 80 women of sexual improprieties (one or two even charged him with rape). Within a week or two the cloud of scandal engulfed him like Pig-Pen's aura, he was fired from his own company, and he became a lightning rod for the anger of women in relation to the archetype of the powerful and influential man who is also a sexual creep.

Weinstein's epic crash was followed closely by similar scandals swallowing up the A-list actor Kevin Spacey and one of America's biggest comedians, Louis CK. Around the same time, Alabaman would-be Republican senator and former judge Roy Moore was accused by half a dozen women of sexual harassment and abuse stemming from events in the late 1970s when these women were all underage (early teens, mainly) and Moore was in his early thirties. The fact that he apparently had a thing for young girls and wasn't exactly asking permission from these girls' parents to hit on their daughters, despite his claims to the contrary, was enough to get him rejected by most powerful members of the Trump administration (though not, notably, by Trump himself) and scorned by the media. Many Alabamans remained loyal to him, a gift the southern states also gave Trump when he got elected president anyway despite having his own accusations of sexual harassment leveled against him in late 2016, and despite his own voice being famously recorded admitting as much (the infamous 'locker room talk' *Hollywood Access* tape). That Moore went on to lose the Alabama senatorial election to Democrat Doug Jones is of questionable meaning, since he lost by only 1.5 percent of the vote.

To be fair, Weinstein's crash and burn may have been the most spectacular, but it had been preceded months before by the various scandals involving key figures at Fox News: Roger Ailes and Bill O'Reilly. Ailes was of advanced age and died shortly after, but O'Reilly was at the peak of his game when the plug was pulled on him. What is remarkable about the current trend in all this is the impact such accusations are having on the careers of these men. In effect, while women are levelling the accusations (and gay men, in the case of Spacey), it is mainly men in power who are lowering the boom and switching off the lights on the careers of the men. These CEOs and their companies and organizations fear the consequences if they don't (loss of advertisers and revenue; reputation or more noble purposes likely run a distant second). In the heat of the battle in late 2017, feminist author Jill Filipovic summed up the sentiment well:

> For feminists, this is a watershed moment. All around us, once-mighty men are being swept up—and sometimes swept out of their jobs—in sexual harassment and assault allegations.[6]

Before Ailes and O'Reilly there were the Bills: Clinton and Cosby. Both men were publicly roasted, but throughout their active careers neither paid any real price professionally. Clinton, despite 'Oral' Office sexual encounters with his young intern Monica Lewinsky, went on to a lucrative career as a speaker and media pundit. Cosby was already old and retired; the dozens of accusations against him by women who claimed his *modus operandi* was to drug them and then assault them at first came to little avail, as he was initially acquitted in court. He was subsequently retried and as of mid-2018 was found guilty on three counts of aggravated indecent assault. His reputation has been largely destroyed. Other cases abound: Hollywood directors James Toback and Brett Ratner, NBC journalist Mark Halperin, literary figures Hamilton Fish and Leon Wieseltier; and even the British Parliament, where some three dozen members have had accusations of misconduct tossed at them. The list continues to grow.

As all this was going on, an older man in my Facebook feed lamented, 'Hell, if these accusations are going to go back 30 or 40 years then all men must be guilty.' He was immediately set on by a pack of angry women in the comment section of his post and ended up feebly recanting some of his views. His last miserable remark was, 'Well, guess I'm wrong.'

Much of this issue hits on the matter of power and its perceived imbalances between the genders. The public perception of the current narrative is largely uniform: men are being accused because they are the aggressors, and because, more to the point, they have (or had) the power in the cited cases. Social media fuels all this because it gives the women a forum for their voice and a chance at some sort of psychological catharsis via safety-in-numbers. The whole matter appears, at first glance, to be much more about power than it is about sexuality, a fact attested to in that all cases involve high-profile men (or those possessed of the Wikipedia-standard of 'notability'). We don't hear of powerless men being accused publicly, because no one would be interested in their cases and there would be no popcorn-eating audience to listen (and probably no one to fire them either). However, examined more closely, this whole matter is as much about *immature sexuality* as it is about power.

'Slut-shaming', one of the conventional terms for pathologizing human nature—making a woman (in this case) wrong for being sexual or dressing in perceived sexually provocative ways—is not just a common way of expressing jealousy between women; it is also a result of centuries of moral programming that makes sex wrong, or promotes the idea that sexuality is immoral or disreputable or dangerous. Men who 'slut-shame' are more in this latter category, making a woman wrong for appearing sexual because he is not comfortable with his own sexual energy, that is, he feels guilty for being a sexual being and is uncomfortable when the attractive woman reminds him of that, just by how she appears. At the root of this we find religious-social programming, insidious in its ability to have lasting effects over many generations of families, keeping men (and women) stunted and immature sexually.

This religious-social programming is based on a simple core idea: sexual energy is dangerous because it can make people independent and powerful. Powerful individuals who do not serve the state or church are not in the interests of—and are no good for—the power structures of the world. For one, soldiers do not make good fighters if they are too immersed in the matters of love and sex—and especially so on the eve of their battles.

To repeat: the core problems here are two, the misuse of power, and the backward, immature relationship with sex that is still so much a part of the fabric of early twenty-first-century Western culture. (This is mostly a global thing as well, but here we're focusing on North American culture.)

Much of North American Caucasian culture is rooted in puritanicalism, which has always involved the need to keep sex hushed behind doors, or (mainly) anonymous as in pornography. A man in power who extracts sexual favors from a subordinate woman or man in exchange for opportunity, position, and status is misusing power, yes, but he's doing it because his relationship with sex is immature. The woman or man he lusts after is an object of gratification, but she or he is no more than an object. Sex is objectified in his mind because he's not integrated with its energy. It is a force that *has him*, not the other way around.

Woman do not get off scot free here either. A woman who sees her self-worth as primarily manifest through her sexual charms is not just carrying on centuries of limited programming about the value of the woman, she is likely *demonstrating* that very limiting belief by projecting an image that reinforces the idea that she is primarily a body, secondarily anything else. Many women thrive on the attention drawn from appearances, but cry foul when men act in response to this image in an aggressive fashion. Of course, a woman must 'cry foul' when the man abuses his power in whatever manner. But the usage of *her* power in all of this is as effective if far less obvious to detect.

An insightful film that illustrates much of this is Jane Campion's 1999 movie *Holy Smoke*, which stars Kate Winslet as a young woman caught up in the community of a spiritual guru in

India, and Harvey Keitel as a 'cult deprogrammer' who is hired by her family to psychologically extract her from the clutches of the 'evil' guru and his cult.

The Keitel character, supposedly around 50 (though Keitel himself was near 60 when he made this picture), initially is effective in intellectually confronting and outmaneuvering the intelligent, attractive Winslet character, who is in her early twenties (Winslet was 24 at the time). But as the movie progresses, it becomes clear that the film is not so much about religious or cult deprogramming, as it is a feminist screed about the intrinsic power of women and, specifically, female sexuality. The Winslet character eventually wins the chess-match by sexually seducing the Keitel character, who in the end is reduced to a pathetic old man chasing her in the desert wearing a dress and one boot, begging her to marry him. She is, of course, repulsed. The movie ends with her leaving the guru's organization (so perhaps the 'deprogramming' worked after all) and finding a new love in India, and with him returning to his wife and writing secret letters to her, admiring her from afar. The bottom-line message is that female sexuality trumps male egocentricity and intellectual charisma. A man is no match for the sexual power of a woman. The only way he can 'overcome' it is to apply the power of his status and position in the world to control her.

But, as we now see, and as so many high-profile men have been painfully discovering, even that does not work anymore. It doesn't work because most of these men are not being toppled by women. They are being *accused* by women, but they are largely being brought down by *other men* who are allegiant to women and their cause. Two vivid examples of why this is a new trend are Roman Polanksi and Woody Allen, legendary figures in the movie-making industry who both enjoyed success and recognition years *after* scandals involving women much younger than themselves—scandals that in the current climate would have almost certainly obliterated their careers. Yes, Polanski did have to leave the United States and live out his life in France, and yes, Allen was excoriated by many, but that didn't stop them from continuing to make successful movies and even to receive prestigious awards.

The point being made in all of this is that both men and women need to be responsible for their sexuality and their usage of power—be that power economic, social, political, or sexual. However, this is a book for men, not women. For a man to be a 'conscious warrior', a man who strives for impeccability in his life, he needs to really know the primitive beast inside of him. He needs to go beyond religious or cultural or family conditioning that tells him he is bad and guilty for being a sexual being. And he needs to have *healthy* outlets for his darkest thoughts. I stress the term 'healthy' here because without that he is little more than an undisciplined, dangerous beast or a secret pervert.

How does a man have healthy outlets for his darkest thoughts? *By having other quality men in his life.* He needs a community of brothers, and preferably solid elder men as well. Alas, it is precisely this that is lacking in the lives of so many men, especially younger ones. Their 'brothers' are too often toxic, and their 'elders' too often uninterested, corrupt, or absent altogether. Needless to say, we have work to do.

Social Networking, the Millennial Generation, and the Importance of Embodiment

The classification of generations is always an approximate business at best but is nevertheless a useful tool for recognizing large-scale social patterns and how they shift over time. A rough outline of recent generations (birth years in parenthesis) looks something like this:

The Lost Generation (1883–1900)
The Greatest Generation (1901–24)
The Silent Generation (1925–45)

The Baby Boomers (1946–63)
Generation X (1964–82)
Millennial Generation (1983–2001)
Generation Z or Next (2002–20)

If we accept the rough dating within this scheme it's clear that the Millennial Generation is the first one to truly grow up amidst the advanced communications technology brought about by the advent of home computers, the Internet, and smartphones. Each generation has had their outstanding qualities, sometimes obvious in their name: the 'Greatest Generation' was so named for their direct involvement in World War II (they were too young for the earlier Great War); the 'Silent Generation' grew up during the Great Depression and consequently inclined toward a certain savviness with finances; the Baby Boomers appeared during the population spike in the relatively affluent aftermath of the Second World War and gave rise to the cultural revolution of the 1960s; 'Generation X' immediately followed them and is marked by a tendency to be less concerned with leaders (the Baby Boomers were more focused on replacing such leaders and instilling more modern ideas) and more concerned with transforming institutions from within.

While late Gen-Xers grew up with home computer technology and the Internet, it is the Millennial Generation that has grown up with both in addition to the smartphone era. Facebook appeared in 2004, at which time Millennials were aged approximately 3 to 21. Gen-Xers, by contrast, were somewhere between 22 and 40, while Boomers were roughly between 41 and 58. Thus while Gen-Xers were exposed to Facebook in young adulthood, most Millennials have not known adult life without social networking, and many of them will scarcely recall life when such things did not exist.

One has only to visit a typical coffee shop in many First World nations to see the results of the combination of Internet technology, social networking culture, and coffee house ambience. The general means by which young people relate in such environments is radically different from what it was in the 1970s, 80s, or 90s. Arguably there is very little relating at all, with more emphasis on an introverted absorption in online life. That is not to suggest that nothing good comes out of online relating. It obviously has some powerful advantages, mainly in rapidity of connections and accessibility to certain people or information that otherwise we would have no access to at all. But it all comes with a price. That price is in depth of connection. Online relating tends to be superficial and to encourage such superficiality.

A large percentage of interpersonal communication is non-verbal, based on body language. Online communication is disembodied. It is like a bunch of minds floating around in cyberspace interacting with each other, which could be very interesting and rewarding if such minds were advanced or even just mature, but this is rarely the case. Accordingly, it's common, even routine, to fail to accurately interpret what someone is saying in online interaction, or at the least, to miss all the nuances.

There is an element of masculinity that is best characterized by the term 'penetration'. Usage of such a term may seem obvious, but I'm more concerned here with the qualities of psychological depth and fullness of experience. A man is psychologically healthiest when he can penetrate deeply into his experiences, and especially in his work. This includes, naturally, his relations with people. He may not be the multitasker that a woman can be, but he compensates (ideally) by investigating deeply and thoroughly whatever it is he is focusing on.

Social networking, as well as texting technology, are in some respects the antithesis of deep and penetrating experience (and, it goes without saying, communication). They are mainly about surface contact; capable of wide scope, without the need for depth. These are forms of communication well suited to the feminine mind. That's not to imply that a feminine mind cannot and does not communicate deeply and penetratingly, but the feminine mind is more naturally attuned to wide-scope communication that it can navigate without trouble, absent the penetrating quality intrinsic to the healthy masculine.

How does all this translate practically? A man can effectively use a smartphone, obviously, and the device itself is remarkably practical and effective on so many levels (many businessmen, especially those who are self-employed, are all but addicted to their smartphones). But the overall quality of his relating to people will suffer if he becomes too habituated to online communication (which, for younger men and boys, includes the vast gaming universe that more than one of them has gotten hopelessly lost in). A man needs to acquire and develop the discipline to put his communication devices aside when focusing on more important matters—such as his livelihood, his health, his important relationships that require his bodily presence, and so on.

The key to balancing a life immersed in advanced communication technologies is *embodiment*. Above all, a man needs to be in good relationship with his body. He needs to *inhabit* his body, in the true sense of that word. This is usually best accomplished by engaging in a regular exercise regimen— martial arts are excellent, or some sort of regular cardio workout—but whatever it is, it should involve the need for significant *effort*. A man who is lazy and always seeks the path of least resistance grows weak and is inclined to fade into obscurity as he ages. Work ethic for men is crucial to well-being (let alone success), and this applies to his relationship with his body as well.

Back in the early 1920s the spiritual teacher G.I. Gurdjieff was running his 'Institute for the Harmonious Development of Man' in Fontainebleau, France, about 40 miles southeast of Paris. Owing to the uniqueness of his teaching and his personal charisma which soon gained him a reputation, he attracted many quality disciples. One of them was the renowned English literary editor A.R. Orage. When Orage arrived at Gurdjieff's school (a large chateau that had been home to both royalty and monks in the past) he was soft, overweight, and out of shape. Seeing this and realizing that Orage was an intellectual who needed to be more mindful of his body, Gurdjieff assigned him the task of digging a ditch. When Orage completed this task, he was told to fill the ditch in and dig another. This routine—dig a ditch, get told to fill it in, and dig again—went on for about a week. By the eighth day Orage was exhausted and felt defeated mentally. He would retreat to his monk's cell in the evening and on occasion break down in tears, so unaccustomed was he to the hard labor. Then, the next day, just when he was about to give up, Orage decided to dig harder. Suddenly he felt some sort of shift internally and realized that he was enjoying the physical activity. For the first time in a long time he began to inhabit his body. Gurdjieff, noticing this, then told him to stop digging and join him for coffee. He had passed his first 'initiation'.

The Masculine Core

Many modern men lack a strong sense of what it means to have a healthy masculine core. What is a healthy masculine core? It implies several things. First, a man with a comfortable masculinity has a natural ability to hold space when interacting with others. To 'hold space' means, in this context, to be able to listen to the other without feeling threatened at the level of identity; to *not take things personally*. Probably more disasters have occurred in the lives of men due to taking things personally and lashing out in vengeance, than for any other reason. Of course, there are times when 'taking something personally' may be appropriate—for example, in the defense of one's body, one's property, one's loved ones, or even one's neighborhood or nation. But these are more appropriate responses to boundary violations. Taking something personally means, in the context implied here, to perceive slights and to react badly, which is deriving from a lack of centeredness and confidence that results in feeling vulnerable when in the presence of people one deems more accomplished or confident than oneself. (It is certainly possible to take something personally and to be offended by someone one deems less accomplished or successful or confident than oneself, but this rarely results in vengeful behavior toward them, unless one has a pathological intent to dominate. If so, this usually requires deeper therapy than can be provided by typical men's work.)

An expression sometimes used in men's groups is, 'A true warrior never engages in battle with a weaker opponent.' It's a generalization, of course, but it's not hard to see how to apply the idea in a workable way. 'Weaker opponents' is sometimes thought to be an indirect reference to women (physicality), but it also applies to men one deems to be one's junior in confidence, success, power, or (sometimes) age. 'Not engaging in battle' does not mean having no boundaries or being a walkover. It rather refers to restraining hostile aggression, much how a practitioner of some martial arts such as jiu-jitsu will, when encountering hostile aggression, simply redirect their opponent's movements, rather than meet them head-on and 'out-bash' them. 'Redirecting the opponent's movements' can be understood as holding space (for example, during an argument) and responding from one's inner core of confidence, as opposed to the anxious and tense fight-or-flight stance. A truly confident man rarely has any need to be reactive or overly aggressive, and if clever enough, can use mature humor to defuse many situations.

We are here describing, naturally, someone who already has that confidence. A man who lacks a good masculine core, or developed masculine confidence, is in no position to respond in some elevated fashion when confronted with hostility, especially from a 'stronger opponent' (as deemed in his mind), or even a weaker one. The viciousness of his response will be inversely proportional to the strength of his masculine core:

Strong Masculine Core = even-tempered, alert, appropriate response to threat

Average Masculine Core = typical lukewarm 'get even' or 'turtling' response to threat

Weak Masculine Core = vicious response to threat, or a cowardly retreat

All rage is a secondary emotion, a defense against vulnerability and fear. The nastier a man is capable of being, the weaker he believes himself to be deep inside. That is straightforward: if a man suspects that inside he is weak, it's a given that he's going to feel it necessary to growl loudly at or bite viciously those who threaten him, in case they find out just how weak he is. Alternatively, he may just flee or pretend he is not offended, if his fear is so strong that cowardice is part of his nature. The cowardly lion is less of a threat to society than the vicious weak man, but the cowardly lion suffers no less mentally than the vicious weak man (who usually ends up having to pay for his impulsive displays of noise or aggression—not unlike a rabid dog that gets put down).

When a man lacks a healthy masculine core, he is easily threatened by the accomplishments or confidence level of the person he is relating to. He becomes competitive and displays a need to 'top-dog' the other—or, he 'plays small' and seeks never to challenge (or offend) the stronger person. Either way he has a hard time being natural, being who he really is, because he does not yet have a strong sense of what that looks like.

How to develop a 'healthy masculine core'? There is no magic pill, no overnight process, no accelerated growth program that will bring about the confidence that arises from resting comfortably in one's masculinity. However, it can be said that a strong and well-balanced masculine core has as its foundation a sense of accomplishment in life. A man who gets in the knack of completing tasks, projects, programs, and in general goals designed to improve his life—and most importantly, does not allow relationships with romantic partners to seriously slow down his progress or distract him—is a man who gradually feels more and more confident about who he is.

Alongside that is the importance of tribe. A man comfortable in his masculinity does not arise in solitude, the proverbial 'he came out of nowhere' stereotyped hero of cartoons. A confident man develops among a tribe of elders and brothers, even if such elders and brothers are few. He has relationships with other men, and he chooses to work *with* them, rather than constantly competing with them, or even worse, avoiding and secretly hating them.

Part Two

Warriors, Junkyard Dogs, and Popular Figures

Chapter 3

A Brief History of Warrior Cultures: Part I

The samurai and the shinobi of Japan remain in the looming shadow of modern fantasy and romance. The samurai is now widely believed to be a knight who charges headlong into death for the love of a lord. They also have a mysterious and shining blade, which can cut through any material. In the day he meditates on loyalty and is gifted with blessed enlightenment, but in the night, he fearfully protects against his famous dreaded enemy—the ninja. This outline is as redundant as the knight fighting the dragon next to a maiden locked in a tower, and it belongs in one place: story books.[1]
Antony Cummins

As a boy growing up in the 1960s I used to watch the campy TV show *Batman*, starring Adam West as the Caped Crusader and Burt Ward as his sidekick Robin. This show, compared to modern TV shows, was bad, very bad. So bad as to seem like pure parody (which, essentially, it was—the camp-factor was for the kids). Of course, back then we had no reference points of note and so these shows were what we saw, and what we got. They seemed cool enough at the time.

There were many riotously funny scenes in *Batman*. Most famous of all is probably the scene where Batman is heroically fending off a shark while dangling from a helicopter ladder over an ocean. The shark—looking like a giant plastic condom with fake teeth—has Batman's leg in the grip of its jaws. Robin is piloting the bat-copter. Batman hollers up to him to fetch him the 'shark-repellent bat spray'. Robin yells 'Holy *sardine!*', puts the chopper in park, gets the repellent (conveniently there in a shiny container), and clambers down the ladder to Batman.

All this time Batman is clobbering the shark over the head

with his fist, throwing in the odd body-shot for good measure (perhaps reminiscent of Gil Clancy, George Foreman's manager, memorably hollering at him to 'go to the body!' when George was pounding Ron Lyle's head in the ring in a 1976 bout generally regarded as the wildest boxing match in history). Finally, back-flipping down the ladder with his flowing yellow robe and green boots, Robin reached Batman, passed on the shark-repellent bat spray, and the rest was history. The dummy shark landed in the ocean with a thud, and then weirdly, *exploded*. Batman's leg mysteriously emerged unscathed.

This scene has been immortalized, like so much else of pop culture, on YouTube. Young men delight in watching these videos and trashing them in the comments section, bewildered at just how bad they are. (Although one commenter, writing, 'This is so bad, it's good', got the point.)

Perspective and context are nine-tenths of everything in our humanly constructed views of reality. But in warfare, and especially in understanding the value of warrior-consciousness, they are particularly crucial. The time we inhabit grows closer to a conceivable future where qualities of the warrior such as battlefield courage will be limited to virtual hologram experience. We men would do well to not forsake the more noble warrior qualities. The following two chapters deal with the alchemy of extracting valuable warrior qualities from the madness of warfare and masculine destructiveness.

* * *

This is not a history book, let alone a comprehensive study of the history of warriors and their cultures. Nor is it a glorification of the values of martial culture. However, a basic premise herein is that healthy and vibrant masculine nature is founded on some of the qualities of the psychologically healthy warrior. Conversely, elements of the unhealthy masculine ego derive from two general areas: the darker and destructive parts of warrior nature, or the denial of and disconnect from the same. Therefore, a brief overview of some of the more noteworthy warrior cultures of history is presented in the next two chapters. These include the Spartans, Knights Templar, Mongols, Shaolin monks, samurai, and ninja. In addition, because in this book we're not shying away from a look at some of the grittier elements of gender issues, we also won't shy away from a direct look at some of the darker elements of the male psyche. And nowhere does the dark side of the male psyche show itself more clearly than in the history of warfare, noble examples of specific military men or military organizations notwithstanding.

From the outset, it could be argued by any intelligent pacifist that all war by nature is primitive and ugly, and so therefore the idea of a 'psychologically healthy warrior' is a contradiction in terms. That could indeed be argued but the argument would soon flounder. For while it is true that war is base and brutal and hard to imagine in a truly advanced, unified global civilization, it is also true that it is an essential part of our history (and current affairs). It is even recognized by some distinguished historians as being (ironically) the main force behind the creation of civilization itself.[2]

That said, I'm not concerned here with promoting the values of the soldier, honorable as they may be. I distinguish between the soldier and the warrior, the latter being more of an archetype that represents very specific qualities basic to masculine nature. A soldier could be a man of greatly varying quality, anything from a powerful and noble warrior to the flabby guy next door who was unwillingly drafted (or who enlisted with vague intentions) to represent his nation. A warrior, however, in the ideal sense, is a figure that embodies many worthy qualities, and moreover, qualities sorely lacking in many modern Western men. Hence in the following sections we'll be looking at the history of certain notable warrior cultures not for the mere sake of just recounting facts, but to mine the finer virtues found in these cultures—as well as taking an honest look at some of their uglier elements.

The Spartans

Sparta was a city-state of ancient Greece, the capital of Laconia, situated in the south-eastern Peloponnese. It has an extraordinarily rich history in the annals of warriorhood. At their peak (around 650–450 BCE) Spartan soldiers were arguably the greatest in history, rarely to be surpassed in categories such as courageousness, fierce commitment to their cause, single-mindedness, and excellence in training. This could be so in part because Spartan culture was based entirely on the training of its warriors. They were the military culture *par excellence*. Slick early twenty-first-century movies such as *300* have served to popularize their mystique, but as always, the truth is more interesting—and it must be said, considerably less flattering.

The title of *300* referred to the famous Battle of Thermopylae of 480 BCE, in which a small but fierce group of Spartans—traditionally recognized as numbering 300 (aided, the truth be told, by a few hundred other Greeks)—defiantly took on a vast Persian army of over 100,000 (the commonly cited figure of 'one million' is exaggeration), succumbing in the end, but not after inflicting serious damage on their enemy. The battle, and the Spartans, became synonymous with extraordinary courage in the face of almost certain defeat and death, thereby immortalized as symbols of valor and of a steadfast refusal to buckle even in the face of insurmountable odds (about 100 to 1 in the case of this battle). That the small Spartan force ultimately lost is irrelevant. It's the fact that they bothered to fight at all that marks them forever with the qualities of courage under fire and the willingness to place a greater just cause before personal gain or even survival.

Of course, 'just cause' (depending on how it is interpreted) 'before personal survival' can also be a formula for madness and senseless destruction, but in the case of the Spartan ideal it speaks more to a deeply impersonal disposition that values, in the words of *Star Trek*'s Mr Spock, 'the many before the one', even at cost of the death of the one. Taken at its best, this is a quality that exemplifies selflessness and confirms the best part of the warrior as protector and defender.

Sparta was the very definition of the elite warrior culture, with a relatively small—by current standards 'tiny'—population that usually numbered fewer than 10,000 official citizens. The entire culture was based on a strange master–slave relationship with a much greater surrounding population of *helots* (state slaves who had originally been conquered by the Spartans). The slaves served the Spartan citizens, and the latter maintained a constant state of military preparedness against their own slaves, who, it was assumed, could and would revolt at any time. Their own status as uneasy masters to a much larger flock of slaves kept them ever alert to possible rebellions. This alertness was the basis for their continuous military and martial training. And the Spartans did not limit themselves to mere military readiness. They declared war on their state slaves every year to ensure that they remained psychologically and physically dominated. The Spartans anticipated by two millennia Machiavelli's famous idea that it is safer for a leader to be feared than loved.

Remarkable combat and warrior virtues aside, the Spartan culture overall was not particularly admirable, permeated with what would today be recognized as a general 'cold war' mindset. Foreigners were regarded with great suspicion, intrigue was ubiquitous, and covert and aggressive oppression of its own slave workforce was ongoing. Great military warriors they were, but socially their culture was fear-based, oppressive, and tyrannical. A particularly extreme form of deception practiced involved Sparta inviting its slave population to nominate their finest members—those who had served the Spartan citizens most effectively and admirably—for recognition and possible freedom. Once this group was rounded up (according to one historian they numbered 2,000) they were duly murdered by the Spartans. In this way, the slaves were prevented from ever building the leadership structure needed for any kind of rebellion against their masters. (One can see the reflection of this practice in far more recent events such as the brutal elimination of the Polish intelligentsia by both the Nazis and Soviets during the Second World War.) There was even a Spartan practice of initiating young men by sending them out at night to hunt for slaves who were breaking curfew. If any were found, the young Spartan men were not only legally able to kill them, they were expected to as part of their training and initiation.

Because the number of Spartan citizens was limited, in terms of survival the entire culture was always on a delicate footing. In 371 BCE Sparta was defeated by Thebes in the Battle of Leuctra and the Spartan citizenry shrank to a mere 1,500. (An interesting facet of the Theban army was an elite fighting unit known as the Sacred Band, comprised entirely of homosexual soldiers — the idea being that warriors would be particularly fierce if fighting alongside their lovers.) The Spartans suffered a second defeat to the Thebans in 362 BCE that led to a permanent shift of power in Greece, soon to lead to the Macedonian triumphs of Philip II. These military defeats were accompanied over time by slave revolts that led to further loss of power. Despite that, Sparta continued as a regional power for two more centuries, though isolated and without the expansive influence it once enjoyed. During the Punic Wars (264–146 BCE) Sparta fought on the side of Rome against Carthage. The Romans conquered Greece in 146 BCE, at which point Sparta was reduced to an isolated culture and tourist attraction for Romans.

A notable and unusual (for the times) element of Spartan culture was the status that Spartan women in general enjoyed. They were educated and had freedoms unknown to women of most other cultures of that time (including Athenians). They could dress as they pleased, exercise, speak their minds and compete with men in ways that we in the modern West would consider normal, but at that time was rare. They also held, in general, as much economic power as did the men. (Aristotle, who held a dim view of the female mind in general, blamed the rapid decline of Spartan culture partly on the material indulgences of powerful Spartan women. Given how many male-dominant cultures faded equally quickly throughout history, we have to take Aristotle's analysis with a grain of Mediterranean salt, but his views do yield interesting insights into just how unusual Spartan culture was, and was regarded as, in his time.)

Mining the Virtues of the Spartans

Sparta was an odd culture for its time, and that was arguably one of its best virtues—it did not blindly conform to mass expectations, but demonstrated the courage to find unique expressions of excellence in training, for both men and women. That the whole thing was tainted by its dependence on slavery, similar perhaps to the legacies of Washington and Jefferson, doesn't take away from those qualities that made the Spartans standout warriors. Mastery and excellence in training are not virtues to be trifled with, and they are also the antidote to the modern tendency of mental laziness above all else. Modern Western men are presented with endless possible forms of physical training, but so often avoid these for the soft life of online interaction and flat-screen observation. We are largely a culture of watchers, not participants. Spartan military training was all about indifference to luxury; the very idea has even entered our language, where 'spartan' means exactly that. The idea of shedding some of our layers of comfort, to engage in rugged participation in life, is relevant and very important to our times.

The Knights Templar

Few so-called 'secret societies' of history have had as many fanciful and romantic tales affixed to their legend as have the Knights Templar. Technically they were less a secret society and more a Christian military order, but owing to their general mystique and dramatic downfall they have come to be associated with the most secretive of powerful organizations. Their full name was 'Order of Poor Knights of Christ and of the Temple of Solomon', though they have been known to history more as the Knights Templar or more commonly as the Templars. As an organization they existed for almost 200 years, being founded in 1119 and forcefully (and dramatically) disbanded in 1312. The association of the Knights Templar with old Western esoteric legends such as the Holy Grail is more than mere retrospective fancy; Chretien de Troyes, the twelfth-century French poet who penned many of the original Grail myths, was born in the same town (Troyes, in northern France) which hosted the first council to sanction the Templars.

According to fanciful esoteric lore the Templars came to be associated with relics, and the transmission of secrets connected to these relics. In addition to the Holy Grail, these also include the Lance that allegedly pierced the body of Christ on the cross, and even the Ark of the Covenant. Trained historians do not take these legends seriously, but they remain interesting as metaphors for masculinity in the context of organized warriorhood.

The Templars were synonymous with the Christian Crusades and were never fully separated from that cause. The origins of the Order lay in the First Crusade of 1096–9. In the seventh century Muslim military dominance had resulted in the capture of Jerusalem and the immediate surrounding Levant. For over four centuries this Muslim control held fast, until the First Crusade was launched by French and German pilgrims in late 1095 as directed by Pope Urban II. The crusade to 'take back' Jerusalem became a drawn-out and highly charged *raison d'être* for hundreds of thousands of people spanning two centuries. Here in the politically sensitive early twenty-first century,

over 700 years since the final major Crusade in 1272, the word
'crusade' is associated with cumbersome and toxically dated
religious and socio-political baggage. It has become synonymous
with fanaticism, aggression, lack of empathy, and an anti-Islamic
viewpoint. (A far cry from the nineteenth century, for example,
an era of marked romanticism where the Crusades were
associated with chivalry—as Thomas Keightley put it in his 1846
study of the Templars: 'the very sound of the word Crusades
conjures up in most minds the ideas of waving plumes, gaudy
surcoats, emblazoned shields, with lady's love, knightly honor,
and courteous feats of arms.'[3] To be clear, Keightley, a fine
historian, was not writing this as a statement of what he believed
the Crusades were really about, but rather as a reflection of the
common sentiments of his time—which he called a 'perversion
of truth'.)

For one group of medieval soldiers the Crusades meant much
more and became an opportunity for something else—a rallying
cry for the birth of an organization that had as its ideal a mix
of adventure, courage, and chivalry, along with organizational,
military, and financial competence, and a deeply committed
spiritual life that was based in part on private ritual and
ceremony. It was this latter ritualistic element that became the
stuff of legends and would find its echo in the rumors attached
to more recent secret societies and fraternities such as the
Rosicrucians, Illuminati, and Freemasons.

The First Crusade of 1095 had been preceded by a disastrous
event, the so-called People's Crusade, led by the charismatic priest
'Peter the Hermit' (1050–1115) and his chief lieutenant 'Walter
the Penniless' and comprised of an impatient, overly idealistic,
loosely organized mob. The People's Crusade ultimately
proved to be a disorganized farce. Despite its initial mandate to
recapture the Holy Land it never made it there, instead meeting
its demise in Turkey. This rag-tag army, comprised of men,
women, and even children (along with a small smattering of

legitimate knights), had left Germany, in several distinct bands, some 40,000 strong in early 1096. Four months later most of them arrived in Constantinople, 10,000 of them having failed to make it that far. In Turkey they fell into disarray, unable to feed themselves or attract sufficient support from locals. Many were sold into slavery or slaughtered. Only a few lasted to join with the properly equipped Crusader armies that came behind them and eventually made it to Jerusalem. The 'second wave'—the first legitimate Crusader warriors—followed the people's army and was comprised largely of several small, independent armies. They joined forces with the remnants of the pilgrims and, some 60,000 strong in total, finally made it to the Holy Land by June of 1099. The group that made it to Jerusalem, though its members were depleted in number and their bodies scarred, was battle-hardened, a quality that is invaluable for any warrior and any army and often a decisive factor in battles of uncertain outcome.

The first Crusader victories in Turkey were, according to legend, accompanied by 'providential signs', such as a comet, meteors, visions of angels, and much more pragmatically, a few Muslims surreptitiously aiding Crusaders in the capture of key sites.[4] The actual Battle of Jerusalem lasted only five weeks, ending by July of 1099. The Crusaders were victorious, and promptly divided the Holy Land into four territories. There were chronic problems of manpower in the ensuing years, as the Franks struggled to safeguard their newly won territory. Many Crusaders returned to Europe and an insufficient number of European settlers arrived. The inevitable result was real difficulties in protecting Western pilgrims who came to pay homage at the sacred sites. This was the usual assumed reason for the formation of a secret Order of devoted knights whose sole mission was to protect pilgrims and provide for their safe passage to and from Jerusalem and the Holy Lands.[5]

The first appointed leader of the Order was Hugh de Payens (1070–1136), a Champagne nobleman and member of the Counts of Troyes. Clear historical records of his background are scant. He had been one of a small group of deeply committed and pious knights who had joined forces in Jerusalem over ten years after the First Crusade had ended. These knights were put up by King Baldwin (the first Crusader King of Jerusalem) and given lodgings near the Al-Aqsa Mosque and the alleged site of the original Temple of Solomon (the present-day 'Temple Mount', which remains, almost a millennium later, one of the most highly charged and controversial holy sites in the world). The knights followed a daily regimen that was very similar to monkhood, thus earning the apropos title of 'warrior-monks', finding their parallel in the Muslim Nizari Assassins or (to a lesser degree) the Chinese Shaolin monks. Like monks they made vows of poverty, chastity, and humility, performed daily spiritual practice (in this case, prayers), and had their needs subsidized by the state (in this case, the king). And like real warriors, they were trained, skillful, and fearless in combat.

Including Hugh du Payens there were nine original knights. The Order was unofficially formed in 1119, 20 years after the First Crusade. In 1125 Hugh was given the formal title of Magister Templi ('Master of the Temple'). From 1119 until 1128 the knights operated quietly, wearing simple clothing. The famous white tunic was not added until 1129 when they were publicly recognized and given an official commission by the Council of Troyes, along with their storied title, the 'Order of the Poor Knights of Christ and the Temple of Solomon'. This council— comprised of French and Burgundian bishops and abbots and a papal legate—commissioned Bernard of Clairvaux (1090–1153), the French Cistercian abbot, to draw up a Rule for the Order that was comprised of 72 articles.

A main rule for the knights of the new Order was not to associate with women, a 'purity' symbolized by the white of their tunics (the red cross, the defining symbol of the Templars, was added in 1145 when Pope Eugenius III granted it as a martyrdom symbol). This chastity rule was written in words that were an echo of older ideas around the dangers of sexual temptation—'the ancient enemy has driven many from the right path to Paradise by the society of women'[6]—a warning that was to be elaborated on in more dramatic and misogynistic language three centuries later in the infamous witchcraft polemic *Malleus Maleficarum*. Married men could be associated with the Templars, but could not wear the white tunic. There were initially two grades: knights and sergeants. The latter wore a dark brown or black mantle that denoted their lesser rank. The Order soon grew as recruits were added. Additionally, various grants (mostly land) were received, a key to the Templars' future financial power.

Within a year of their official recognition the Order had some 300 knights. The initial Templars were French but the recruiting campaign involved forays across France, England, and Scotland. The spiritual and philosophic basis of the Order was given literary expression by Bernard, whose screed 'In Praise of the New Knighthood' was written in 1135 in reply to a request from Hugh de Payens to provide intellectual justification for a monk becoming a warrior (this obviously needed some explaining owing to biblical injunctions such as 'Thou shalt not kill'). Bernard did not write his treatise lightly; he claims in his prologue that Hugh de Payens had asked him three times to write an exhortation for the knights— evidently as early as 1129 owing to morale issues suffered by knights who wondered if their martial life equipped them for salvation[7]—but that he delayed for some time because of the gravity of the task and because he did not want to be perceived as taking it anything less than seriously. Bernard characterized the Templars thusly:

This is, I say, a new kind of knighthood and one unknown to ages gone by. It ceaselessly wages a twofold war both against flesh and blood and against a spiritual army of evil in the heavens.

And in a further passage that in all ways seems indistinguishable from the doctrinal justifications of an Islamic jihadist, Bernard pronounced:

> What a glory to return in victory from such a battle! Rejoice, brave athlete, if you live and conquer in the Lord; but glory and exult even more if you die and join your Lord. Life is indeed a fruitful thing and victory is glorious, but a holy death is more important than either. If they are blessed who die in the Lord, how much more are they who die for the Lord![8]

The idea of warrior-monks was not to take hold exclusively via the Knights Templar, but also to spread across Europe. Over the remainder of the twelfth century new Orders of fighting monks were to appear, including several Spanish Orders and the German Order of the Teutonic Knights. In addition, the older Knights Hospitaller (or Knights of St John), inspired by the Templars, also acquired a military arm. Along with the Templars, the Hospitallers were the primary military force protecting Christian pilgrims during the centuries of the Crusades. They were also responsible for rebuilding, developing, and administering the largest of the famous Crusader castles in the Levant, the Crac de Chevaliers in western Syria (which at its peak in the early thirteenth century housed a garrison of some 2,000 knights).

As the fledgling Templar Order slowly gained in prestige and fame, the seeds of its downfall were also being sown. These lay in the special dispensations issued by the papacy between 1139 and 1145, in which Templars were accorded certain exceptional privileges, such as the right to all spoils gained on the battlefield, the appointing of a Grandmaster who was accountable to none but the pope, as well as certain spiritual rights such as control of their own churches and the burial protocols of their members. In effect, they were slowly becoming an independent state within a state, answerable not to kings, but only to popes. This would ultimately backfire 150 years later when one king (Philip IV) turned against them with deadly consequences.

In addition to their military and political advances, the Templars had extraordinary commercial and financial successes as well. The main ideas of banking—money lending and changing, making deposits, and so forth—did not begin with the Templars, such activities being found, in isolated forms, as far back as Assyria, Babylonia, Rome, Greece, China, and India of antiquity—but the Templars (along with the Hospitallers) were involved in the beginnings of modern banking in Europe throughout the twelfth to fourteenth centuries. This arose, in part, due to security concerns. In order to avoid robbery while traveling across the various highways and wastelands of Europe and the Near East, the Templars used demand notes to represent money, which later grew into the typical bank notes that we recognize today (this applies to the West only; bank notes were invented by the Chinese over four centuries before the Templars).

Heresy and the Fall of the Templars

The demise of the Templars was probably not caused by actual heretical practices. But it certainly was brought about by the *accusations* of heresy leveled against them by King Philip IV. In this connection, it is important to understand the concept of heresy, and with that, its great power to incite fear and trigger punitive acts from those in power. As has been pointed out by historians, witchcraft, sorcery, or black magic, while considered criminal acts and condemned in most of Middle Age Europe, were regarded as of minor significance compared to the danger presented by heretics.[9] It was thought that a witch or magician consorting with dark forces could cause great mischief, but only in a limited sense. A heretic, however, was potentially far more troublesome as he struck at the very root of the ruling religion and its influence on royalty and politics. The term 'heretic', from the Greek *hairesis* ('choosing'), originally meant any philosophical, political, or religious doctrine that opposed the dogmas of the Catholic Church. At the time of the arrest of the Templars in October of 1307 the situation facing convicted heretics was grim. To be accused of heresy was like being accused of treason, and the results were also similar — all the more so if the group accused had prestige and wielded considerable power and influence.

The reputation of the Templar Knights as great fighters was reinforced by certain of their victories, such as the battle of Montgisard (in present-day Israel) of 1177. Reminiscent of the Spartans' Battle of Thermopylae — only different in that the Templars were victorious — they were massively outnumbered by a force of Mamluks led by Saladin — the numbers recorded were 375 Templars versus over 25,000 Mamluks. These numbers are almost certainly not reliable, but they do give some hint as to the courage and tenacity of the well-trained Templars and their purpose as fighting men driven by a (in their minds) divine purpose.

The 'spiritual warfare' element of the Templars was articulated by Bernard in 1135 when he wrote:

A Templar Knight is truly a fearless knight…his soul is protected by his armor of faith, just as his body is protected by the armor of steel. He is thus doubly armed, and need fear neither demons nor men.

The fall of the Templars was connected to more than just accusations of heresy, of course. The prime cause was internal conflicts as well as the rising power of Muslim armies, leading to the ultimate failure of the Crusades. The Templars lost Jerusalem in 1187 to Saladin. The Holy City was regained by Crusaders (without the Templars) in 1229, whereupon it was lost a final time in 1244 to the Turks. The Templars gradually retreated from the Holy Land following a series of further military setbacks, culminating in 1302 with a final loss to the Mamluks in present-day western Syria.

As their military purpose faded, the Templars declined in popularity and lost much of their political support. They remained a powerful, legendary, and somewhat mysterious organization however, with privileges of wealth and status envied by many, not least of whom was King Philip IV. The last Grandmaster of the Templars, Jacques de Molay (1243–1314), was tortured and burned to death by Philip under the pretext of heresy. The actual reason was that the king was deeply in financial debt to the Templars; this, combined with the general unpopularity of the Templars by the early 1300s, led to the king's decision to destroy them and appropriate their wealth.

Mining the Virtues of the Knights Templar

Shorn of their fanaticism, brutality, and racism, the Knights Templar had noble intentions buried in the mix. These intentions were related to the idea of *teamwork in the service of a greater cause.* The cause in this case is hard to justify, let alone respect, as it was rooted so thoroughly in prejudice and the belief that one's religion or god is superior to another, with no consideration for the merits of these 'others' at all. Certainly, there was much to reject in the Knights Templar. However, the energy mustered in the face of encountering difficulties is virtuous in and of itself, and the Knights Templar did encounter extraordinary difficulties in mounting their original crusades. These difficulties were surmounted only via the power of focused intent and cooperative teamwork. No adventure for a higher cause has any hope of success if it is populated by self-centered men who lack the ability to operate as a team.

Of course, horrific events in history have been engineered by excellent teammates, so teamwork in and of itself means little if not supported by a framework of truly worthy ideas and intentions. Most modern men *do* have easy access to worthy ideas and noble causes, however. What they more often lack is the ability to function effectively on a team. A joint venture can be a powerful and exciting thing, or it can be annoyingly stifling. If the venture is worthy, then it will likely be experienced as 'annoyingly stifling' only by one who lacks the ability to function as a teammate.

The question must also be asked, how is killing in the name of a god (or in the case of the Templars, Jesus) justified? By at least *some* modern sensibilities this seems impossible. But for the Crusaders the moral and religious justification arose from the belief that a 'crusade' was ultimately a defensive act—that is, it was based on righting a historical wrong (the same position that has always been, and continues to be, the motivating justification for revolutionaries, tyrants, terrorists, or any leader or group that decides something must be done about a major historical injustice).

The other factor at play is that for some Templars the Crusades were also regarded as acts of penance. By warring and even killing for Jesus a Crusader could discharge himself of personal sins and thus achieve redemption or even salvation, so he believed.

For twenty-first-century educated men such ideas will seem crude, not to mention dangerous. But more useful is to examine our own personal prejudices that remain—if our way of viewing things, be that religious, atheistic, political, or from whatever viewpoint, necessitates dismissing or condemning the viewpoints of others. We are always learning to expand our capacity for tolerance and empathy, while at the same time not abandoning boundaries or a common-sense approach to safety and security. This is what it means to be a warrior with heart.

The Mongols

The average person of current times who has not studied history in any serious fashion may be surprised to learn of just how big the Mongol Empire was at its peak in the thirteenth and fourteenth centuries. It ranks first in history as the largest continuous empire on land, at its greatest reach spanning from the eastern borders of present-day Germany and Austria to Korea and the Sea of Japan, with most of the entirety of Asia (except for India and parts of southeast Asia) falling within its realm. From 1206 to 1370 it was ruled by a series of seven Great Khans, the most renowned being the first, Genghis Khan (1167?–1227) along with his son Ogedei Khan (1186–1241) and his grandson Kublai Khan (1215–94).

The Mongols were the ultimate conquerors, although how exactly they accomplished what they did — minus any significant military technologies beyond the bow and arrow along with the steeds they rode on — remains something of a mystery to historians. One thing is certain and that is that their first supreme warlord, Genghis Khan, must have had extraordinary charisma, force of presence, and political acumen to bring together the nomadic and unruly tribes of the rugged Mongolian steppe grasslands. This unification of his own people was perhaps his greatest accomplishment, and undoubtedly the main key behind his subsequent wildly successful military campaigns.

Mongol tribal culture was not based entirely on blood-relations, but also on the concept of *anda*, or 'sworn brotherhood'. This bonding of warriors not of the same family was a key to Genghis's successes in unifying the tribes — in addition to being a courageous warrior he was also an astute politician. Add to that, the Mongols had the concept of what they called the *nöker*, a term that was originally closer to 'comrade' or 'associate'. Over time it came to denote 'follower' and eventually 'slave'.[10] The original meaning of the word suggests further hints into the factors that lay behind the Mongol military successes. A wise leader understands how to empower his lieutenants. Hierarchy functions best when those in the pecking order feel important in their role, as they have a greater vested interest in performing with excellence.

The *nöker* system, whereby a particular leader could gain aides and associates and 'brothers' to his cause, was central to the young Genghis Khan's rise to power. The central point of it was that a personally impressive and charismatic young leader, who had no particular political pedigree or connections, could attract 'associates' from rival clans and tribes merely on the basis of his personal connections with them. This was an important step in the transition of the Mongolian steppe tribes from small, bickering groups whose loyalty was based largely on blood-relations, into a large, powerful organization based preeminently on individual quality or merit.

Mongol warlords had to earn the respect and confidence of their followers; their rank and position was not always hereditary, and even when it was, they could easily lose their position via displays of weakness and incompetence. In addition, they had a relationship with their officers and soldiers that was remarkably mature: all their orders were to be obeyed without question, but only in wartime. During peacetime, they did not meddle in the lives of their men, requiring only that their followers not act in ways that were counter to the warlord's greater purposes and interests. In this way, the Mongol warlord avoided the complications and problems of a full-fledged personality cult.

Nevertheless, Genghis Khan cannot be called a completely self-made man. He was in fact born into the noble class, around 1167. He was given the name Temujin. His father, Yesugei, was a minor warlord and was killed by Tatars when Temujin was nine years old. Young Temujin and his family were then abandoned by their father's followers and left to scratch out a bare existence. Rival tribes had the opportunity to kill the young future Khan, but for unknown reasons opted not to do so. Temujin rose to power gradually by establishing himself as a courageous young warrior, and then using his natural political acumen, as well as his legitimate claim of noble blood, to draw other warriors to his standard. All this was possible because of the lack of a central ruling tribe or governing body at that time.

The transformation of young Temujin into the powerful leader known as Genghis Khan was not overnight. His path was full of drama, treachery, intrigue, and finally, triumph. By the year 1206 when the dust had settled, one of the major tribes (the Tatars) had been largely wiped out, and another, the Merkits (who had kidnapped Genghis's main wife), were similarly decimated. All the other tribes were simply absorbed. The late twentieth-century TV show *Star Trek* featured a particularly powerful alien race known as the 'Borg'. Their main motto was 'resistance is futile—you will be assimilated'. That part of Borg philosophy was in some ways a sci-fi dystopian version of the thirteenth-century Mongols. Genghis Khan had a particular savvy that recognized the value of assimilating cultures so as to add to his war machine. However, he did not stop from obliterating those that refused to submit to his rule.

At around 40 years of age, and made Great Khan of all the tribes of Mongolia, Genghis was fully armed with a powerful battle force comprised of his unified tribes. He merely had to use this force in some fashion—if he didn't, there was every possibility that it would sooner rather than later become unstable due to infighting. Like a gang of restless gladiators his fighting men needed a cause and an opponent to justify their unification with each other.[11] That first opponent was to be China.

At that time China was not a unified nation. It, much like the Mongolia of Genghis's early years, was split into three regions—the Chin Empire of the north, the Hsi-Hsia (mainly of Tibetan stock) in the north-west, and the Sung Empire of the south. Of these three the Sung was the most developed culturally; its city of Hangzhou (just south of present-day Shanghai) was at that time probably the most advanced and populous city on the planet.[12] The northern Chin Empire was the most problematic—they had every incentive to undermine Genghis's hold on power— and so they were the first natural target. However, the decision was made to attack the northwestern Hsi-Hsia instead as they were a lesser opponent, providing a good practice run, and affording the strategic advantage of another entry route to the Chin. The Hsi-Hsia government was overrun in 1209, although not destroyed (they were 'assimilated'). The Chin Empire was then assaulted in 1211, but they proved no easy foe to conquer. The campaign against them stretched out for some 23 years. In our era of modern warfare where powerful technologies tend to make for shorter wars (exceptions such as the various Afghan wars notwithstanding) it may be hard to imagine just how much suffering and carnage a war that lasts for a quarter of a century can involve.

Those familiar with the antiquity of northern China's 'Great Wall' may wonder how the Mongols breached it. Construction on the Great Wall began as early as the seventh century BCE, and by 206 BCE—some 1,400 years before Genghis Khan—large sections had already been built. However, in the thirteenth century CE when Genghis was launching his attacks on northern China much of the old walls had crumbled; the newer sections, and most of what we see today, were not built until the Ming Dynasty of the fourteenth to sixteenth centuries, largely in response to the incursions of Genghis Khan's successors.

The Mongols captured Beijing in 1215 but the overall conquest of China was slow and Genghis Khan was involved in Western campaigns as well. Many of the Chin Empire defected to the Mongolian side when it was clear that their defeat was inevitable. Meanwhile Genghis had established an uneasy friendship with a powerful Muslim civilization to the west (in present-day Uzbekistan). After a serious breach of diplomatic outreach (the Muslims killed one of Genghis's ambassadors over a dispute about alleged Mongol spies), the Mongols attacked and quickly conquered them—in an evidently violent and unforgiving fashion—and thus began the gradual expansion of Genghis Khan's empire westward, as well as the birth of his fearsome reputation to those of the West who remained within the path of his armies.

After a further decade of Mongol conquests of Islamic cultures in Central Asia, Genghis Khan returned home to Mongolia in 1223. Now around 60 years old and doubtless weary, he nevertheless remained ever the conqueror, devoting his last years to the full subjugation of the northwest Chinese government. At his death in 1227 he stood as one of the most successful military commanders in history, comparable to Alexander the Great, although Genghis's conquests went on for almost twice as long as Alexander's.

A successful warlord is also a ruthless warlord, exercising brutality, often fueled by a desire for vengeance as much as territory or booty, to a degree perhaps hard to fathom for a modern man whose main adventures take place in front of his flat-screen TV on his couch armed with beer and potato chips. Emperors such as Genghis Khan dominated and ruled in such a fashion as to inspire fear in most of those who happened to be in his path. In was not uncommon for entire centers of population to capitulate even before his armies loosed their first arrows. In the end the records of contemporary historians suggest that his invasions in Central Asia and China killed millions of people, and although some modern historians believe these numbers may be somewhat inflated, he and his Mongol armies were without question among the most fearsome and destructive forces in history.

The so-called *Pax Mongolica* lasted for over a century after Genghis Khan's death in 1227, until about the year 1350. To give some idea of just how vast this roughly formed empire was at its peak in the late thirteenth century, it encompassed the land area of no fewer than 38 present-day nations. Astonishingly, no Mongol army was ever defeated on the field in direct combat until 1260, when in present-day Israel a Muslim Mamluk force overcome a Mongol army, thus preventing the Mongol Empire from expanding through the Middle East into Egypt. (This famous battle, known as *Ain Jalut*, involved the first known usage of primitive firearms, called 'hand cannons'; in this case, by the Mamluks, mainly to frighten the Mongol horses with explosive sounds.)

As might be expected, the *Pax Mongolica* reign was not especially stable, with battles of succession commonplace, including civil wars. Genghis was succeeded by his son Ogedei, who ruled from 1229 to 1241. At Ogedei's death his wife ruled as regent from 1241 to 1246. Ogedei's eldest son Guyuk Khan then ruled for just two years until his death in 1248; Guyuk's wife then ruled as regent until 1251, whereupon Mongke Khan (from a rival bloodline) was elected Great Khan and ruled until 1259 (conquering Iraq and Syria while he was at it). Genghis Khan's famed grandson Kublai Khan then assumed power in 1260. Kublai's reign was long, until 1294; during that time, he successfully conquered all of China, and was established as Emperor of China alongside his status as Great Khan of the Mongol Empire. In 1271 Kublai founded the Yuan Dynasty, the first foreign-run empire of China. It lasted nearly a century, until 1368. During his life, Kublai established two main capitals: one on the spot of present-day Beijing, and the other in Inner Mongolia (*Shang-tu*, or Xanadu) which was visited by Marco Polo in 1275 and became the focus of the famous poem (written in 1797) by the English Romantic poet Samuel Taylor Coleridge.

Kublai Khan's successors were not as successful as he, although one of them, Toghon Temur, did rule for 37 years. The Yuan Dynasty founded by Kublai collapsed in 1368, after which the Chinese resumed control of their territories.

Reasons for Military Success and Decline of the Mongols

It's acknowledged by most historians that while Mongol armies were large—in the order of hundreds of thousands of soldiers—they were not as large as some of the Muslim armies to their west, or those of the Chinese emperors.[13] And yet they defeated these battle forces of superior size. How did they do it? Apart from their efficient organization and powerful bows constructed from horn and wood, they were also highly resourceful, using whatever their immediate possibilities provided. One technique was to overrun a town, then use some of the captured soldiers of that town as the front line of their next assault on a second nearby town, the logic being that those of the second town would be reluctant to kill these front-line soldiers who were their compatriots.

The Mongols were, in effect, accomplished at psychological warfare. The main technique they seemed to employ was terror by reputation. When conquering a city, they would be so thorough and ruthless in their destruction that word was soon spread, resulting in numerous towns and cities surrendering wholesale before the Mongols fired an arrow. They thus achieved, on many occasions, Sun Tzu's prime recommendation to win battles without fighting. (As has been pointed out by historians, President Truman used a similar—if far more destructive—approach at the end of the Second World War; rather than risk immense numbers of American casualties by invading Japan he opted to drop two atomic bombs on Hiroshima and Nagasaki, sufficiently intimidating the stubborn Japanese so that they agreed to surrender before the invasion.)[14]

Warlord–Guru Relationship with Tibet

The Mongols were also influential in the fate of Tibetan Buddhism. Tibet, as with Mongolia and Siberia, was originally the home of various forms of shamanism stretching back to ancient times. Buddhism was introduced into Tibet around the ninth century CE, and eventually spread to China and further east. It was adopted in part by the Mongols of the thirteenth and fourteenth centuries, before being once again superseded by indigenous shamanistic traditions. However, by the sixteenth century Altan Khan, ruler of what remained of the Mongol Empire, formed a unique relationship with the spiritual leaders of Tibetan Buddhism. The Gelugpa or so-called 'Yellow Hat' sect, founded around 1400 by the famed Buddhist master and scholar Tsongkhapa, was adopted by Altan Khan in 1578 when he was initiated into the tradition by Sonam Gyatso, senior master of the sect. Altan then awarded Sonam Gyatso with the title of 'Dalai Lama'—he was to be the third, with his two predecessors being conferred the first and second Dalai Lama titles respectively—so beginning a lineage that exists to this day in the person of the famed fourteenth Dalai Lama, Tenzin Gyatso (b. 1935).

It has also been pointed out that the Mongols of the thirteenth and 14th centuries, despite their occasional flirtation with Buddhism or Taoism, were largely irreligious or shamanistic, and thus were free of high moral imperatives or the orientation toward what the historian John Keegan called 'concerns with mercy' or 'personal perfection'.[15] The decline of the Mongols by the sixteenth century is usually ascribed to some key military defeats (especially as inflicted by the Mamluks) and to the limitations of a horse-based culture, but the adoption of pacifist Tibetan Buddhism by Altan Khan cannot have been said to be supportive of the aggressive conquests of other people. Trying to imagine the current Dalai Lama beside Genghis Khan would be a study in contrasts, to put it mildly. One would have to change for both to work together, and according to history, it was not the Dalai Lamas who changed. In short, it can be said that many of the Mongols eventually came to adopt a more advanced form of warriorhood—conquest of one's mind.

Mining the Virtues of the Mongols

Outstanding traits of the Mongol warriors were battlefield cooperation, loyalty to a comrade, fierceness and endurance, mental fortitude, strategic intelligence, and (as counter-intuitive as this may sound) tolerance of others (via not enforcing religious doctrines on their conquered cultures).

As touched on in the discussion of the Knights Templar, battlefield cooperation—the ability to do 'good teamwork'—is an essential aspect of masculine nature precisely because of the masculine tendency to lean toward competitive individualism. Men need to learn how to cooperate with each other, thus countering their deep competitive instincts.

It's naturally difficult for modern men to grasp the higher principles of marauding warriors such as those who made up the Mongol hordes, as brutal and fearsome as they were in their combined military force. Masculine force in its more aggressive forms can be likened to electricity, a neutral power to be used to some end. It can be destructive, creative, or protective. Many of the warriors of the past, be they the Spartans, Knights Templar, or Mongols, as products of their times clearly used this power toward destructive ends. Men of the twenty-first century face different challenges, but that doesn't mean that the sword must be thrown into Hades never to be seen again. Rather, the sword must be refashioned and directed toward forging a life full of passion and the capacity to engage in meaningful and powerful teamwork.

Chapter 4

A Brief History of Warrior Cultures: Part II

The Shaolin Monks

In 1972 an American TV show appeared that was utterly unlike anything presented in that entertainment medium before. Called simply *Kung Fu* and starring an American actor in his mid-thirties named David Carradine (1936–2009), it lasted for three years before being cancelled in 1975. Two decades later a reboot of the show was made (*Kung Fu: The Legend Continues*, 1993–7), where Carradine played an aged kung fu master who was the grandson of the Kwai Chang Caine character that he'd played in the original series, but most agreed that the reboot didn't match the quality and originality of the 1970s show.

Kung Fu was not just about a master of that particular martial art, but a very particular master: a Shaolin monk. It's safe to say that in the early 1970s few North Americans, outside of certain martial art circles, were aware of the illustrious history of the Shaolin temple and its extraordinary masters of hand to hand combat.

The Shaolin temple is a real place. It is a Chan (Zen) Buddhist temple in Dengfeng county, within Zhengzhou (a large city in the Honan province of east-central China). Dengfeng is near Mount Song, one of China's most sacred places of pilgrimage. In addition to the Shaolin temple the area also is home to Taoist and Confucian centers of practice and learning.

The Shaolin temple has a history that stretches back some 1,500 years. This history invariably mentions the legendary patriarch of Chan Buddhism, Bodhidharma, who sometime around the year 500 CE is reputed to have traveled from India (his alleged country of birth) to eastern China, where he ended up in Zhengzhou. According to the legend Bodhidharma spent many years in solitary meditation at the Shaolin temple before accepting a disciple, to whom he eventually transmitted his teachings. The more fanciful legends attached to this event have the disciple demanding a reluctant Bodhidharma to teach him, only to be refused. The disciple then cuts off his hand and throws it at the master, to which Bodhidharma replies with words to the effect of 'ah, so you have finally come', and proceeds to accept him as his first disciple. The moral of course being that only extreme commitment can demonstrate the worthiness to be instructed by a great teacher.

The legend of Bodhidharma is not just inseparable from the Shaolin temple, it is also closely connected to the history of kung fu. Modern critical scholarship sees little but myth in the story of Bodhidharma, some even questioning whether he existed. Myth however can be as potent as historical fact, if not more so. The legends attached to Bodhidharma's life are fanciful, reflecting the human tendency to embellish and imagine, borne out in the tales of most founding figures of ancient traditions. However, hidden within all the fancy and romance are teachings, which if interpreted usefully, can yield profound insights.

According to the legends Bodhidharma was also supposed to have transmitted or invented certain physical exercises—which eventually grew into Asian martial arts as we've come to know them—to keep the monks active and physical. All these legends have several problems, not least of which is that there is no record of Chan Buddhism in China before the eighth century CE (a few centuries *after* Bodhidharma).[1] Far more likely is that Bodhidharma was the recipient of the age-old practice of attributing teachings and doctrines to certain quasi-mythical individuals (a very common practice in the West as well, via figures such as King Solomon or Hermes Trismegistus, who were credited with having written all sorts of esoteric doctrines that were certainly not written by them. The concept of 'intellectual property' didn't develop until the seventeenth century, and remained rudimentary until the twentieth century).

The person of Bodhidharma may not stand up that well to historical analysis, but the legends associated with the martial arts he was credited with starting are certainly rooted in physical realities. Shaolin temple is known to have originally been a center for swordsmanship. The name Shaolin derives from Shao Shi, which is a mountain peak that is part of the Song mountains. This association with a mountain is revealing, in that one of the legends ascribed to Bodhidharma was his extraordinary discipline in meditation—to, effectively, sit like a mountain, grounded and focused. The mountain is often associated with the masculine polarity, with the solidity and steadfastness central to the healthy masculine core. In Hindu tradition, Shiva, the masculine expression of the divine, is thought to dwell on top of a mountain (Mt Kailash in Tibet). The expression 'Mountain Man' suggests a rugged masculine individualist, and the quasi-phallic form of mountains themselves relates not just to form but also to the idea of masculine connections with the element of air, fire, rising force (volcanoes) and 'rising' consciousness, in contrast to classic feminine associations with water, earth, the body, nesting, and the instinctive.

The Shaolin monastery that exists now is not the original. The monastery has been rebuilt numerous times. Around 1355 the monastery was laid waste during the so-called Red Turban Rebellion, and three centuries after that it was sacked again. In both cases the fighting monks were decimated by bandits and government forces respectively, a sobering dose of reality to counter fanciful notions of trained fighters who are immune to defeat in combat. It is a hard truth that all warriors and armies sooner or later face defeat (or at the last, aging and fading away).

Shaolin monastery teachings and methods migrated to parts of Japan in the 1700s, shaping and influencing certain of the karate schools. In some ways this pattern followed the transmission of Chan Buddhism from China to Japan (where it became known as

Zen). This connection is important because Shaolin philosophy cannot really be understood without grasping the basics of Zen.

Zen as a teaching developed when the brilliant idealism of Indian Buddhism met the pragmatic nature of Chinese culture, resulting in an approach to enlightenment that focused more on the importance of practice and direct experience, over theory and cosmology. When the Japanese added their contribution to the mix, the pragmatic and simplistic elements of Zen were developed further, resulting in the classic schools of Zen we know today. Of course, Shaolin was Chinese, not Japanese, but the elements of Chan (Zen) found in their philosophy lent themselves well to fighting systems that were based on a deep understanding and harmony between the mind, body, and forces of nature.

Shaolin philosophy, having been birthed in China, was naturally influenced by Taoism as well, incorporating Taoist ideas and teachings connected to the cultivation of chi energy (life force), the alchemy of yin-yang (the significance and resolution of opposites), and the transcendent wisdom of Lao Tzu's classic *Tao Te Ching* (considered by some the most sublime doctrine ever penned on the teachings of spiritual enlightenment). As is common in most wisdom traditions, two strands developed from Taoist philosophy, one concerned with the purity of spiritual transcendence, the other more focused on the practicality of controlling elements of one's life and one's world (via teachings of alchemy and magic). Shaolin philosophy was, to some extent, influenced by both of these strands. The 'darker' forms of Shaolin teaching, utilizing cultivated mind-powers to influence events or harm enemies, was likely part of the roots of ninja training in Japan in later centuries.

The Shaolin temple was destroyed and rebuilt numerous times between 1300 and 1800, with the exact history being difficult to trace (historians rarely agree on the details). But in a sense the historical confusion is appropriate, as Shaolin is really an 'inner school' more than anything, despite its real objective existence. Legends of the Tibetan land of Shamballa, or even the Western Rosicrucians and Illuminati, while mainly literary and fantastical, carry significance inasmuch as they point seekers toward the inner realities, and the importance of cultivating qualities of character and being, above all else. Both Zen and Taoism are concerned with inner development, and Shaolin, as a training school for fighters, is unique in its insistence on basing martial development on inner growth and harmony.

Mining the Virtues of the Shaolin Monks

Extracting the gold from the lead, in the case of the Shaolin monks, is not a difficult task. Shaolin monks, while not comic book characters of moral and physical perfection, nevertheless represented one of the more advanced systems of masculine development that combined a rugged discipline with advanced training in meditation and philosophic wisdom. In this connection it's useful to make some observations about the TV version of the Shaolin monk touched on above, the character Kwai Chang Caine from the early 1970s show.

As rendered by David Carradine, Caine was a man of many admirable qualities. He had an essentially peaceful disposition, due mainly to his meditation and moral training. He was a manifestly good man, a kind of Robin Hood minus the 'stealing from the rich' part—although he would many times play the protector of the poor and weak against powerful or ignoble authorities. He was a man of superb physical condition and— although his walking only barefoot was obviously overdone for TV drama—his attention to detail in diet and communion with Nature reflected the ideals of the man who lives a quintessentially healthy life. He was gentle but extremely powerful and even deadly when he had to be. He was never vengeful, and forgiving by nature. He was curious and capable of humor.

There was, however, another side to Caine as was portrayed

by Carradine that does not necessarily hold up so well as a model for modern men. It has to do, ironically, with his moral virtue. Put simply, he was too good to be true. When men push that hard to be that pure, they run the risk of repression of their darker nature. By 'darker' I refer here not to moral quality, but rather to natural expression and embodiment of *desire*. The problem with simplistically applying some of the grander Eastern philosophies (Buddhism and Hindu yoga, mainly) to a Western life based on the need to work and form relationships is that the idea of 'desire' as problematic gets too easily misused.

When the Buddha referred to 'desire' (or 'craving') as being the major impediment to enlightenment, he didn't mean that we should divide ourselves in two (the good and the bad), followed by some artificial attempt to repress, deny, or ignore the bad. He was pointing rather to the profound idea that desire is based on being fundamentally ignorant of our true nature, which is already connected to all things (and thus, in theory, 'desire-less'). However, this understanding is only possible for one who is already psychologically healthy, not given to denying or repressing elements of their nature. Most modern men (and women) are not living from that natural place, but rather from a more conflicted and divided mindset that has them struggling against their natural desires (see the work of the early twentieth-century novelist Herman Hesse for many good treatments of this issue in his characters).

The Shaolin monk as an archetype of the warrior-mystic is a tremendously appealing image to aspire to, for so many reasons. But modern Western men need always to be mindful about any tendency to artificially repress their 'inner beast' in the service of attaining the sublime heights of the true warrior-mystic. Understanding the psychology of the modern man and his need to remain balanced, is the necessary foundation for developing the admirable wisdom of the true Shaolin conscious warrior.

The Samurai

The word 'samurai' has an etymological origin that might surprise those who associate it with fierce and independent warriors. It derives from the Japanese term *saburau* and originally had to do with the idea of devoted and loyal service to the noble class, a type of specialized karma yoga, accompanied by key skills (mostly related to protection). The word *saburau* eventually came to be pronounced as 'saburai', and then 'samurai'. A samurai was, therefore, both a servant and a warrior—in principle, a warrior who served a noble cause (although, it goes without saying that the people or person he served may, on occasion, have been anything but noble).

Samurai were given a popular boost of Hollywood star power via Tom Cruise's role in the 2003 film *The Last Samurai* (though many would argue that it was Ken Watanabe's charismatic presence as the samurai lord, along with Hiroyuki Sanada as his brave and loyal captain, who anchored the movie). Historical quibbles notwithstanding, the movie did a good service in representing the samurai as a three-fold figure: courageous and accomplished fighter, a fierce loyalist to his cause, and spiritual man (he regularly meditated) who also had a love of the arts and the omnipresent beauty of Nature. Melodramatic romanticism aside (and the movie did have that) it was a clear and moving statement about the old values of honor and discipline in the face of modern deadly technology and the less than honorable men who too often wield it.

Japanese mythology is closely intertwined with martial symbolism. Legend has it that the entire country was created by a weapon—a spear wielded by the god Izanagi and the goddess Izanami. They thrust the spear into the ocean, and upon lifting it, four drops fell into the sea and formed the islands of Japan. The descendants of the current race of Japanese occupying the islands arrived about three thousand years ago, although where they came from is still a matter of speculation (Asia, Korea, or the south Pacific). There was an indigenous population already there (the Ainu) who were soon conquered and pushed to the northern island.

The samurai have their roots in the feudalism of Japan's past, taking form during the reign of the first recognized shogun, Minamoto no Yoritomo (1147–99). It was during this time that the professional class of warriors, the samurai, truly came into their own. In several respects they were parallels of the knights of Middle Age Europe of that same time. The golden age of the samurai lasted until around the middle of the fifteenth century. Much like the Mongols of that time their main weaponry consisted of the simple bow and arrow, wielded with deadly accuracy and speed. The period from the sixteenth to the early seventeenth century involved a great deal of domestic warfare as Japan shifted from a tribal society ruled by warlords to a unified nation, which naturally involved struggle and bloodshed as the changes were resisted. Guns made their appearance at this time, intensifying the overall bellicosity of feuding clans, although the samurai code was interpreted at the time as requiring the rejection of guns.

The warrior-clans who originally dominated Japanese culture promoted certain values that later became synonymous with the legend of the samurai. First among these was deep loyalty, especially to their leaders. The second was a remarkable courage in battle that was based crucially on the 'never retreat' discipline. This 'discipline' can of course be severely double edged: either decisively brave or maniacally suicidal. But it forms the essential attitude of the samurai brand of the warrior.

These twin qualities of loyalty and utter fearlessness were married to a third, that of a refined sense of aesthetics. Samurai warriors have always been unique in their sense of artistry, from their elaborate dress and armor to their appreciation of various forms of art and writing, to their traditional association with the bamboo flute. This latter instrument perhaps captures the ideal of the 'inner samurai' as much as anything: solitary, soulful, and in tune with the softer rhythms of Nature—even as the 'outer samurai' brandished his weapons and bristled with a pit bull-like eagerness and readiness for battle.

These are of course ideals. The real samurai was an imperfect human being. Much as many accomplished Zen masters got caught up in the politics of Japan's involvement in the great wars of the twentieth century, so too did the samurai of old get entangled in the politics and tribalism that drove much of Japanese history.

In some respect the samurai were the very embodiment of romanticism, in that they held fast to old and cherished values and often refused to relinquish them even in the face of sweeping modern changes. The best example of that occurred in the sixteenth century when gunpowder and firearms became openly available in Japan. The samurai resisted the new technology and conspired to remove the firearms from the country and keep them out for over two centuries, during which time the samurai and his iconic two swords—perhaps the ultimate symbols of masculine power—remained sovereign over the land.[2]

Bushido and the Code of the Samurai

Bushido is the warrior code of the samurai, similar in some respects to the English term 'chivalry' (especially as it applied to European knights of the Middle Ages). The word itself translates as 'military-knight-ways' or more simply as 'the way of the warrior'. Bushido applied to not just any warrior, but rather to aristocratic warriors, and the ways in which these warriors should comport themselves when not engaged in battle. The French expression *noblesse oblige* is key here; meaning 'nobility obliges' it refers to the importance of living up to one's station in life—earning it, by demonstrating quality behavior and good works in the world, thereby showing that one has gone beyond mere entitlement.[3]

There were many tracts and codes written in the last millennia on Bushido and samurai ethics. One of the more well-known of these is Daidoji Yuzan's *Code of the Samurai*, written in the sixteenth century. Yuzan was himself a samurai as well as a military strategist and advisor. His work was first translated into English in the early 1940s. Although not as renowned as Sun Tzu's *Art of War* it has held equal value and influence on military men over the centuries.

The Samurai code—Bushido, the Way of the Warrior—has been most commonly represented by two preliminary points and eight general points:

A. Awareness of Death. The key defining feature of a samurai warrior was thought to be his ever-vigilant stance, and a perpetual awareness of his mortality. This kept him sharp, alert, on purpose, excellent in his performance, and humble.

B. Contemplation. A samurai warrior held much in common with a Zen monk, such as marked abilities in focus, concentration, and discipline. A warrior who was tuned into his deep spiritual nature, and the cosmos around him, was far more advanced than one who merely mastered the physical martial arts.

1. Integrity. Sometimes this word is rendered as 'rectitude', 'justice', or 'knowing right from wrong'. The modern expression of it is 'do the right thing'. It was thought to be the most important of all qualities for a samurai to exercise. Bushido itself was defined as this quality, so important was it regarded. It included, naturally, the understanding of when was the right time to die, not simply when it was right to do something for one's advantage.

2. Courage. This is not a blind courage. It is courage backed by clarity and understanding of what is right in each moment.

(Hence the importance of point 1 of the Code.) For example, to see what is right and to fail to do it is symptomatic of the opposite of courage, cowardice.

3. Compassion and Mercy. A true warrior is not cruel. The greater his skill and power in life, the greater is his need to demonstrate mercy and compassion.

4. Politeness. This kind of behavior is easily misunderstood as affected or inauthentic, but in fact to be courteous—to treat others well—is a form of empathy and reflects higher spiritual awareness that one is ultimately not separate from anything, even one's enemy.

5. Honesty and Sincerity. This typically referred to the importance of a samurai shunning greed and materialism. He was not expected to understand the ways of commerce or business, but if he did, was expected to be humble, simple, and to disdain unnecessary wealth.

6. Honor. A samurai was expected to conduct himself with dignity. He was not to be too reactive or to get involved in petty matters. He was encouraged to associate with those of similar lofty character. For those reasons, he was encouraged to not form friendships casually, in case he became entangled with small-minded affairs.

7. Loyalty. This was originally meant as loyalty to one's samurai superiors—to honor the chain of command—but applies also in the general sense of being loyal to a good and just cause greater than oneself.

8. Character and Restraint. The character and restraint spoken of here represented, for the samurai, an absolute moral code, having its roots in an understanding of right and wrong that was beyond intellectual debate. This 'moral code' was not a mere doctrine, however; it rather had its basis in a refined and developed sense of what was right for any given situation.

Mining the Virtues of the Samurai

As with the Shaolin monks, mining the virtues of the samurai is not difficult, if only because the samurai character was very black and white, lacking in ambiguity. 'Kill or be killed'—the essential battle cry of the samurai—is not any shade of gray. Such a code has no chance of working *literally* in the life of a conscious warrior (barring, obviously, exceptional circumstances). But as a metaphor it is very powerful. 'Kill or be killed'—or 'never retreat and take no prisoners'—can be understood as a profound commitment to one's life and work in which the key feature is *totality*. This totality is sometimes summed up in the modern two-word expression 'all in'. To be *all in* is to be so committed that all escape hatches are sealed and all run-away bridges burned. It is a discipline of mind in which one is utterly committed to true effort and a refusal to allow apathy, fear, thoughts of unworthiness, thoughts of giving up for fear of failure or of what others will think of you, and so forth, to control one's forward movement.

The 'all in' attitude also makes for a standout teammate. It is disquieting and distracting to operate on a team of any sort all the while doubting the attitude of a colleague. The proverbial weak-link in a company or on a team can be enough to not only cause problems but to sink the entire ship. The samurai attitude of *totality of intent* is an essential piece in the character of the trustworthy warrior and how he operates in community of whatever sort.

The famed loyalty of the samurai is also a prized virtue. In its best sense, it is not a dumb loyalty, blind to the realities under its nose. (To be loyal to an obviously corrupt cause or criminal is what the legal system calls an 'accomplice' and is usually a bad thing.) Loyalty in its purified state is an egoless stance that sees the value in supporting a vital cause, even if it means that one's personal stature is not recognized or rewards for such loyalty are not immediately obvious. (It is here where such loyalty is tested; if rewards are immediate, we have no way finding out how grown up we are.) The male psyche, in its more egotistical manifestations, is inclined toward boasting, exaggerating his value in the eyes of others to inflate his confidence and quash his insecurities. The confidence achieved by boasting is, however, artificial, and sooner or later collapses as the deception is detected by others. True loyalty to a worthy cause is an excellent, and often vitally necessary, antidote to the problems of pride, boasting, and narcissistic tendencies.

The third element of the samurai, his developed aesthetic sense, is a vitally important element for a conscious warrior because it prevents him from becoming out of balance (hyper-masculine). A hyper-masculine man has disconnected inner centers (his mental, emotional, and physical bodies). His emotional body is not well developed. He is out of touch with his human side and struggles to relate to people from a position of equality. He tends to impose his mental or physical centers on others, seeking to dominate in some fashion. By developing some aesthetic sensibilities, the conscious warrior stands a better chance of achieving a harmonious balance between his inner centers. That, in turn, will tend to be positively reflected in his outer relationships.

Covert Warriors: Ninja and Black Ops

The ninja were the stealth warriors of Japan. They differed from the samurai most notably in ethics, and particularly honor, which was essentially irrelevant to their purpose. They were trained mercenaries, spies, and assassins. Their prime function was gaining intelligence against enemies and when necessary, quietly eliminating them.

Throughout history the ninja underwent something of a transformation in the eyes of the public. Although they were chiefly hired assassins, with their decline (around the eighteenth century) their legend shifted more into folklore, and they were re-imagined as more than just assassins: they were dangerous wizards with exceptional powers. Clad in black and covered entirely (except for their eyes) they became in the mind of the average person a symbol of mysterious and rebellious power carrying out appropriate justice, like the fictional Western legends of the Lone Ranger or Batman.

The true history, as usual, is less flattering. Ninja were required in Japan because the samurai, highly trained in field combat but guided by strict ethical codes of honor, could not be expected by their lords to perform covert warfare operations. For this a different breed of warrior was required—a stealth soldier who was not concerned with giving his opponent a 'fair fight'. His sole objective was to get the deed done no matter how unethical his means.[4]

In some respects, the ninja were the forebears of modern covert ops organizations such as the American CIA and Delta Force, the British MI6, Russia's FSB (formerly the old Soviet KGB), Israel's MOSSAD, or China's Ministry of State Security. The ninja were organized into clans with very structured hierarchy. The main difference between them and more overt military organizations—as it always is with covert ops—was the element of secrecy. Much of their affairs operated on the 'need-to-know' basis, and at times this even included (or excluded, more precisely) their own family members. It was common for a man high up in a ninja clan to operate in such a fashion that his own family was unaware of his espionage activities.

A typical ninja clan was headed by a *jonin*, who was responsible for executive decisions and overarching strategies and agendas. The *jonin's* lieutenants were known as the *chunin*, who were involved in directing the practical business of the organization. The *chunin* in turn oversaw the field agents, known as the *genin*. These were the soldiers who did the actual hands-on dirty work, and are the ones most commonly recognized by the public as ninja.

Ninja soldiers were highly trained in deadly combat techniques, as well as espionage and infiltration tactics. They also on occasion utilized 'Trojan horse' methods such as garbing themselves in the attire of the enemy to escape detection as they infiltrated an enemy location. They were entirely unconcerned with ideas such as 'honor' or ethical codes of combat. Their sole purpose was to undermine, defeat, or destroy an enemy via whatever means necessary.

Accordingly, ninja *modus operandi* was based entirely on stealth and secrecy. Legends of their powers of invisibility had not just to do with their black garments. They had more to do with the ninja's ability to pass undetected, and more to the point, to be a master of disguise. At first glance, it may seem hard to find much worthy of admiration in ninja or covert ops culture of any sort, but to dismiss it as dishonorable, unseemly subterfuge or mere secrecy would involve hasty judgment.

Mining the Virtues of the Ninja

The word 'disguise' literally means to change one's guise, that is, to alter one's appearance. In covert ops, this is done for deception. However, there is another realm in which changing one's appearance is not only a good thing but is sometimes necessary to function effectively in the world. Castaneda in his works referred to this idea as 'changing routines' or 'erasing personal history'. Gurdjieff referred to it in what he called the way of the 'Sly Man'. It all has to do with how to be 'in the world but not of it', meaning, how to live a conscious life without having to broadcast to others this fact. A Sly Man (in the Gurdjieffian sense) goes about his everyday business with practical efficiency and responsibility, but at the same time is always working on himself, endeavoring to 'remember himself'—to maintain a center of grounded self-awareness—as much as possible. He is an undercover mystic. He does this because most people are not especially interested in the development of consciousness, or in aspiring to something beyond the traditional values of mainstream culture, and therefore most people will not understand and will even seek to actively undermine such ideas. More to the point, the 'undercover mystic' keeps his own ego in check by avoiding the pitfalls of spiritual pride or what is commonly known as the 'spiritualized ego'.

Granted, here in the early twenty-first century we inhabit a different time. Ideas related to inner development are more widespread and commonly accepted than they were in the mid or late twentieth century, where to even pursue a path as innocuous as yogic meditation was to be thought a member of a quirky subculture. That is no longer quite the case. However, while yoga studios may now be as ubiquitous as Starbucks, that doesn't mean that deeper forms of inner work have been accepted or even understood. Consequently, the idea of Gurdjieff's Sly Man, Castaneda's 'changing personal routines', and the ninja's stealth and mastery of disguise, are not irrelevant. A conscious warrior can adapt to the environment he finds himself in, to 'do in Rome as the Romans do', without any loss of inner integrity. In fact, he saves energy in doing so as he waits for the right time and place to communicate with specific others more openly about who he is. He masters the arts of discernment, discrimination, and quiet purpose.

Chapter 5

The Dark Side of the Male Psyche: Secrets and Junkyard Dogs

Back in 1974, during the Bruce Lee craze (Lee had died under mysterious circumstances the year before) and when the original TV show *Kung Fu* with 'Grasshopper' Caine was airing, my father enrolled me in a karate class. I was 15 years old. A few of my buddies enrolled also. I was very passionate about martial arts then, had seen all the Lee movies, never missed an episode of *Kung Fu*, and even on occasion skipped school classes to catch the latest Hong Kong martial arts flick, complete with spectacular acrobatics and terrible dubbing, playing at the local arts theatre in downtown Montreal.

I trained ferociously. I used to put on my heavy ski boots, go into my backyard, and lumber around like Frankenstein's monster practicing my kicks in those boots. After an hour, I'd take the boots off, and it seemed as if I could almost fly. My kicks were lightning fast.

Our martial arts classes were held two or three evenings per week. I used to attend as much as I could. Within a few months, I'd passed my yellow, orange, and green belt levels. All that was left was blue, brown, black, and immortality. Then I too could boast about having to have my hands registered with the police as dangerous weapons.

Rumors passed between us boys about what was required to pass the black belt level. We were told, by older members in hushed tones, that we'd have to go into a pitch-black room, blindfolded, and fight against three black belts at the same time. It was a given that we'd get the crap kicked out of us. 'Heck,' one of us muttered to the other, 'if we can't see, neither can they. That about makes it even.'

Of course, it was never even. It was a hierarchy, as these things so often are. Older men with darker, more intimidating belt colors shouted at the younger men. The lighter your belt color, the bigger target you were for this shouting and berating, which at times bordered on abusive. The white belts got the worst of it. They were fresh meat for the seasoned lions to eat—bewildered young boys, chubby, skinny, pimply, and wondering why the hell their parents had enrolled them in *this*.

One of the 'advanced older guys', a brown belt and assistant instructor, was a known alcoholic. Jokes were frequently directed at him by the head teacher, jokes which always featured the punchline of a '48-ounce bottle waiting for *you*'. Years later, after I'd left the dojo ('dojo' is the name for a karate gym), I ran into this assistant instructor on a Montreal subway. He gave me some sort of death-stare. But I'm getting ahead of myself.

In time, I became the premier fighter of my dojo, mainly by virtue of my fast and skilled kicks. The head teacher was clearly proud of me and once proclaimed me the 'number one fighter' of his group. I regularly won my sparring matches. Not due to size—I was somewhat smaller than average for my age—nor by power, as I was slightly built. It was entirely due to speed and coordination. I had very good control of my legs and could conduct fast and complex kicks that would usually surprise my opponents.

Alas, my exalted status in the dojo did not last. One night I was offering some offhand advice to one of our novices when suddenly the head teacher turned viciously on me. 'If you ever say anything like that *again*, you'll be out of here fast, mister!' He had bellowed the words at me with extraordinary intensity. Such a rebuke, coming in front of about 35 men and boys, all standing in stunned silence at this angry display by the master, was humiliating. To make it worse, I had no idea what he was referring to. I was only trying to help a newcomer.

I dropped out that night. This 'lesson', if it was one, was too much for my 15-year-old psyche to integrate. The head teacher was himself about 30 years old, a large and powerful man. He was a very skilled and intimidating fighter. However, he was not a skilled teacher in any other respect—he was generally impatient, intolerant, and lacking in any sort of discernable philosophical wisdom. But he was not stupid. He knew his craft. He was just perpetually angry, like some sort of powerful, foul-mannered lion with a huge chip on his shoulder.

It took me years to properly evaluate and understand what had gone so severely wrong in the dynamic between him and me. In one ugly moment, I had gone from being his star student to being attacked and shamed in front of the entire school, for what appeared to be a simple misunderstanding. He apparently thought I was trying to undermine him, based on what he *thought* he heard me say to the novice, when in fact my intention was innocent and good and I'd said nothing wrong.

Perhaps he struggled with some form of paranoia, or perhaps he couldn't handle the power and responsibility that comes when one's organization grows. Or perhaps it was nothing more than a simple misunderstanding. Regardless of what was going on for *him*, the lesson for me was to grow beyond the victim-position and take responsibility for my own feelings toward him, and toward male authority figures in general.

About a decade later I began a long journey through many years of depth therapy. What I came to see during that time was just how much hatred I harbored for authority, and for male authority in particular. And this hatred was certainly not put there by my karate teacher of many years before. It long preceded my association with him. As I put the pieces together, I began to understand that he, and my violently ruptured relationship with him, was *symptomatic* of factors within me, not the cause of them.

That's not to excuse his behavior. From the perspective of where I stand now, as a 60-year-old man, I see that he was an insecure young man with nasty unhealed anger-issues. He had trained his body but hadn't done his psychotherapy. But none of that has anything to do with what I was to ultimately make of the whole experience. Much as I began to understand the roots of my own anger and hatred, I began to see the key point that any man who wishes to escape the conditioning of his past or upbringing must begin with becoming accountable for his own tendencies. And the truth was, I always had a temper as a boy and a great deal of anger. My karate teacher was, really, a kind of mirror reflection of me.

Moreover, I could be bossy and arrogant, even at that age, and my teacher probably was sensing some of that and giving me a lesson in needed humility. Did he do it with skill? No, but that wasn't the point. The point was to see into the depths of my own character and be accountable for my darker angels.

Unfortunately, we men often struggle in this area. We can be very good at demonizing what we don't understand, refusing to get off our proud positions, and deeply competitive with each other. As Pogo said, 'We have met the enemy, and he is us.' The problem is that this inner enemy so efficiently takes on an outer guise.

This chapter looks at some of the darker angels of masculine nature, including historical realities, and ways in which modern men can come to terms with these parts of their nature.

Junkyard Dogs?

Justin Sterling, the American seminar leader whose men's community—a sort of 'personal growth warrior's society'—I was involved with in the early 1990s, once characterized the dark side of men as akin to a 'junkyard dog'. The term summons images of a nasty beast that is not well cared for and cares even less for human beings. Something like a neglected pit bull, I imagine.

Alas, if one bothers to research some of the history of warfare one soon realizes that any junkyard dog, no matter how feral or rabid, rapidly pales in comparison to the utter depravity that men—and in particular organized groups of fighting men— are capable of. And I stress the usage of the word 'men' here, not 'human', for there is only scant evidence in the records of the human race of women being seriously capable of the monstrosities perpetuated by men throughout history. Yes, men have written the philosophy books, set down the laws, made the great scientific discoveries, produced most of the great art, built most of the material infrastructure of civilization, and are even the best cooks. But they have also demonstrated an inhumanity to their fellow humans to an almost unfathomable degree. They have burned their own books, broken their laws, condemned those who have made scientific discoveries (while burning other heretics), destroyed their own art and the civilizations that have housed them, and created fast food.

In the short outline that follows, several of the warrior cultures of the past that contained especially barbaric elements are listed, in approximate order of extremity (which is, of course, the subjective appraisal of one writer—the facts, however, are real).[1] By citing these cultures, it is obviously not intended to paint all members of them with the same brush. The existence of extremist elements among the Aztecs of, say, the fifteenth century, does not imply that all Aztecs – or even many of them – ate humans, but only that the practice existed.

1. Nazi Death Camps. Information on the Holocaust of World War II is widely available and need not be recounted here in detail. Despite the odd fringe element of historical revisionism that seeks to downplay or even deny outright the horrors that happened, the evidence is incontrovertible. Perhaps even more disturbing than historical revisionism, however, are recent reports that more than 1 in 5 Millennial Americans (born after 1982) are unaware of the Holocaust, and that over 40 percent think that only 'two million' were exterminated, rather than the actual number of close to six million Jews.[2] This genocide eradicated two-thirds of the Jewish population of Europe. It is arguable that the subculture within the greater culture (Nazism) that engineered this monstrosity was not a 'soldier culture', let alone a warrior culture, but the fact is that the Holocaust was perpetrated leading up to and during a great and terrible war, and so is forever associated with warfare and the men that are behind it. It therefore takes a valid place in the 'heart of darkness' of warrior nature. The sheer scale of what happened in the Nazi death camps boggles the mind.

2. Roman Persecutions of Early Era Christians. Roman soldiers engaged in some of the most gruesome practices imaginable when torturing early Christians. The fabled 'thrown to the lions' scenario, while true in some cases, was actually one of the milder forms of punishment for these unfortunate Christians. Some were literally cooked to death. Others had molten iron poured down their throats or even into their anus. Other forms of torture involved ripping off the skin, or being placed in boiling oil, being fed to hungry animals, broken on wheels, and so forth. Crucifixion itself was plenty barbarous, the crucified man generally dying a slow, agonizing death by suffocating under his own weight.

3. Aztecs. Certain of the Central and North American Indian cultures, along with some Polynesian tribes of the South Pacific, are generally recognized by anthropologists and historians as demonstrating some of the most barbarous behaviors known in human history, specifically in the area of what is sometimes generously termed 'simple cruelty'. This 'simple cruelty' is distinguished from, say, the mass depravity of the Second World War Holocaust, which is generally understood to have been a one-time severely aberrant event. Cultures such as the Aztecs, and some of the North American Indian tribes, demonstrated extraordinary cruelty as part of their cultural standards, and most of this was connected to the capture of members of enemy tribes, alongside the idea of human sacrifice to appease the gods—or, as equally likely, to intimidate their enemies. And many of these activities went on for a long time, in contrast to the horrors of the great Western wars which were largely punctuated events in history.

The main job of Aztec warriors was to capture victims for usage in rites of human sacrifice. On occasion, when an Aztec tribe triumphed over an enemy, thousands of men might be rounded up, with many if not most of them sacrificed in elaborate rituals, some of which involved forcing them to climb the steep steps of a tower whereupon at the summit they would have their heart ripped out while still beating. (Mel Gibson's popular and notorious 2006 film *Apocalypto*, which featured a cast of Maya and Native American actors and was filmed in a Mayan dialect, may have seemed to the casual moviegoer as exaggerated history and over-the-top entertainment, but in fact Gibson and his team had done their homework. His film dealt realistically with the themes of ritual sacrifice, including the tearing out of the heart of the victim while still alive, as these occurred in history. Gibson was criticized for making a movie about the Maya, when it was the Aztecs who did more of the gruesome stuff, but in point of fact the Maya did have some edgier elements to their culture, as they were influenced during some periods of their history by the Aztecs and the older Toltec culture.) Historians estimate that the Aztecs of the fifteenth century, for example, sacrificed thousands per year as part of their rites. One account has them sacrificing, at one event alone, well in excess of 10,000 people captured from an enemy tribe. In many cases these practices of human sacrifice ended with the remains of the captured victims being eaten by the general population of the conquerors. These sacrifices would on occasion even involve children or newlywed couples.

4. Plains and Iroquois Indians. It may surprise some, but certain of the Amerindian tribes, particularly of the southern and northern plains and the eastern parts of North America, were not uniformly the gentle and spiritual folk that the late twentieth-century New Age community loved to depict them as—a somewhat more cosmic version of Rousseau's 'noble savage', brutally oppressed by the white man, living in harmony with the land and the flora and fauna, and that's all there was to it. Not exactly. (One is reminded of the well-worn late twentieth-century New Age saying attributed to a certain Chief Seattle about 'what you do to the Earth you do to yourself'—only problem being that it was never said by Chief Seattle.) There are events in the history of the Pawnee, Huron, Seneca, Mohawk, Algonquin, and further southwest in particular with the Comanche, that involve specific acts or rituals based on exacting vengeance from enemy tribes or trespassing whites that are ghoulish in the extreme. Most of these involved slow torture and eventual death, and many involved cannibalism. In one example from seventeenth-century Iroquois, a beautiful young woman of an enemy tribe is captured, and after a few days of misleading good treatment, she is stripped and hung up between two poles, where she is then impaled repeatedly by arrows. Another involved a captured male of an enemy tribe who is slowly tortured with hot axes and various other atrocities for an entire night before being killed, dismembered, and eaten. Some Iroquois tribes (the League of the Iroquois was comprised of the Onondaga, Mohawk, Oneida, Cayuga, Seneca, and Hiawatha) regularly practiced ruthless torture of war prisoners. This would, often, be followed by eating the remains of the enemy prisoner, particularly the heart. Most Iroquois reserved torture and slow deaths for men; women and children of the enemy were killed quickly. It is also worth noting that those executing the various tortures—lopping off fingers, pulling out nails, branding with hot axes, lancing with knives, etc.—were, in this case, not just men. Women and even children also participated in the brutalities.[3]

In the southwestern plains, the fearsome (and arguably even worse) Comanche regularly demonstrated extreme cruelty in punishing enemies or mere 'outsiders'—common tactics being to tie men to wagon wheels and roast them alive, cut off genitals, or to beat, rape, and disfigure women.[4] It should be added that in many cases captured prisoners were not tortured but adopted into the family. Much of it depended on the word of the matriarch of the family—if her grief over the loss of one of her own family in battle was too great, she would often demand retribution, which the male warriors would then exact on her behalf. (To be fair, some historians believe that the practice of torturing and killing enemies, although pre-Columbian, was accentuated with the arrival of the white man, which seems common sense. Many Europeans were subjected to the fates mentioned above. In the case of the Comanches, there is some evidence that their cruelties were intensified in the decades following their interactions with the Spanish.)

5. The Korowai of New Guinea. The Korowai are a small tribe (they currently number a few thousand) that until the 1970s lived more or less in complete isolation, dwelling in elaborate treehouses in the rainforests of southeastern Papua (western New Guinea). They have been reported to have ritual practices of cannibalism that involved (especially in the case of accused sorcerers) torture, killing, and the consumption of the brain. As with other cultures that practiced torture and cannibalism, this is usually a revenge ritual. The cannibalism is almost secondary to the torture, the cruelty of which gives it its infamy. They do not, however, believe that they are torturing and eating a person, but rather a particular demon that has assumed control of the person (typically a sorcerer). These practices have been reported to still occur in present times, although only by Korowai tribes that remain isolated from the outside world. The practices seem, of course, primitive and barbaric, but the Korowai persecution of sorcerers is arguably only different from the Early Modern European persecution of witches in that the victim is eaten.

Cannibalism

Cannibalism is not at all rare in human history. It has been practiced in numerous cultures around the world, from the tribal West Indies to certain Amerindian tribes in all of the Americas, to Melanesia (the islands northeast of Australia, including New Guinea), Fiji, parts of Africa, and among some of the Maori of New Zealand. Many cultures within these territories long had a practice of eating their defeated enemies or even unwelcome guests—usually part of a revenge ritual against enemy tribes or invaders.

Cannibalism is certainly an old practice as well, undertaken by both very early *Homo sapiens* and Neanderthals. Much of it appears to have its basis in the idea that eating an enemy was a way to gain power, although in some scattered cases it may actually have been related to dietary needs. 'Cultural relativism' is an important idea in anthropology: you can't necessarily judge, let alone clearly understand, the values of an alien culture if you yourself are not a full member of that culture, experiencing the world via its perceptual filters. That said, I think we can safely categorize these kinds of practices, especially by warriors, as among the darkest and most brutal of human behaviors. Round about here it's natural to raise the point that a World War II Commander-in-Chief who gives the order to vaporize an entire Japanese city with an atomic bomb is more savage than these mere tribal barbarities we've just outlined, and what to say of the Nazi death camps of that same war? Certainly, on order of magnitude these events make Aztec or Iroquois atrocities pale in comparison, but our discussion here is not limited, or even focused on, quantity. We are here more interested in the potential dark side of the individual warrior, and what exactly he's capable of. It's not within the scope of this book to take anything more than a cursory glance at these examples, for they are certainly found in all cultures and races throughout history, including particular cases of conquering soldiers representing supposedly relatively advanced cultures (from the Romans to the Allied Powers of World War II).

Suicide Bombers

The idea of the suicidal warrior—the young man (and in certain Islamic cultures, occasionally a woman) who effectively uses his body as a weapon to hurl against the enemy—is not a recent phenomenon, even if Islamic extremism has given it wide press. One has only to go back to the Second World War and recall the *kamikaze* pilots of the Japanese Imperial Navy who attempted to fly their warplanes into American warships in a desperate attempt to ward off looming Japanese defeat.[5] Precise statistics have not been easy to come by but the estimated figures are extraordinary—almost 4,000 Japanese pilots gave their lives in *kamikaze* missions, although of that number only about 730 (just under 20 percent) actually made it to their target.[6] The majority were shot down. So not only was the whole enterprise incredibly brazen and reckless, it was also largely futile. And it certainly didn't save the Japanese from defeat. It's not that the *kamikaze* attacks could not cause exceptional carnage. They could. In one attack alone two young *kamikaze* pilots managed to fly their bomb-laden planes into an American aircraft carrier, killing or maiming one-quarter of its entire crew, 650 sailors of 2,600. By the end Japan's *kamikaze* campaign had sunk over a hundred American ships and killed over 7,000 servicemen. It failed to stop the American advance, due mainly to the powerhouse American industries that churned out ships and weaponry at a pace the Japanese could not cope with.

The origin of the *idea* of suicide attacks (if not the psychological impulse) is generally rooted in religious indoctrination. The

Japanese word *kamikaze* translates as 'divine wind', finding its genesis in legends of the defeat of the thirteenth-century Mongolian invasion fleets destroyed by typhoons. *Kamikaze* can be rendered as 'the wind of God'—in effect becoming the 'fist of God'. The idea is straightforward. If you are backed by the divine or by divine cause, then surely you cannot be defeated and even if you are, in the afterlife you will be redeemed in one way or another. In the case of the Japanese it was also rooted in the *bushido* code of the samurai, founded on extreme loyalty (to both Japan and its emperor) and a notion of honor that preferred death over the shame of defeat.

The psychological background of *kamikaze* warriors, in addition to the expected peer pressure and winning of honor for their families, was often based on the idea that they were the 'last line of defense' against a ruthless foreign enemy that might exterminate their entire race. The propaganda surrounding them was decidedly less flattering, usually founded on carefully crafted deceptions. For example, Japanese youth and children were routinely told tales of heroic and successful *kamikaze* campaigns when in fact the stories were wild exaggerations or outright fabrications. But the desired result was achieved, that being the indoctrination in the minds of youth that dying for one's nation—even if such required transforming oneself into a human missile—was both worthy and desirable.

In other words, *kamikaze* pilots were young men that had been typically programmed by older men (and on occasion the patriarchs and matriarchs of their families) to develop a construct of reality in which sacrificing their lives was not only appropriate, but exciting and desirable. Viewed objectively this may seem insane, but for those operating within the social construct it was not only sane, but practically obligatory, as the consequences of avoiding the call to attack the enemy involved a humiliation or emasculation, the anticipation of which amounted to something worse than death.

Islamic Extremism

Since 1980 there have been almost 5,000 suicide attacks in the world (as of 2018) in over 40 countries, although the majority have occurred in the Middle East, Afghanistan, Iraq, and Pakistan (with some in India, Sri Lanka, Africa, and more recently, Europe), in which over 45,000 people have been killed. Most of these attacks—in part inspired by the spectacular 1983 destruction of an American-French military barrack in Lebanon in which nearly 300 American and French servicemen were killed by a suicide bomber—are based on notions found within Islamic martyrdom, or perhaps more accurately, on how these notions are interpreted.

Suicide attackers have not been limited to Japanese or Muslim cultures. The Chinese revolutionaries of the Xinhai Revolution of 1911–12 (a civil war in which rebels overthrew China's last imperial dynasty) were motivated by the ultimate soldier's credo of Huang Xing who wrote, 'We must die, so let us at least die bravely.' The notion of such extreme bravery is, ironically, connected to (and takes advantage of) the masculine impulse toward the lust for life. The idea, twisted as it is, is that only in the face of death can one experience life in its most vivid sense, and achieve a fierce aliveness not possible in a softer, more yielding existence. To know this fierce aliveness even if only briefly, and especially the honor it confers in the eyes of one's peers and superiors, is worth the loss of one's life—that is, for one conditioned by that idea. (That said, it should be noted that not all suicide attackers are male—about 15 percent in Islamic cultures are female, and their effect is often deadlier than attacks carried out by males, as they tend to evade detection more effectively.)

The psychological background of modern suicide bombers— insofar as it has been known—is, needless to say, complex. Studies have been done showing that many of them suffered from psychopathologies such as depression, post-traumatic stress disorder, as well as other physical and material hardships, although many come from relatively educated middle-class backgrounds.[7] We see here an issue deeper than that of religious indoctrination or mere peer pressure (or 'groupthink'), one rooted in self-loathing and the deep-seated belief in one's worthlessness and the pointlessness of one's existence. That such conditioning is both transmitted and reinforced by elders is a given. Young suicide bombers are being taught the doctrines that drive them by *someone*, and that someone is not usually a peer, but more commonly an older male who inhabits some position of assumed moral authority. In a twisted version of Bly's Iron John myth, in this case the 'hairy wild man' is supremely dangerous and the younger man would indeed have a good reason to distrust him — if he could but understand the dangers that lurk under the doctrines as blindly transmitted.

Western Home-Grown Terrorists and Aberrant Cases

The Western version of the suicide bomber is the home-grown terrorist, although he's usually more interested in exacting mass casualties than he is in giving up his own life in the cause. He is a psychopath, demonstrably incapable of empathy, and devoid of even the religious concept of an honorable death. (Technically a 'psychopath' can be distinguished from a 'sociopath' in part due to the meticulousness of planning. Sociopaths enact crimes spontaneously and without organization; psychopaths usually plan carefully.) His mission is destruction and he usually prefers to be alive to witness both it and the after-effect of it. A few examples will suffice: Timothy McVeigh (aided by Terry Nichols), who in 1995 managed to kill 168 citizens and injure over 600 in the bombing of a federal government building in Oklahoma City; Anders Breivik, the Norwegian right-wing extremist who in 2011 decided to take into his own hands what he perceived to be unacceptable European permissiveness of Muslim immigration, and accordingly killed 77 Norwegian citizens with bombs and guns (most of whom were adolescent boys at a summer camp whom he hunted down and shot one by one); Ted Kaczynski, the intellectual psychopath who had a major grievance against modern technological civilization, and who killed 3 and maimed 23 by mailing bombs to them; Seung-Hui Cho, the Virginia Tech senior who in 2007 shot and killed 32 (and wounded another 17) on his campus; Omar Mateen, a 29-year-old security guard who, inspired by the radical Islamic organization ISIS, took it upon himself to use an assault weapon to mow down over a hundred people in a gay nightclub in Florida in 2016, killing 49 of them in the process; and last but not least, Steven Paddock, the infamous 'Vegas Shooter' who in October of 2017 rained bullets down on a large crowd of country music fans from the 32nd floor of a nearby hotel, wounding over 500 and killing 58 in what is (as of 2018) the largest mass shooting in US history.

Profiles of such individuals do not necessarily yield comforting answers. McVeigh may be the poster child for American home-grown terrorists, but his history as a Gulf War vet and self-proclaimed bullied child who came to perceive the American government as the 'ultimate bully' does not explain such destructiveness. The truth is that young men (in particular) have throughout history performed occasional acts of violence to such a degree that their effects are irreversible and their consequences extreme. McVeigh had access to certain technologies that enabled his brand of 'vengeance' (at least in his mind) to be especially ugly, but such men have always been around, even if their means of attack were limited by mental or technological capability.

Paddock, the Vegas shooter, is perhaps a particularly odd duckling in this motley collection of ugly ducklings. A far older man (64) than most perpetrators of such crimes, financially comfortable (he was a millionaire and professional gambler) and lacking in any significant criminal history, his motives remain largely a mystery to investigators or the cable TV talking heads who cover such events for the public. By all accounts he was a depressed older guy who obviously was sitting on years of rage and hate and wanted to go out in a blaze of gunfire and death. But it was the sheer magnitude of his act that left stunned investigators scratching their heads. Where does such demonic hate come from? As Private Train muses in Terrence Malick's brilliant 1998 war movie *The Thin Red Line*:

> This great evil, where's it come from? How'd it steal into the world? What seed, what root did it grow from? Who's doing this? Who's killing us, robbing us of light and life, mocking us with the sight of what we might have known? Is this darkness in you, too? Have you passed through this night?

There was, however, one obvious signpost in Paddock's case, and that was the man's father. He'd been a notorious bank robber and at one time found himself on the FBI's Most Wanted list. Mentioning this well-known fact is not meant as some sort of facile justification for Paddock's psyche and the sheer brutality of his actions at the end of his life. But the cliché 'chip off the old block' did not appear randomly out of thin air. The sins of the father are too often in life carried on by the son, sometimes in a greatly reduced version, other times magnified, as if the son seeks, in some tacitly unspoken fashion, the perverse approval of his father's ghost. In a best-case scenario, such pathology may get redirected into creative brilliance—as played out in *Amadeus*, the superb (though historically exaggerated) 1984 film version of Mozart and his tortured relationship with his father—but far too often it happens that the son carries on some version of the family patterns and legacy.

The other thing about Paddock worth mentioning is the sense of isolation about him. He had a partner, a Filipino woman who seemed rather clued out about her relationship with the man, and snippets of reports came out from people who saw him in public treating her in a disdainful fashion. In the wake of the shooting, one of Paddock's brothers made a few spontaneous TV appearances, and in my eyes his histrionic reactions and freaked-out demeanor about the carnage his brother had wreaked seemed weird. Not *inauthentic*, mind you, just weird. I take note of these things because the key to individual psychopathology is usually found in the dusty secrets of the family system.

I mention the isolation factor, because in my experience this has been the single-greatest cause behind the downfall of so many males. The sheer inability to connect, to communicate, to share one's consciousness with another male (let alone female) has plagued many throughout history and continues to do so. Men who commit acts of sudden violence to a disturbing degree have years of introverted brooding behind them, constructing entire worldviews in their heads and on occasions seeking the means to justify certain actions in order to respond to the detached and demented narrative they've fashioned and fed inside of them.

In the men's groups I've participated in and led for the past quarter-century, I've seen and heard many cases of men defusing the rage and hate inside of them merely by learning the art of sharing their minds and stories with other men, and then finding out that they were never as strange, alien, or alone as they feared they were. 'I've got your back' is one of the mottos that my own men's community has and strives to live by (we even have a T-shirt with those words on the back). I'd be willing to bet that this one simple idea, of men caring about and supporting other men, free of political ideologies or the need to form crusades against some evil Other, is a key to unlocking the troubled psyches of some of the next mass killers who are walking the streets at this very moment.

In the case of Westerners who are radicalized, that is, become allegiant to an extremist branch (in modern times this usually involves the Islamic faith), studies have suggested that such individuals are not driven by the desperation of Middle Eastern or other terrorists, but rather are motivated by a desire to forge an identity. Identity-weakness is always a challenge for the young, and especially men. This is because while young women often lack a strong identity as well—and arguably struggle more than men to establish their individuality free of peer influence—they tend to be better at deriving *group* identity-strength, and support, from their peer tribes and social networks. Young men are, generally speaking, not as good at this, being more given to being various shades of loners. (Even when a guy has a social circle of reasonable size, he may still remain 'alone' in his mind, not communicating on the more personal levels that women are usually more at ease with.) A young man in search of a cause, something to sink his testosterone and considerable vital energy into, is vulnerable to radicalization if he carries significant unresolved anger toward authority, and especially the father, and all the ways in which that can be projected onto structures of authority. Whether he attacks his own nation and people in the name of some cause (be it well articulated in the case of Kaczynski or poorly so in the case of McVeigh or Mateen), or whether he goes overseas and adopts a Muslim name and identity, does not change the central point that he *lacks* a structured, let alone healthy, identity to begin with. A man with a reasonably solid sense of self is not given to being easily threatened or angered by figures of power, unless such figures are themselves directly threatening him or his loved ones.

Where does this problem of identity-weakness begin? It is natural to assume that the psychological health of a boy's parents is the main cause behind the quality of his masculine identity, and indeed it's not rocket science to surmise that. Ideally the masculinity of a boy or young man is supposed to be confirmed and endorsed by both his father *and* his mother. But as has been touched on in this book several times, what is often lacking in current times is the process of initiation. A boy who is not *properly* initiated into manhood (via whatever means) tends to feel alienated from his surrounding culture, and seeks his identity-formation via subversion in endless possible ways. Of course, such 'initiation', or the lack thereof, cannot be pinpointed as the sole cause of aberrant behavior (early-life trauma or abuse can obviously be a powerful factor). But in general a young man who has been made to feel *welcome* by the family of his ancestors and by the culture of his 'tribe'—assuming the tribe itself is reasonably healthy—is less inclined to act out in severely antinomian ways later in life. He has, you could say, more interesting things to direct his energy toward.

As touched on at the top of this chapter, men are creatures capable of manifesting the extremes of human behavior. This capacity for focused intensity, for explosive creativity or destructiveness, has biological roots, but we're more interested here in the psychological factors. What leads to one man producing great works of art or philosophy or science, and another to destroying and maiming and killing? Cultural factors are dominant, of course, so much so that any sort of generalized psychological analysis of this matter may seem too out of touch with the grassroots causes. But for Western men—the most likely readers of this book—the causes of male rage and blind explosiveness are relevant and important to look into, for two reasons. First, many men can identify easily with the idea of explosive frustration, and second and perhaps more importantly, many men know of someone in their lives who either shows such potential or who is already acting it out in some fashion, however subtle.

A key factor behind aberrant behavior, often hiding under such rage, can be defined as the harboring of secrets, to the extent that such secrets cause a psychological pressure that ultimately requires outlets.

Eight Secrets

The Jungian psychotherapist James Hollis once outlined what he saw as eight essential secrets that men carry within:

1. Men's lives are as much governed by restrictive role expectations as are the lives of women.
2. Men's lives are essentially governed by fear.
3. The power of the feminine is immense in the psychic economy of men.
4. Men collude in a conspiracy of silence whose aim is to suppress their emotional truth.
5. Because men must leave Mother, and transcend the mother complex, wounding is necessary.
6. Men's lives are violent because their souls have been violated.
7. Every man carries a deep longing for his father and for his tribal Fathers.
8. If men are to heal, they must activate within what they did not receive from without.[8]

The list is predictably negative (most secrets are) but therapist Hollis has worked in the trenches for many decades and knows human nature. I believe his list is mostly on the mark, something I can attest to after over 30 years of field work myself. Of particular note are Hollis's points 2, 5, 6, and 7. Put in capsule form, these are: *men are governed by fear, men are wounded in their transition to manhood, men's souls have been violated, men long for older man guidance.* That, you might say, is a formula for the creation of a destructive man, a kind of Frankenstein's monster who is disowned by his creator. One can find endless examples of such men across all cultures throughout history.

There are many good men, obviously, many of whom never get any limelight precisely because the general public finds junkyard dogs compelling even as they pillory them. Good men tend to be perceived as dull—unless they become famous by dint of talent, opportunity, and originality. And even then, their charisma is more a persona, a glittering front created by their accomplishments. In private they are often seen as distinctly lacking in charm.

What does it mean to suggest that a man's 'soul has been violated'? The language is dramatic, perhaps overly so, but what it points toward is valid, namely, that men have been through a transition point in their psychological development that is unique to males. Quite simply, this is the realization every young boy goes through when he understands that he's a different gender from his mother. He's supposed to bond with males at that point, his tribe of elders, but if that tribe is of low quality, or lacking altogether, the boy remains 'stuck' to his mother with apron ropes (never mind strings) and sees the world through her lenses — often well into his adult years. He remains alienated from the community of men. He doesn't particularly care for them, hates older men with authority, hides out in the world. Or, more dangerously, he deeply resents the control his mother wields over him, and begins to hate women and the covert power that he senses they embody.

The Latin root of the word 'violate' is *violat*, which simply means to be treated violently, with aggressive force. The issue boils down largely to power and its abuse. The idea that men are 'violent' because their souls have been 'violated' relates to the key initiations into manhood that men undergo. These initiations can be healthy, as when the elders of a tribe welcome a young boy into manhood (even if such 'welcoming' is of a rough or 'tough love' nature). They can also be toxic, based on rejection or abandonment. When the latter is the case, the boy learns to shut down his emotions and lose his capacity for empathy. This rejection or abandonment can take many forms, but they have as their shared essence the experience that the boy is being mistreated unjustly, cruelly, capriciously, or because he in some way presents a threat to the older male who violates him. He is, essentially, a dumping ground for the frustrations and wounds of the older male who mistreats him.

This cause-and-effect line of transmission has ancient roots, found in biology and in the primordial struggle of human beings to survive in the face of harsh elements and powerful competing animals. The masculine is the guardian gender, part of a universe based on consumption, where entities eat other entities in order to exist and propagate. But for the common man, the problem lies not so much in the cosmic background as it does in his relationships with the male elders of his immediate tribe. Once the younger male has been abused by the older male, his path forward will be fraught with challenges. If he faces his pain, finds quality guidance, *seeks* quality guidance, he may transform much of his pain into higher values and skills and become a helper and healer himself. But if he doesn't, he grows into a resentful man, harboring the secret belief that he is special in some freakish way, in a way that prevents him from ever being truly understood by others. And his alienation from older men, or from authority figures in general, serves to keep him isolated and ineffectual for much or most of his life. He then requires a target to expel his anger on. Occasionally that target is an outer figure, but more often it is the erosion of his self-image.

The Deep Masculine and the Wild Man

When a man is overcome by his inner darkness, he has the potential to be far worse than any junkyard dog. He can become demonic in the true sense of the word, a narcissistic psychopath unable to feel empathy, unable to imagine himself in the shoes of the other. This kind of savagery is polar opposite to the true wild man.

A basic idea of masculine psychology is that a man who feels inwardly weak, inwardly impotent, will tend to compensate outwardly by emphasizing a more stereotyped masculinity. He will beat his chest, disdain weakness, may be uncomfortable around gay men, and incline more toward macho. In more extreme cases he may even be prone to violence and a general sociopathic indifference to the fate of others. It's not hard to see all this in the spectacle of young disenfranchised men who act out violently, often with only marginal just cause (even by the terms of their own warped construction of reality).

The concept of the 'deep masculine' is an important part of the teachings of the mythopoetic men's movement in general, and it also applies very much to the ideal of the conscious warrior. The main thing that differentiates the deep masculine from the more conventional ideas of masculinity is balance, and in particular, the integration of a rich-feeling, sensual, embodied life into a healthy masculine core.

A man who has very developed classical masculine traits (strength, bravery, sense of direction, purpose, etc.) but who is disconnected in other ways—say, he's too emotionally shut down, he's clued out in interpersonal relating, he lacks empathy and is emotionally tone-deaf, and so forth—is not fully masculine. A man truly developed in his masculinity is strong but not threatened by softness; can reason clearly about the big picture but is not deaf to the emotional particularities of a given moment; can lead a company or group but is also sensitive to the needs of an individual.

The deep masculine is the wild man harnessed to the practical needs of a man who has to work for a living, pay bills, and keep relationships. The main quality of the wild man is boldness and courage, and in particular, the courage to face the darkness of his own heart. When a shaman or a magician raises spirits in the wild or in the inner sanctum of his magic circle, he is also confronting the dark side of his own nature. To 'tame' a spirit, or to 'bind a demon', is a metaphor for taming one's own shadow side. The main difference is that this shadow side is not to be abused; it is rather tamed much as a horse is tamed, at which point it can be ridden joyously and celebrated as two minds working together.

Masculine Competitiveness

A facet of masculine nature—and one that easily deteriorates into a difficult shadow element—is competitiveness. While this tendency should not be denied or spiritualized away (something that usually leads to disempowerment and identity-confusion) and can be integrated in a healthy fashion (via passionate engagement in life), it easily results in serious problems even for the most intelligent and seemingly conscious men.

Masculine competitiveness can be overwhelmingly intense, egocentrically focused, and brutal in consequences. It can also be far subtler, and often plays out in fascinating ways in the spiritual realm. Below are a couple of examples: the rival Karmapas of Tibetan Buddhism, and the 'struggle of the magicians' exemplified by the Greek-Armenian spiritual teacher G.I. Gurdjieff and his three chief disciples.

Rival Karmapas of Tibetan Buddhism

Perhaps one of the strangest stories found within the culture of religious community is that of the 'dual Karmapas' of late twentieth- and early twenty-first-century Tibetan Buddhism. The Karmapa—more informally known as the 'Black Hat Lama'—is a continually 'reincarnating' office within the Karma Kargyu lineage of Tibetan Buddhism (the concept of reincarnation being, of course, a core part of Tibetan Buddhist cosmology). It is similar to other reincarnating offices, the most notable example of which is the Dalai Lama (the current one, the famous Tenzin Gyatso, born in 1935, is the 14th Dalai Lama). The Karmapa is the oldest of these offices, predating the Dalai Lamas by several centuries. (The first Karmapa died in 1193; the first Dalai Lama in 1474, recognized posthumously.) The well-known 16th Karmapa, Rangjung Rigpe Dorje, passed away in 1981. As is the custom, a search was made for his reincarnation.

The technical name for a 'reincarnating office' in Tibetan Buddhism is a *tulku*. The Dalai Lama and the Karmapa are both *tulkus*. But they are only the two most famous ones. There are some 500 *tulku* lineages in the Tibetan tradition, each of which is regarded as an advanced teacher of Buddhist principles who, it is understood, differs from the average Joe on the street (or the average Tibetan monk or nun) in that he is able to consciously choose whether to reincarnate or not. He returns to human life again and again based on the Bodhisattva ideal, which is that the enlightenment and emancipation of all other beings in the universe is more important than one's own salvation. A Bodhisattva is preeminently motivated by compassion. He is believed to come back (as opposed to disappearing into some ethereal realm) because he cares about humanity. The office of the Karmapa is the oldest of Tibet's *tulku* lineages, dating back to the twelfth century CE.

Given the lofty principles and personages associated with the *tulkus* it was, to put it mildly, something of a shock to see the weird series of events within the lineage of the Karmapa unfold in the late 1980s and 90s (and still going on as of this writing in 2018). At issue has been the true identity of the 17th Karmapa. In this case two, not one, Karmapas have been identified and proclaimed by rival Tibetan Buddhist factions, something virtually unheard of in the annals of the tradition. The two candidates have been Trinley Thaye Dorje (b. 1983) and Ogyen Trinley Dorje (b. 1985). Both have been enthroned into their office and both continue, to this day, to function in their duties. They have not met each other. A majority of Tibetan Buddhists accept Ogyen as the true Karmapa—he was the one endorsed by the Dalai Lama, even though the Dalai Lama is not traditionally involved in the endorsement of the legitimacy of a Karmapa—but the minority that reject him and accept Trinley Thaye as Karmapa has been of sufficient size to cause real problems.

Imagine if there were two popes. (In fact, there once was. Back in 1378, during what is called the 'Western Great Schism', a second pope, Clement VII, was elected by the College of

Cardinals in Avignon, France, while a first, Urban VI, was still enthroned. A number of other men claimed or were elected pope by various factions over the next few decades until the matter finally resolved itself by 1429.) Not dissimilar to the pope, the Karmapa is an extremely important office within Tibetan Buddhist hierarchy, head of one of the four main Tibetan Buddhist lineages, the Karma Kargyu. The others are the Gelugpa (led by the Dalai Lama), the Sakyapa (led by the Sakya Trizin), and the oldest of the four, the Nyingma (led by a number of teachers, all of whom trace their spiritual lineage to Padmasambhava, the great Tantric adept).

It is to be noted that this entire history of Tibetan Buddhist spiritual politics is almost exclusively patriarchal. There *are* some female *tulkus*, but they are comparatively rare. It has been the men who have dominated the ranks of religious leadership in Tibet since the Buddhist tradition was first kick-started there around the eighth century CE. Such religious predominance within the culture of Tibet—at one time it was estimated that one in four Tibetan males was ordained as a monk—is perhaps ironic given Tibet's earlier history as a nation of fierce and semi-nomadic warriors (similar, in some ways, to the Mongols under the Great Khans, although without their geopolitical ambitions).

From a strictly psychological perspective the saga of the two Karmapas is rife with the darker shades of masculine competitiveness. This cannot, of course, be directed at the two Karmapas themselves, who were ensconced in their positions as young boys oblivious to what was going on around them. Their fates were manipulated by scheming and competitive men—in particular, by the four 'heart-sons' of the famed 16th Karmapa, Rangjung Rigpe Dorje (1924–81). The odd thing is that these four men—themselves all 'reincarnating' *tulkus*—were highly trained *lamas*, masters of meditation and with an understanding of the mind equivalent to Western PhDs in psychology and philosophy. (Two of them have passed on as of this writing. The

3rd Jamgon Kongtrul died in a car accident in 1992 at age 37; and the 14th Shamarpa, the senior regent of the four, died in 2014 at age 61. The other two are the 12th Tai Situpa, b. 1954, and the 12th Gyaltsab Rinpoche, also b. 1954.) Yet despite their rigorous training and the dignity accompanying their elite status within Tibetan Buddhism, they still found themselves mired in scandal and a stubborn unwillingness to resolve with each other a profoundly important issue within their tradition. Even the Dalai Lama expressed his frustration with the four of them when he met with them in person in the early 1990s, remarking that he encouraged them to at least try to cooperate as ordinary people, let alone spiritual leaders—and he invoked the imagery of the father, suggesting that the four 'sons' should act honorably in light of Karmapa's passing.[9]

The details of the luridly fascinating story are beyond the scope of this book but have been presented in several works; three that can be pursued and that present differing views are *Rogues in Robes* (1998, Blue Dolphin Publishing) by Tomek Lehnert; *Karmapa: The Politics of Reincarnation* (2004, Wisdom Publications) by Lea Terhune; and *Buddha's Not Smiling* (2014, Motilal Banarsidass) by Erik Curran. None of these books are impartial, perhaps appropriately reflecting the intense masculine competitiveness and startling spiritual dysfunction that is their theme.

Gurdjieff and His Three Wayward 'Sons'

The renowned and notorious Greek-Armenian spiritual teacher G.I. Gurdjieff (1872?–1949), a rugged and masculine man, had many students during the four decades his teaching career spanned.[10] Many of his most loyal students were women, such as Jeanne de Salzmann, Olga de Hartman, Sophie Ouspensky, and his wife, Julia Ostrowska, as well as the famous group of lesbian intellectuals known as 'the Rope' who studied closely with him in the 1930s (these included Margaret Anderson and Jane Heap among several others). That said, it's generally recognized that Gurdjieff's three highest-profile students were men—Peter Ouspensky (1878–1947), A.R. Orage (1873–1934), and John Bennett (1897–1974). His relationship with these three men was fascinating, mainly because (seen through Gurdjieff's eyes) the three failed him due to similar causes at play between all four men, which could again be reduced to 'masculine competitiveness'.

Ouspensky, himself an accomplished writer and teacher of esoteric material, met Gurdjieff in 1915 in Moscow.[11] By all accounts he was excited to finally find what he deemed to be a worthy teacher of the mysteries. Ouspensky's seeking had not been limited to trips to the library or visits to a local Theosophy chapter. He had traveled extensively in the East, visiting India, Sri Lanka (then 'Ceylon'), and Egypt, but he apparently never got out of the tourist trap and failed to connect with legitimate teachers. (Undoubtedly those teachers were there, Ouspensky's suggestions to the contrary, but his main complaint was that what teachers he found 'required too much of him', and that didn't refer to money, but rather the need to abandon his conventional life.)

Ouspensky progressed to become Gurdjieff's leading student, but within a few years began to fall out with him due to reasons related to power, respect, status, and resistance to facing into deeper elements of his ego—all the usual reasons for masculine dysfunction in the field of transformational work. That said, Ouspensky still went on to author what many believe to be the best book ever written on Gurdjieff's teachings, *In Search of the Miraculous* (1947). When Gurdjieff got his hands on the book— he was an old man at that point in the twilight of his life—he remarked, 'For a long time I hate this man. Now I love him.' The master was impressed, and the book is indeed an excellent and lucid presentation of Gurdjieff's ideas and work.

The two men, however, never repaired their relationship.

Ouspensky had even reached a point where he asked his own students to never mention Gurdjieff by name. He once remarked, 'Most men have a crowd of selves inside of them. In Gurdjieff, there are only two. However, one is very good, and the other is very bad.'

Both these men proved influential and both acquired significant followings that lasted well beyond their deaths. However, the reasons for Ouspensky's withdrawal from his teacher's community seem rooted in the competitive instinct. The records suggest he was clearly attached to his own role as a teacher and had no desire to further humble himself with his master. Gurdjieff, for his part, seemed reluctant to empower or endorse his student and showed signs of that territorialism that powerful men so commonly demonstrate, in ways that all too often ends up degrading their work.

A.R. Orage had been a well-known and respected literary editor in England when he first decided to abandon his career and go 'in search of God' to study under Gurdjieff in France in the early 1920s. Soon after, Orage advanced to become Gurdjieff's point man in America, his key ambassador there when Gurdjieff made a number of visits and established teaching centers in New York, Boston, and Chicago. Orage ultimately left Gurdjieff when he got involved with a woman nearly 30 years his junior (Jesse Dwight), and was made to choose between the two. He chose his woman.

The records indicate that Gurdjieff and Jesse Dwight detested each other, for different reasons. For Dwight, Gurdjieff was a threatening menace, the authoritarian guru who wielded influence over the very man that she herself sought to influence. It would be safe to say that Gurdjieff's view of her would have been more or less identical in that regard. He was, however, the elder and wiser figure, who had something substantial to offer the world, so history has tended to frown on Jesse Dwight for being too self-centered. The main point here, however, does not really concern Dwight but rather the relationship between male teacher and male student, and the ways in which it so commonly goes astray.

The third 'wayward son', John G. Bennett, met Gurdjieff at a young age and was immediately recognized by the master as a young man of exceptional quality and potential. At the time of the meeting Bennett was 23 years old and already a military intelligence officer. They met in Turkey in 1920 (Bennett was a linguist and fluent in Turkish). He studied under Gurdjieff for a short period until 1923, when he withdrew. He then returned to Gurdjieff after World War II, in the late 1940s when Gurdjieff was an old man living out his last years in Paris. Bennett resumed his studies with him and after Gurdjieff's death in 1949 went on to become one of his prime exponents. He did, however, follow other teachings as well and never could be described as a Gurdjieff-purist.

Bennett's overall life was commendable, but the interesting point here is how, again, Gurdjieff was unable to direct the work of one of his key male students in ways that he wanted to. When Bennett was young Gurdjieff had even offered to support him, telling him, 'I don't need your money, but your work.' But Bennett declined the offer, feeling more driven to strike out on his own and explore without being attached to a powerful older male personality—even though the benefits of becoming Gurdjieff's disciple were clear, even by Bennett's own account.

This theme is quite common among men in positions of power, be it spiritual or worldly. Perhaps the archetypal story in that regard is Jesus and Judas. Although the reasons for Judas's 'betrayal' are, according to the gospels, limited to cowardice and greed, the causes were doubtless more complex and probably had male competitiveness as part of their core. The irony of course is that men feel compelled to prove themselves, and part of this proving often involves the impulse to surpass, overcome, or otherwise win over, important male elders or father-figures.

Judas represents something different, however, and that is the behind-the-scenes scheming of the man driven by fear. Greed is a function of fear, of course, as are all other negative emotions and mental states governed by the failure to grasp that one is not that important in the grand scheme of things. Men who feel self-important (in the egoic sense) often feel the need to validate themselves in all kinds of strange and destructive ways. Deep down they feel worthless, and fear facing into this core of worthlessness, and so avoid it by wreaking havoc in the world or seeking to undermine those more accomplished than themselves.

How is the darker face of competitiveness transformed? The root of the problem seems to be pride, and its main manifestation as righteous attachment to a position. Deep down many men fear the sense of worthlessness that will come from admitting defeat, being crushed by the father or brother or opponent, or losing the girl or the property or the land to the other guy. This ego-demolition can seem worse than death, leaving the man with no purpose at all. He cannot bring children into the world as a woman can, so there may seem nothing of import to fall back on. His default ego-worth is founded on the drive to prove himself in contrast to other men.

The key, as it is with most things, is in the establishment of right relationship. A man must learn to truly connect with other men, and in so doing, begin to understand that they are not the enemy. This can take time, naturally, and in the case of 'worthy enemies' may seem insurmountable, even over the course of a long lifetime. A nemesis can be sustained forever. But at what cost? And for what purpose?

Buddhist teachings present the idea of cultivating the 'big view'; in Zen, this is sometimes called 'big mind'. This big view or big mind sees beyond petulance, personal position, or the need to be eternal combatants in defense of a point of pride. As Jacob Bronowski said at the close of his magnificent *The Ascent of Man*

1970s documentary on the history of science, 'We have to touch people.' He'd uttered those words while standing in the mud on a rainy day at Auschwitz, site of one of the major Holocaust concentration camps (Bronowski was a Polish Jew). It has been the failure of men to *connect* with men, to truly know them, that has fueled so many divisions of heart and mind between male leaders—and between civilizations—throughout history.

Chapter 6

Mythology and Revisioning the Code of the Warrior

Perceval, the Quest for the Holy Grail, and Modern-Day Warriors

The original 'Holy Grail' stories were written in France in the twelfth and thirteenth centuries CE. The first to create fictional treatments of the myth seems to have been Chretien de Troyes, whose stories about Perceval and his quest were written around the mid-twelfth century. Chretien had himself been influenced by the Welsh cleric Geoffrey of Monmouth who, writing in the early twelfth century, had fashioned the original King Arthur myth via his fanciful *History of the Kings of Britain*, published in 1136. Geoffrey did not have a 'Holy Grail' in his legends. Chretien took the idea of a legendary king and his brave knights and added the idea of a romantic quest for a sacred object. Chretien did not finish his tales, but others did, resulting in the fully fleshed-out Grail myths we know today.

In Chretien's original story—*Perceval, the Story of the Grail*—a young man, named Perceval, is being raised in a secluded Welsh forest. After his father's death—when he is being raised by his mother—he starts encountering shining knights in armor passing through the forest. Drawn to these mysterious and powerful-looking men on horseback, he soon realizes that he wishes to be one as well. However, this will require him to leave the forest and his mother. She does not want him to go, and she has a good reason. Perceval's father, who was also a knight, had been gravely wounded in battle and then died of grief upon hearing about the death of his other two sons. Perceval's mother, naturally, does not want to lose her last son. (This theme was echoed in Steven Spielberg's 1998 World War II drama *Saving*

Private Ryan—although in a twist reflective of the twentieth century, the young hero was not in search of any Grail, but rather was merely fulfilling his honorable duty as ordained by old military men sitting around strategy tables.)

The time to 'leave the mother' in search of a destiny is a key point in the journey of every young man in his transition from boyhood. That transition, while ideally occurring early in life (say, by 20 years of age), often does not occur until considerably later, especially for those born after 1975 or so (late Gen-Xers and Millennials). It's relatively common for early twenty-first-century men to not move out until they are well into their mid or late twenties. Part of this is simply due to the vastly inflated cost of real estate (including rental rates) as compared to earlier decades. I recall my first rented apartment in a major Canadian city (Montreal) in 1980. It cost $110 per month for a bachelor's suite. After a year there I moved down the street into a spacious one-bedroom apartment for $225 per month. These same units now cost (four decades later) six to ten times as much or more. Cost of living colors the fate of many twenty-first-century would-be Percevals.

Arguably this makes the myth of Perceval all the more relevant for young early twenty-first-century men. In Chretien's fable, he must break away from his mother. The mother represents more than just the matriarch or the female head of the household. She also represents the ties to home, village, and tradition. Her instinct is to preserve continuity and thus she tends to discourage anything too radical, anything involving wandering and adventure and uncertainty. These are arguably more masculine tendencies, and therefore the mother in general works counter to the development of the masculine spirit. It's not that she opposes it due to any nefarious motive. It's just her nature to restrain things, to temper things with practicality. And this is why the boy needs sufficiently inspiring older men upon which to model himself. A man can help him escape the forest and go on his adventure, not his mother. Even in the case of a mother who outwardly encourages him to go, inwardly her pull is very often to hold him back, because she does not want to lose him and, in so doing, lose her identity and purpose as mother and guardian of the hearth.

The problem in current times is that there are so few shining knights for the young man to model himself upon or aspire to follow. An interesting modern parable from popular culture is the 'Batman' tale, especially the early twenty-first-century reboots directed by Christopher Nolan. In his first one, *Batman Begins*, released in 2005, the young future Batman (Bruce Wayne, as portrayed by Christian Bale), having passed through a rather traumatic childhood (his parents were murdered by a mugger in front of him), ends up in the Bhutanese Himalayas where he is trained in martial arts and mind-control techniques by a shadowy organization fittingly called the League of Shadows. This 'League' is full of highly trained fighting men with various advanced and mysterious powers—an edgier version of the Jedi Knights. As his training ends, Bruce becomes aware that the League is involved in the business of eradicating what it judges as corrupt centers of civilization. It plans to destroy Gotham City, which it has deemed irredeemable. Our hero then takes it upon himself to stop the ruthless plan, and—in the most absurdly unrealistic part of the film—promptly destroys, singlehandedly, the entire League temple where he trained. This temple had been run by powerful older men, in particular by the mysterious Ra's al Ghul (played with appropriate gravitas by Liam Neeson), who had been Bruce's main mentor for training.

The reason the whole tale is a fitting reflection of early twenty-first-century times is that the 'shining knights' who inspire Perceval (in this case, the future Batman) are themselves corrupt, or at the least, run by dark ideals and agendas that are reminiscent of Nazi ideas of racial purity and the desire to eradicate, wholesale, bodies of population judged as undesirable.

The League of Shadows is convinced Gotham City is evil, and so wishes to erase it.

What Bruce's plight reveals, in part, is how twenty-first-century young men view the power structures of the world (run, mostly, by older men). The screenplay for *Batman Begins* was written by Nolan and David Goyer, both at the time in their thirties. The way they conceived of the older male mentor figures in the League of Shadows reflects well the mindsets of the time. Even the name, 'League of Shadows', is hardly reminiscent of a home for noble, virtuous, and shining knights. While Perceval had resplendent knights to follow and emulate, Bruce Wayne must kill his mentors and then retreat to an underground lair where he decides to fight crime as a shadowy figure himself. Despite his best intentions, he has unavoidably become something of a chip off his mentors' blocks.

To continue with the tale of Perceval. He eventually heads off to the court of King Arthur. Once there he proceeds to establish himself — after being taunted by fellow knights — by killing a particularly troublesome knight who had been a problem for the king. After killing him, Perceval takes his armor. (This theme, a distilled version of the ancient tradition of eating the heart of a slain enemy, is often echoed in modern culture — a good example being Tom Cruise's character in *The Last Samurai*, who after killing a particular samurai, ends up not only with the samurai's armor, but with his woman also.) He is then accepted by the community and trains under an experienced knight. We can note the key difference between this tale and that of *Batman Begins* — Perceval must kill only one corrupt knight and then he's accepted by the community of legitimate knights, whereas Bruce Wayne has to kill them all, and then has no one to accept or embrace him. He is orphaned from the community of older men, something many modern men can relate to.

Traditionally and historically, most young men sooner or later have encountered some sort of test in life that required them to prove themselves to other men. However, the modern man more commonly finds himself in a situation where he is proving himself to *women* more than men. This is in part because of the central importance his mother, and women in general, have held for most of his early life. His father just did not carry that much significance, because his absence, or his fatigue after working, has bred the remoteness that makes him less consequential a figure than the mother (and thus, the female).

Few modern men meet the challenge Perceval did and was required to tackle (killing the troublesome knight). Of course, we need not take Perceval's tale literally in order to mine its virtues. We are not required to find some bad guy to eliminate in order to become a man worthy of initiation. But at the same time, our initiation cannot come from a woman. Not the kind of initiation that enables the entitled and self-important prince to transition into a worthy knight.

Initiation

What does it mean to be 'initiated'? The word stems from the Latin *initiare*, meaning 'to begin'. Nothing too mystical there. It was only in sixteenth-century France that the term began to be associated with the idea of undergoing participation in secret rites, secret doctrines, or secret brotherhoods. Although the idea of 'beginning' may seem banal, it is anything but. Biologically, the masculine polarity has to do with *fertilization*, the stimulus needed to spark the creation of life. The best automobile engine, resting in the most wondrous autobody, goes nowhere without some sort of ignition and starter.

Since the early 1990s I've participated numerous times in West Coast Native Indian sweat lodges. The tradition of the sweat lodge—a kind of spiritualized sauna—though found in different forms around the world, seems to have had its North America genesis with the Plains Indians. Apparently, it was originally intended as a purification rite (and doubtless a bonding event) for warriors about to go into battle. By the time the sweat lodge had migrated to the West Coast it had become available to both men and women (and there are now sweat lodges only for women). The mixed sweat lodges that I participated in—attended mostly by Caucasians (though led by Native Indians)—had the men sit on one side and the women on the other, doubtless an attempt to preserve some semblance of tradition.

What I found interesting was the tradition the 'keepers of the lodge' or the 'pipe-holder' (the man or men who ran the sweat lodge) had of referring to women who entered the lodge as the 'life-givers'. The men were given no title. Upon reflection, I found this somewhat puzzling in that it seems, at least from a biological perspective, equally appropriate to refer to men as 'life-givers' since it is male seed that fertilizes female egg.

Male self-image tends to be, in many respects, poor in this time we inhabit. I have certainly encountered many young modern men who lack a healthy image of the masculine ideal, but have no shortage of examples they can draw on that define male stupidity and destructiveness—the 'life-taker'. One has only to observe the typical destructive force in a Hollywood science-fiction or fantasy film, which is invariably portrayed as some male monster whose sole purpose is to eradicate life—or as a master villain who wishes to subjugate the universe. Admittedly there are exceptions to the rule—the creature in James Cameron's 1986 *Aliens*, the sequel to Ridley Scott's 1979 *Alien*, was apparently female, and Japanese monster movies have an entire category of female *kaiju* (monster) in their canon (not to mention, the gender of Godzilla has long been disputed)—but these are hardly the norm. In television shows, movies, and popular culture, the bad (or stupid) guy is usually just that, a guy.

A poor self-image, be it personal or related to one's history—or one's gender—is never a good thing, except in the more extreme cases of men who really need their ego deconstructed, but even there the remedial possibilities of such deconstruction are either marginal or overridden by the need to punish the ego-inflated man. He gets his ego dismantled but almost never emerges a better man. More commonly he ends up like the Iraqi dictator Saddam Hussein: a scared old dog found hiding in a ditch, later to be ignominiously hanged—the footage of his execution was even available for entertainment on YouTube—for his crimes.

The gift of masculinity—as well as its challenge—is to *initiate* things, to infuse them with vitality and energy, and to spark life into what it focuses on, not unlike the iconic image in the Sistine Chapel of God sparking Adam with life. The paintings of the nineteenth-century Dutch impressionist Vincent van Gogh perhaps express this quality of energy as well as any art has ever done, in the vigor and sheer intensity of his brush strokes, all suggestive of a powerful movement of energy that is both expression and release—expression of 'lust for life' and release into freedom. Van Gogh was no example of healthy-mindedness to emulate; he was the archetypal troubled soul and ended his own life at just 37. But his troubles were in large part related to the circumstances of his time (as it was with Jesus), and his tortured self-expression was both his grounds for learning and the means by which his gifts became manifest.

Chretien's Grail legend was paralleled by the Welsh romance *Peredur*, in which the young hero had six older brothers, along with his father, all killed in battle. Peredur's mother then absconds with him into the wilds, determined to raise him away from worldly, and certainly warrior, ways. Again, it is virtually impossible to find fault with the mother's actions. She is simply doing her instinctive duty to preserve the life of her son. (And this is why all male issues are ultimately never truly 'about' the female, but rather about a man's inability to manifest his maleness.)

Peredur was raised not just in Nature, but ignorant of his heritage. He thus embodies a kind of innocence and purity of heart. Eventually he meets three great knights, Gawain, Owein, and Urien. In keeping with Peredur's naivety his mother tells him that these knights are in fact angels, but the boy soon finds out otherwise, which motivates him to follow them and seek to become a brave knight himself. His mother, doubtless recognizing the futility of restraining him, bids him to go to King Arthur's court, accompanied by her motherly advice, part of which involves the instruction that if Peredur hears the wails of a damsel in distress he should attend to her.

This 'white knight' quality, perhaps one of the central defining features of chivalry, is on occasion basic to the inheritance of modern, dysfunctional feminized men. It often carries the shadow issue of instinctively rejecting other men in favor of protecting women at all costs. There is a bar fight scene from the action movie *Knockaround Guys* (2001) that speaks well to this. The 'hero' of the piece, played by Vin Diesel, responds to a local bad guy's mistreatment of a pretty blond woman (he'd slapped her in the face) by delivering a vicious beating to the bad guy. Diesel's character doesn't quite kill him, but beats the guy so badly that his ego, as well as his body, is crushed. The demolished bad guy was anything but honorable and, as portrayed, it's hard to find fault in Diesel's character for initially challenging him and physically punishing him. However, it's the savage nature of the beating that gives pause; that, along with the gratuitous nature of the bad guy's original bullying of the woman. It's not to argue that these two elements are not common in the bad old world out there—men who bully women and men who wreak vengeance on them for doing so are, and always have been, commonplace. What is more noteworthy, and troubling, is the modern focus on these kinds of men in popular culture. Vin Diesel's character at first appears to be the good guy in contrast to the bad boy he beats up, but by the time he finishes his over-the-top beating, neither one is admirable.

The Short Lives of Bruce and Brandon Lee

A more admirable embodiment of masculine intensity in a skilled fighter can be found in the legendary martial arts master and actor Bruce Lee (1940–73; his birth name was Lee Jun-fan). The cause of Lee's sudden death at age 32—he lay down for a nap and never awoke—is still disputed. Theories range from cannabis misuse to brain swelling caused by allergic reactions to painkillers or tranquilizers. It was even speculated, as it so often is with prominent families plagued by misfortune, that his family was the subject of some weird curse. This notion received more currency when Lee's son Brandon, a talented martial arts practitioner and charismatic actor following in his father's footsteps, died tragically on the set of *The Crow* in 1993 at age 28 (in a spectacular display of film production incompetence he was accidentally shot to death by a gun that was supposed to be harboring blanks).

Bruce Lee's legacy was remarkable in part because he only made five films: *The Big Boss* (1971); *Fist of Fury*, titled in North America as *The Chinese Connection* (1972); *Way of the Dragon*, titled in North America as *Return of the Dragon* (1972); *Enter the Dragon* (1973); and *The Game of Death* (released posthumously in 1978). In an odd coincidence Lee's son Brandon also made five films. He was finishing up his fifth when he was killed.

Prior to this work Lee's most notable turn was in the 1960s TV show *The Green Hornet*, where he played Kato, the martial arts expert sidekick to the main character. The show lasted only one season (1966–67) before being yanked by ABC due to low ratings. The 'Green Hornet' himself was a vigilante businessman and publisher named Britt Reid, who clandestinely moonlighted as a successful crime fighter. The tandem of the Green Hornet and Kato was arguably a more interesting tandem compared to other dynamic duos such as Batman and Robin or the Lone Ranger and Tonto. This was mainly because of Lee's exceptional athletic ability and fighting prowess. Kato was unlike anything seen on screen at that time. As an interesting side note, the character of Kato in the original 1939 and 1941 film versions of *The Green Hornet* was played by Keye Luke, the same guy who later played Master Po, the blind old martial arts master who famously christened Kwai Chang Caine (David Carradine) as 'Grasshopper' in the early 1970s TV show *Kung Fu*.

The connection between Lee and *Kung Fu* doesn't end there. When the show was being conceived there was some consideration about casting an Asian in the lead role, and in that regard Bruce Lee was the leading choice at the time (owing mainly to his role as Kato). However, the creators of the show (Ed Spielman, Jerry Thorpe, and Herman Miller) wanted David Carradine, as he had a more 'serene' disposition. And, to be frank, he was a good actor; Lee, for all his physical prowess and martial arts mastery, was not.

Bruce Lee—and indeed his son Brandon must be included in this assessment even if he didn't have the time to mature to his father's level—was the very epitome of intensity; and specifically, of the warrior who smolders with passion and commitment to his craft. What was mesmerizing about him was not just his athletic skill, which was obviously marked— he had extraordinary speed and agility—but also his charisma. His eyes alone were remarkably expressive. And the shrieking sounds that emerged from him while he fought were strangely animalistic and hypnotic, not unlike a bird of prey.

Back in the mid-1970s when I was training in shito-ryu karate, my instructor once sparred in front of our class with a visiting black belt. The visiting black belt was perhaps in his late twenties, tall and slender, and probably no match for my instructor if the two were to have some sort of street brawl. But the visiting black belt had excellent skill and the two ended up fighting to a draw. Aside from those details the only other thing I recall about the fight was the extraordinary sounds the visiting black belt made as he fought—strange screeching sounds that were very reminiscent of Bruce Lee (who, having died just a year before, was probably his influence). The atmosphere and quality of the whole fight was greatly amplified by these sounds and made for a spellbinding experience.

Charisma is a powerful force in this world—in male warriors it's perhaps the equivalent of stunning beauty in a female. It gets people places in society, because it carries the message that individuality trumps commonality. The magnetic appeal of such a force can never be underestimated.

Bruce Lee was a force of Nature, but his death at only 32 may have precluded the development of deeper wisdom, in particular the refinement of philosophical understanding that almost always requires the help of Father Time. Lee was renowned for his study of philosophy and his general wide reading. However, his grasp of the Japanese word *mushin*—loosely translated as 'no-mind', and an important concept in both Zen and martial arts—was apparently not complete. He is reported to have once remarked that if he'd killed someone in a real fight he would plead not guilty because his fighting moves would be arising from within, from *mushin*, and thus '*it* killed him, not me'.[1]

The understanding of 'no-mind' is central to deeper meditation practice, and is also closely related to an idea that any accomplished athlete can relate to: at the moment of truth, whether it be an archer firing at his target, a boxer throwing his best punch, a baseball batter hitting a 100 miles per hour fastball out of the park, or a hockey player making a successful blind pass, there is a mysterious last, split-second 'letting go' that happens. Psychology might explain this as the unconscious mind taking over in a timely and appropriate fashion. A successful athlete is therefore one who is not just finely honed physically, but who also has a good relationship between his conscious and unconscious minds (something we might simply call 'good reflexes', but in all likelihood there is far more than just that going on). When a baseball player gets into a hitting slump, he's often described as 'squeezing the bat too much'. An athlete who loses their groove is described as 'pressing'. What these terms point toward is the tendency of the conscious ego to try to exert too much control over the more powerful, more efficient unconscious mind. The result is interference. The unconscious (or instinctive) part of the mind cannot do its job as effectively, and so the athlete performs poorly.

Mushin, or 'no-mind', carries deeper connotations than just the relationship between the conscious and unconscious minds, however. It's also related to the idea of transcendence, or what other Western psychological systems (such as Roberto Assagioli's Psychosynthesis) would refer to as the 'higher' or 'transpersonal' self. The awareness arising from this part of consciousness is not like the unconscious mind—which while similar to an immensely powerful computer is also childlike (and childish) in places—but is rather more like a kind of 'cosmic consciousness' in that it takes in the greater picture and sees clearly the intrinsic connectivity (or even Oneness) of all things.

Of course, all this leads to the obvious question: how can a direct experience of the connectedness or Oneness of all things allow for any sort of competitive, let alone aggressive or even violent, actions? Questions such as these were front and center during the World War II years in Japan, when Zen masters were commonly involved in the practice of endorsing or even encouraging young men to embrace the times they lived in and fight the good fight for their flag and land. The tradition of warrior-monks is very much concerned with this issue. While few monks sought to be warriors, and few warriors sought deep spiritual enlightenment, there *is* in fact a meeting ground for the two mindsets, and it lies in the modern so-called 'integral' model of reality. The integral model accepts all dimensions of human existence and recognizes that any sort of avoiding of life circumstances, direct human lessons, and the conditions of our time and culture in the name of seeking supreme spiritual transcendence, tends to result in spiritual bypassing and, all too commonly, a dissociated holier than thou-ism.

Bruce Lee may have been a work in progress, but his fire and charisma alongside remarkable wisdom were obvious to those who knew him. A particularly good interview of him with the Canadian journalist Pierre Burton, done in 1971, can be seen on YouTube (as of 2018). Younger viewers of this interview frequently comment on Burton's 'arrogance' or even 'racism', but I could see neither. One had to know Pierre Burton, himself a legend, and his style of interviewing, in order to recognize the goodwill of the interview and the charming rapport between the two men. One excerpt from that interview, where Lee is dramatically rhapsodizing about the spiritual qualities of water, has been used in a segment juxtaposing it with Lee apparently playing ping-pong, using his famous nunchakus, with some guy. It's not actually Bruce Lee playing ping-pong (it's a lookalike, and the segment was filmed in 2007 as part of a Nokia commercial, but many were fooled), which is all perhaps a fitting testament to Lee's mystery—was he an authentic warrior and philosopher, or just a charismatic actor? I submit he was all of those, and that's not a bad thing.

Killer Tulku

Another example from the Silver Screen bears mentioning. Steven Seagal (b. 1952) has been making martial arts movies since his 1988 breakout role in *Above the Law*. As of 2018 he has made close to 50 films. He usually plays a similar character in each movie—a hero who has a background in martial arts, is defending some hapless person or cause, and invariably must defeat an army of bad guys. Seagal's films are notable in that he rarely gets a scratch in any of his onscreen fights. He always wins decisively, and usually quickly, without the other guy even putting in a decent showing. In point of fact, Seagal actually does have a seventh-degree black belt in aikido, an old Japanese martial art that is not quite as popular as its flashier cousins such as karate or sumo wrestling. He even trained in Japan in the early 1970s and was the first foreigner to open an aikido dojo there.

A repetitive feature of Seagal's films is his vicious beatings of stupid, stubborn, bad boys who never once seem capable of recognizing a lost fight before it starts. Many of these scenarios involve him defending some helpless, and often morally virtuous, woman against a bad man who is accompanied by an army of stupid henchmen. The few good men in his films are usually relegated to the characters of old, wise Asian martial arts teachers (only briefly seen in opening scenes), or the occasional bumbling but likeable sidekick.

That Seagal has made a brand (and a living) out of inhabiting this stereotype—while fighting against the cardboard stereotype of the stupid, bad man who never knows when to raise a white flag (which is why Steven must kill, or break the limbs of, so many of these guys)—is a somewhat disturbing commentary on our times. Popular culture via the movie-making industry may be mainly in the business of reflecting current values and trends, but it's also involved in sustaining, and more problematically, in occasionally creating them.

One could be forgiven for concluding that Seagal's movie characters just don't like men very much—and certainly not the meatheads he keeps encountering. Yes, we all know that these dummy characters are simply thrown at him so that he can demonstrate his combat wizardry. But the sheer repetitiveness of it is yet another meta-message to younger men that most men are really stubborn and really stupid, cannot be trusted, and are almost always of worse moral fiber than women.

A strange twist in Seagal's story occurred in 1997 when he was recognized by an established Tibetan Buddhist master (Penor Rinpoche, 1932–2009) as a *tulku*. As mentioned earlier in this book, in Tibetan Buddhism, a *tulku* is a lineage-holder and a custodian of wisdom-teachings. It is a highly esteemed institution. To be recognized as a *tulku* — in effect, an advanced and very special being — is no trifling matter.[2] Predictably, Seagal's recognition by a respected Tibetan Buddhist teacher was met with skepticism and derision, with the biggest objection relating to Seagal's role in violent movies (Buddhism is supposed to be a religion of non-violence). Penor Rinpoche met these criticisms with the argument that Seagal was merely making movies, and was not acting violently in real life; and that further, some *tulkus* from the past were recognized late in life, or before they began their training and teaching careers.

Seagal is noteworthy because he was really the first Silver Screen martial artist to project an essentially invulnerable persona. Even Bruce Lee, who otherwise came closest in this regard, did take the occasional choreographed blow or scratch. Other notables such as Jackie Chan (b. 1954), Jet Li (b. 1963), and Tony Jaa (b. 1976), although invariably triumphing in their 'battles', also took their shots and might even on occasion seem close to losing. Jaa — who briefly left his acting career to train as a Buddhist monk in 2010 — in particular is renowned for his spectacular fighting technique; his 2003 movie *Ong Bak* has been highly acclaimed among martial arts critics. But he was not portrayed as an invincible machine the way Seagal typically is.

Seagal's onscreen legend, although undeniably entertaining to behold, is one step shy of the comic book superhero whose powers render him more than human. This appeals to the part of the male psyche that fears vulnerability and fantasizes about triumphing over the hordes of bad men out there. It doesn't take Freud or Yoda to see the connection here with the father-wound.

A man's first experience in life of the masculine polarity is of course his father, but if that father is mostly an absence from the boy's life in later years — in effect, a void — he begins to fill up the emptiness with mostly negative perceptions. This easily becomes transferred to men in general, or to the organizations — be they socially acceptable (say, Freemasons) or not (the Underworld)—that they run. A man with a father-wound is looking to conquer bad guys; either on his own, or more conveniently, vicariously through a superhero.

Bond. *James* Bond

A hip, modern, and very Western version of the ninja—and a classic stealth warrior—is the renowned fictional British secret agent 007, James Bond. First appearing as a character in 1953 in the novels of the English author Ian Fleming (1908–64), his status grew to such an extent that as of this writing in 2018 he has appeared in no fewer than 24 movies, far more than the number of actual Bond novels that Fleming wrote (12, along with 9 short stories).

Six actors have portrayed Bond on screen in the major films, beginning with Sean Connery in *Dr No* (1962). Six of the first seven films (from 1962 to 1971) featured Connery as Bond, with one of those starring the forgettable George Lazenby in the role (1969's *On Her Majesty's Secret Service*). Connery's last was *Diamonds Are Forever* (1971), after which he was replaced by Roger Moore who starred in the next seven (the most of any actor to date), from 1973's *Live and Let Die* to 1985's *A View to a Kill*. Moore was followed by the short-lived reign of Timothy Dalton, who did just two, 1987's *The Living Daylights* and 1989's *License to Kill*. The next four films found a new Bond in Pierce Brosnan, from 1995's *GoldenEye* to 2002's *Die Another Day*. Brosnan gave way to the most recent Bond incarnation, Daniel Craig, who thus far has starred in four, from 2006's *Casino Royale* to 2015's *Spectre*.

My personal favorite of this lot was the first, Connery, although each actor carries very different qualities that in part seem to reflect the zeitgeist of when his movies were shot. Daniel Craig is doubtless the roughest of them all, even more robust than Connery, reflecting the angry times of the early twenty-first century in which young men—or men of any age—have grown bored with tamer forms of choreographed martial aggression. One has only to compare the martial arts sequences of a twenty-first-century Tony Jaa film (such as *Ong Bak*), with the slow-mo sequences enacted by David Carradine in his original *Kung Fu* role in the early 1970s. Or better yet, the campy fight sequences of 1960s TV shows—perhaps the all-time classic example of which was William Shatner (as Captain Kirk) fighting the Gorn alien in the 1967 *Star Trek* episode 'Arena'—a sequence deservedly titled on YouTube as 'worst fight scene of all time' (and doubtless the funniest).

Fleming's real-life models for Bond were several, including himself (he had been a commander in the Naval Intelligence Division and assistant to its Director, and thus had direct espionage experience), alongside many actual secret agents and commandos he'd known during his war years. Perhaps the most interesting connection was between Bond's agent number (007) and that of the sixteenth-century magus and polymath John Dee (1527–1609), who had been, at times, Queen Elizabeth I's court wizard, astrologer, adviser, and secret agent in the 1580s. Dee used to sign his letters to the Queen as '007'.

Secret agents have traditionally been almost exclusively male, but this is no longer the case, in real life or in popular culture. A good example is the character of Carrie Mathison, a CIA field agent as portrayed by Claire Danes in the successful TV series *Homeland*. That said, the modern secret agent has its roots in the idea of gathering intelligence about an enemy, something practiced by warrior cultures of old. Sun Tzu, renowned author of *The Art of War*, devoted a whole chapter of his iconic book to espionage. He particularly valued spies who acquire knowledge of the enemy that proves useful and practical. He famously wrote:

> If you know the enemy and know yourself, you need not fear the results of a hundred battles. If you know yourself but not

the enemy, for every victory gained you will also suffer a defeat. If you know neither the enemy nor yourself, you will succumb in every battle.

There is a very interesting idea contained within this passage, something that arguably speaks to the best qualities of the warrior mindset, and it is this: a would-be mystic or monk seeks to know himself, but in many cases, this amounts to a type of insularity or worse, self-absorption and fear of life. (A 'successful' mystic or monk transcends such limitations, but it is a given that many who set out on such a path do not.) The warrior, however, has the advantage of gaining insight into not just himself, but the other as well, thereby avoiding too much introversion. Additionally, this 'other' is not just anyone, but the enemy, and as such he retains an active curiosity about a difficult subject (most people prefer to avoid or ignore their enemies).

The secret agent throughout history was not interested in conscious values, however; his job was to gain information about an enemy that he and his superiors wanted to defeat or destroy. The higher value that can be extracted from the spy-mindset is awareness of the global context outside of one's own self-congratulatory spirituality. To be truly conscious we must indeed know the enemy, because in the deepest sense, he is *us*. To know the other is to know ourselves.

Iron Mike

Mike Tyson (b. 1966), the notorious boxer who ruled the heavyweight division during the mid-to-late 1980s and parts of the 1990s, is another interesting example. A beast in the ring, he was probably the most feared boxer in history in his prime, owing to a combination of speed (almost unmatched), power (like that of Shavers or Foreman), and killer instinct. He won his first 19 bouts, 12 of them by knocking out his opponent in the first round; some of these guys lasted less than a minute with him in the ring—one was knocked out in eight seconds.

Tyson's downfall began when reports of his mistreatment of his young female mate began to surface in the late 1980s. His subsequent (and predictable) decline as a fighter began when, sporting a perfect 37 wins (33 by knockout) and 0 defeats record as a professional, he was knocked out by journeyman fighter James 'Buster' Douglas in 1990 in Tokyo. The fight has an interesting back story in that Douglas's mother had died just a few weeks before the bout. No one gave Douglas a chance in the fight; Las Vegas odds makers were reluctant to give him odds at all (he ended up a 42–1 underdog). Years later Tyson was interviewed by Oprah Winfrey. She said that she knew he was in trouble before the fight started. 'Why?' asked Tyson. 'Because the man's mother had just died,' replied Winfrey. 'He had an angel over his shoulder; there was no way he could lose.' 'In that case,' said Tyson, 'he must have had a whole army of angels, he fought so good.'[3]

The exchange is classic on many levels. Winfrey—probably *the* pop culture goddess in the Western hemisphere of the late twentieth century—is admonishing her contemporary Tyson, the supreme but tarnished gladiator, that his masculinity is no match for the power of another warrior fighting for the memory and honor of his mother. (She proved right—20-20 hindsight notwithstanding.)

More relevant to our discussion is the cause of Tyson's decline, almost certainly not to be found in the bruising blows of a man supposedly fighting for the memory of his mother. It is known that Tyson had already been slacking off prior to the Douglas fight, having grown overconfident and lazy in his training. But the psychological source of his sputtering can probably be traced to his failures in his relationships with women, and further back, to the incompetence of his parents (his mother had been a crack addict, and his father, a pimp). That is not to justify Tyson's real failures as a man. His behavior in the years to follow was, at times, poor and inexcusable—something he openly admits numerous times in his raw 2014 autobiography *Undisputed Truth*. But for our purposes here it bears looking at the back story of his failures with women.

In 1988 Tyson, riding off his spectacular successes as a modern gladiator, had somehow married Robin Givens, a talented young actress, and a graduate of the prestigious Sarah Lawrence College to boot. (I used the word 'somehow' flippantly; Tyson was by then a multimillionaire.) The marriage lasted but one tumultuous year, punctuated by a miscarriage, bitter accusations, conflict, and the usual high drama. Tyson's decline continued when in 1991 he was arrested and charged with the rape of an 18-year-old beauty pageant contestant. (In Tyson's autobiography, he flatly denies the charges. Given his highly self-critical and surprisingly honest approach throughout the book, his innocent plea does give one pause.) During the trial Tyson's behavior was, by his own admission, arrogant and unrepentant, which doubtless contributed toward the jury convicting him and the judge sentencing him. He served three years of a six-year term; while in prison he converted to Islam.

When he got out of the joint he launched a comeback that was initially successful but ran into problems with the notorious Evander Holyfield bouts of 1996–97, the second of which was stopped when an enraged Tyson, frustrated by what he claimed was Holyfield's intentional head-butting, bit off small parts of Holyfield's ear lobes. He was subsequently stripped of his boxing license, although perhaps surprisingly for only a year. His second comeback was less effective, marred by further legal infractions including an assault on two motorists that ended with Tyson serving another nine months in jail. He managed to easily beat three lesser fighters (one in 38 seconds) before eventually losing badly to then-champion Lennox Lewis (after yelling at Lewis, in a boorishly theatrical press conference, 'I want to eat your heart and your children!'). By 2003 the previously wealthy Tyson had filed for bankruptcy. He won a few more fights against lesser opponents, but by 2005, following his loss to journeyman fighter Kevin McBride, he was done at 39 years of age. He ended his career with a record of 50 wins—44 of those by knockout—and 6 losses.

A psychological analysis of Tyson is beyond the scope and purpose of this book, but his life is a worthy cautionary tale as well as a reflection of modern times in which a man's relationship with women is central to his overall well-being. Why? In large part because so many modern men, bereft of male role models, have not been initiated into real manhood by older men. Accordingly, they grow into men who badly need the affirmation, approval, and attention of women to have peace of mind (and this is confirmed repeatedly in Tyson's autobiography, where he is constantly becoming romantically and sexually entangled with women and constantly running into trouble with them). The thing about Tyson is that when you listen to him talk in interviews you don't see a great deal of male energy. He sounds youthful, remarkably open, boyishly feminine, even naive. Yet his physical power, and his manner in the ring in his prime, was suggestive of a menacing animal. Men much larger than him were frightened of him. His masculinity seemed entirely contained in his physique and his fighting aggression. Yet his character did not radiate mature masculine strength.

According to his birth certificate Tyson's biological father was born in Jamaica but seems to have been unknown to him. Tyson was raised by his mother in Brooklyn. At some point, she met a man named Jimmy Kirkpatrick, with whom she had another son (Tyson's half-brother). But Kirkpatrick abandoned the family when Mike was born. He was therefore raised entirely by his mother. She herself died when he was just 16. And it's not even completely clear who his real father was. (As an interesting side note, apparently about 1 in every 135 Western European men are unknowingly raising a child who is not their biological offspring—something confirmed by modern DNA tests.[4])

Tyson did have at least one role model, an old man named Cus D'Amato (1908–85), who in his heyday had managed the storied boxer Floyd Patterson. D'Amato became Tyson's manager and effectively his parent (he adopted Tyson after his mother had died, thus fully taking him under his wing). In a 2008 documentary on his life, as well as throughout his autobiography, Tyson clearly indicates that D'Amato was the only real father-figure he ever had. D'Amato's death in 1985 when Tyson was just 19 left a gap in Tyson's psyche that seems to have never been properly filled by any other quality role model.

Tyson's autobiography is ultimately impressive because of his raw and defenseless honesty—perhaps grandly ironic for a fighter who in his prime was not just an unrivalled attacker but was also a fortress defensively. Tyson's ego was so dismantled by his self-sabotaging arrogance, consequent life circumstances, and losses (not just in the ring), that the man who emerges in later life is strangely likeable, even as he still struggles with his self-loathing. One is reminded of Richard Nixon, so effective, so loathed, and yet in his later years, after his ego had been exploded in a spectacular fashion, emerging as a man of humble wisdom. Or Bill Clinton, widely humiliated as president by the global exposure of his sexual dalliances, gradually reappearing later as a sage-like and respected (by many) public figure.

Tyson has a valuable message, even if it's tritely or not always cleverly formulated, and it's something that many younger and older men can learn from. The message is, quite simply, about humility combined with honesty. Male pride can be brutal and its most common manifestation as an arrogant disposition is probably responsible for more bloodshed and destruction than any other human character trait. Lord Acton famously wrote that 'absolute power corrupts absolutely', which is often borne out, but more problematic is the underlying pride that fuels it, the vicious attachment to being right about things that has caused tyrants and corrupt leaders throughout history to make bad decisions that ended up costing untold millions of lives.

More on Chivalry

In the case of our young would-be knight Peredur, he did, however, locate worthy role models—knights of Arthur's court—and proceeded to train under one of them. He had noble ideals to aspire to. And his attitude toward women—as trained by his mother—was to be entirely chivalrous.

What is 'chivalry'? The word, first used around the thirteenth century CE, derives from the old French *chevalerie* ('knighthood'), itself stemming from the Latin *caballarius* ('horseman'). By the fourteenth century the word had come to be associated less with knighthood per se, and more with a code of behavior, based on qualities such as honor, courage, noble intentions, and courtly courtesy. The main idea was that a man's job was to grow to embody these qualities, in so doing becoming chivalrous, worthy of his gender, and by extension, worthy of women. It was all a variation on the theme of the male as *initiator* in life, perhaps based on the first man (and first human), Adam.

Gurdjieff once said a provocative thing: 'A woman does not need to work on herself to become a real woman. All she needs to do is to find a real man, and then she will become a real woman naturally. But the problem today is that there are so few real men.'[5] It may be surprising to realize that he said these words in the 1920s in France. The 'Roaring Twenties' were a sort of precursor to the New Age 1980s–90s, where feminism had become defined, and the notion of the tentative, feminized man was taking hold.

Of course, Gurdjieff's words would be denounced today as sexist by educated feminists, who would doubtless see in them a barely concealed patriarchal arrogance hiding behind the apparent disparagement of men. For although Gurdjieff was heavily criticizing the modern men of his time, in the same breath he is suggesting that women cannot really develop on their own. They are dependent on men. This sentiment appears to be echoed in the closing lines of the apocryphal Gospel of Thomas:

> Simon Peter said to them: 'Mary should leave us, for females are not worthy of life.' Jesus said, 'See, I am going to attract her to make her male so that she too might become a living spirit that resembles males. For every female that makes itself male will enter the kingdom of heaven.'[6]

Even the Buddha was reputed to have initiated women into his *sangha* only reluctantly, hard as that may be to reconcile with the purity and loftiness of his teachings. Some have attempted to get around this by declaring all seemingly sexist passages in religious scriptures (and there are plenty in Buddhism) to be later editorial insertions from patriarchal priesthoods. That may be entirely so, but we cannot be completely sure. What we can do, however, is examine our emotional reactions to such words. Reactivity of any sort often points toward unfinished business. (For what it's worth, statements like those from the Thomas gospel probably can most usefully be interpreted alchemically, that is, the terms 'man' and 'woman' representing inner qualities rather than gender, with the former denoting the airy-conscious, and the latter the earthy-unconscious—from that perspective, our unconscious does indeed have to become conscious to enter the higher realms of being. It can also be understood as Jesus' decree that women disciples would have to undergo the same disciplines as the males, and so, in a sense, 'make themselves male'.)

The ideal of the chivalrous knight does not preclude a strong and healthy masculinity. In fact, it requires it. The whole point is that a man cannot be good to women, good *for* women, or attract the kind of woman he dreams of partnering with, unless he is first and foremost a man himself. For a man to become 'spiritually developed' he must first *be* a man. Equally so, for a man to have comfortable and enjoyable relations with women, and particularly one woman, he must first *be* a man. The key point, however, is that if he attempts to become a 'real man' only to gain the approval of women, he will almost certainly fail, because his manhood is not based on real camaraderie with other men. It is designed to get him something, a motivation that rarely works in any inner realm.

The radical American spiritual teacher Adi Da Samraj (born Franklin Jones, 1939–2008) was once addressing his community of students. Frustrated with their progress and lack of accountable behavior, he bid them all to 'be manly—man or woman'. It was a simple and straightforward directive, but also very revealing of the connotations we have with the word 'manly'. The word implies accountability. It is perhaps the single most important quality for a man to attain to.

Battle-Hardened

'Battle-hardened' is a term that we commonly hear when military leaders, or more commonly the press, are describing soldiers who have fought in wars. It is not just a cliché, however. There is indeed something that happens to the character of a man who passes through extreme fires, both literally and figuratively.

Sometime back in the mid-1990s I had the opportunity, via a mutual friend, to meet and have coffee with a retired American Green Beret who had fought in Vietnam and had—so he claimed—killed around a dozen people in that war. Based on the quality of his demeanor and general authenticity I had no reason to doubt his claim. He did not report this information in the spirit of boasting; he was both understated and matter-of-fact about his feats. Nor, however, did he sound remotely apologetic. In reporting that he had killed many enemies he sounded more like a 911-dispatcher casually discussing a night of emergency calls. (Of course, perhaps he was a simple liar, although for a mysterious reason, as our meeting was unplanned, and he showed no particular interest in me as an individual beyond being responsive to my questions about his years as a Green Beret.)

Nonchalance aside, there was something about this guy that was not common, however. He radiated an extraordinary *hardness*, for want of a better descriptor. And that was not related just to his voice (which was, granted, baritone-ish). He had a natural 'don't mess with me' disposition, and a coldness in his glance that spoke of an utterly pragmatic detachment. You just knew this guy had both seen and *done* some dark stuff— and more to the point, he didn't especially care about it. He was doing a duty; at least, a duty toward which he had been efficiently trained.

What is admirable in any of this? Not all of it, to be sure. But what stands out about the 'battle-hardened' man—be he a soldier, businessman, academic, athlete, or your wife's hairdresser—is his combination of humility and gravitas. He has the humility because he's seen the darker shades of true battle—that is, he's seen real defeat in some fashion. He has the gravitas because he has the life-experience of having lived in the raw trenches. A man with a finely developed balance of humility and gravitas is a man to be reckoned with.

Modern Cultural Taboo: Criticizing the Feminine

Over the years I've occasionally watched parts of the annual American White House Correspondents Dinner. This event, traditionally held at the end of April, has been going on since 1920 but until 1962 it was a men-only affair. It was John F. Kennedy who brought about a change when he threatened— at the prompting of journalist Helen Thomas—to boycott the dinner unless women were also admitted. He got his way. Then in the mid-1980s the dinner changed again when it shifted from being an evening of entertainment (big name singers, mostly) to one of comedy, featuring a prominent comedian who essentially conducted a roast of the President.

As typical with all roasts there is more than one target. Not only the President gets mocked, but many associated with him get it as well. Pretty much everyone is fair game except for one: the First Lady. She is absolutely off limits. And I think this well represents, in some fashion, the modern Western cultural taboo around criticizing the feminine. There are some sound reasons for that—when something is just emerging from centuries of oppression, there is a natural tendency to treat it with kid gloves, just how you would not ill-treat a newborn. But the shadow side is the tendency many softer modern men have to hold back, be passive, and in general not challenge their ladies in ways that not only might be appropriate but might actually increase the respect they have for him, not to mention the passion of their connection. (Of course, this 'shadow element' has its sporadic violent releases via certain pop-cultural outlets—standup comedians who find anything fair game, some elements of Hollywood films, or darker pornography—but most of that is outweighed by the modern passive man who has been conditioned to regard the feminine as something off limits for open criticism, and in so doing, loses his backbone in his personal dealings with the women in his life, becomes absorbed and lost in the constant need for her approval—or, on rare occasions, becomes explosively dangerous.)

American culture (and I include Canadian in this, although there are certainly differences between the two) is not entirely mature in many obvious ways. One is that despite all boasts concerning democracy, advanced technology, human rights, and gender parity, there has not yet been a female American president. (Canada to date has had one female prime minister, Kim Campbell in 1993, but she was not elected, having assumed office on the retirement of Brian Mulroney, and was soundly defeated in a general election six months later.) Technically, there has not yet been a black president either (Obama's mother was white; thus, he is biracial). Even so, America was readier to elect a biracial president than a female one. Even such (in some ways) culturally backward nations as Pakistan have had a female president (Benazir Bhutto, 1953–2007), who ran her country from 1993 to 1996. She was chased out on corruption charges, lost the 1997 election, and then went into exile for a decade in Dubai. She eventually returned to Pakistan and was preparing for another run at office when she was assassinated in 2007 at the age of 54.

There have been other powerful female heads of state, Indira Gandhi (1917–84)—who was Prime Minister of India for some 15 cumulative years over two stints, before also being assassinated in 1984 at the age of 66—being a prominent example. Not all of these rare women were bumped off. Golda Meir (1898–1974) was Prime Minister of Israel from 1969 to 1974 and died of natural causes at age 80. Margaret Thatcher (1925–2013) had a long run as Prime Minister of the UK from 1979 to 1990, dying of a stroke at age 87. And there have been other 'Iron Ladies' throughout history who have led nations, even if their number is very small compared to representatives of the male gender. (A good, and sad, example is Myanmar's Aung San Suu Kyi, b. 1945, who legitimately won an election in 1990 but who was promptly quarantined and put under periodic house arrest over some 15 years by the ruling military junta—not, it should be added, for being a woman, but for energetically and eloquently representing a powerful democratic movement in a country run by military dictatorship.)

It's always easy to poke fun at the big boy in the room, and America does get mocked, judged, and derided more than any other nation, it being the Roman Empire of current times. But it's hard not to notice the double standard implicit in much of its culture on the topic of the feminine. As much as any nation, it loudly leads the way in championing female rights, yet it retains a thinly veiled patriarchy that surreptitiously demonstrates its real regard for women by, in general, keeping them out of power positions (scattered exceptions notwithstanding).

The ideal of chivalry in its best sense is ultimately not about the feminine, or how it is to be regarded. It is about masculinity that is comfortable with itself. In that very comfort the best qualities of the feminine are then acknowledged and appreciated, often in many colorful ways. But the main point is that a man grounded in a healthy masculinity is not threatened by women, or the feminine quality in men (as with gay men, for example). This is the meaning of a functional chivalry. Dysfunctional chivalry is 'white knight-ism', the tendency to go looking for a troubled woman to play the rescuer and savior for her. As Hume pointed out three centuries ago, most people are driven by their passions (or what modern terminology would call the 'unconscious'), with their rational minds creating scripts to justify their inner, hidden impulses. A white-knight man is already wired to rescue women, and so a healthy, generous woman will be useless for him (or unattractive, as he will likely not eroticize her qualities). A troubled damsel in distress will, however (given other attributes), turn him on, and he then sets about forming a relationship with her. He needs her to play the role in his already formed script. How can he be a shining white knight without a damsel in need of rescuing? (The Darth Vader version of this character is something we could call the 'dark knight'—a manipulative guy who needs a woman with a father-wound to abuse, just as she requires him to play the bad guy role in her script.)

Einstein's List

The iconic twentieth-century German physicist Albert Einstein had an interesting and noteworthy relationship with women. I say 'noteworthy' because Einstein is a good example of a man who did not squander his energy in endlessly seeking the approval of women regarding his life path and activities. He is also an example of a man who accomplished much of what he dreamed about, even if his work was ultimately a work in progress. Notwithstanding the popular image he was a mortal man, not some scientific god, and to his last days his greatest ambition—the 'unified field theory'—remained unrealized, despite his previous spectacular and highly successful work in other branches of physics.

All that said, Einstein, when it came to women, was a regular guy—that is, his brilliance in physics and mathematics did not mean he had somehow figured out the mystery of the opposite sex. In this area, he was as capable of being vexed, frustrated, neurotic, and unforgiving as the next guy. But what he did have was a certain backbone that belied his wild-haired, teddy bear exterior. This backbone was most in evidence in his relationship with his first wife, the Serbian scientist Mileva Maric. In 1914 when their relationship was floundering Einstein drew up a list of his requirements for them to stay together. The infamous list was as follows:

You will make sure:

1. That my clothes and laundry are kept in good order.
2. That I will receive my three meals regularly *in my room.*
3. That my bedroom and study are kept neat, and especially that my desk is left for *my use only.*

You will renounce all personal relations with me insofar as they are not completely necessary for social reasons. Specifically, you will forego:

1. My sitting at home with you.
2. My going out or travelling with you.

You will obey the following points in your relations with me:

1. You will not expect any intimacy from me, nor will you reproach me in any way.
2. You will stop talking to me if I request it.
3. You will leave my bedroom or study immediately without protest if I request it.
4. You will undertake not to belittle me in front of our children, either through words or behavior.[7]

Although this list is obviously a last-ditch effort by a man to remain living with his wife so that he can retain a live-in relationship with his children (they had two young sons at that point) while in the same breath acknowledging that the intimacy in the relationship is dead, the list nevertheless will produce very different reactions depending on who is reading it. A modern feminist would probably be inclined to brand it, and the person who wrote it, as cold, controlling, and cruel. A henpecked husband might frown at it to please his wife while secretly cheering Einstein on. A young single guy who has been free of family responsibilities might shrug and wonder what the fuss is about. A person with some amount of experience in intimate relationship might suspend judgment until more facts are known. But one thing I suspect for sure is that many modern Western men might be inclined to admire, if nothing else, Einstein's firmness in the matter, other aspects of it notwithstanding.

Einstein's first wife was not a simple or easy woman to deal with. She was intelligent—as mentioned, she had an academically trained mind (also in physics), and she did assist Einstein in his initial work by acting as a sounding board for his ideas (it's an urban myth that she did anything more than that)—but she was certainly a match for Einstein in stubbornness. Einstein's 'list' did not appear out of thin air; it had been preceded by years of struggle and acrimony between the two of them. As it happened Mileva agreed to Einstein's frosty conditions, but only for as long as it took her to realize that he really was serious about the separation. At that point, they agreed to live apart and divorced several years later. He went on to marry Elsa Lowenthal, his first cousin who was six years his elder. (Prominent marriages between cousins are not as uncommon as one might think; one need only do a Google search on this matter to read some interesting stories.)

Einstein was no exemplar of stellar skill in intimate relationship, but his list is worth citing if only because it is a reasonable example—albeit one inflexible and cold—of a man who has prioritized his work and is simply refusing to allow his true calling to be sidelined by endlessly processing a relationship that was unhappy and not working for either party. If in this one regard only, Einstein proved more of a lion than a lap dog.

Alas, many men go the lap dog route, typically because they desperately fear the loss of their love-attachment, although probably most such men would deny or scoff at such an idea. A fair percentage of men do poorly on their own, ending up choosing the domesticated lap-dog route rather than risk the terrors of a solitary life. Many men are already alone in their heads, so to speak, lacking the fuller social or feeling life of most women, and many fear the prospect of growing fat and old with nothing to be consoled by except for the flat screen TV, porn, and the beer in the fridge. Best put up and shut up, then.

Another famous, though far less contentious example, was the important eighteenth-century German philosopher Immanuel Kant. A studious, highly intelligent man, he lived his whole life unmarried and unattached, alone with only a servant to attend to his basic needs. He was an academic, a professor of philosophy in a small German town, but he was intellectually ambitious, even if pedestrian in pace (his great works were not produced until he was well into his fifties). His *A Critique of Pure*

Reason, published in 1781, is an extraordinarily rich and dense philosophical treatise. Although parts of it have been surpassed by later thinkers, it remains a seminal document, perhaps the philosophical equivalent of Newton's *Principia Mathematica* if only in terms of its influence. As his equally famous follower Arthur Schopenhauer once remarked, 'Anyone interested in truth is a child until they have understood Kant.'

What has any of this to do with the masculine spirit? Outwardly Kant was no paragon of masculinity. He was a very small man, about five feet tall, and lived a quiet and routine life (for 80 years he never left his home town, except for one brief trip). Appearances to the contrary, he was not antisocial—he had a weekly dinner party, mostly for his students. (If he was gay, there remains no evidence of it.) The main point being illustrated here is that Kant manifested and completed his life work, his *magnum opus*—and by that, I'm not referring to a particular book, however famous Kant's primary work was fated to become. I'm referring to a man's primary life-work, and the need to have structure and discipline to bring it about. Kant's life was a vivid demonstration of structure and discipline—his neighbors were known to set their watches based on his precisely timed daily afternoon walk. Robotic? Perhaps. Pathologically afraid of feminine aliveness and apparent chaos? Possibly. However his life is interpreted, though, it can't be argued that Kant underachieved, or breathed his last regretting that he never exercised his intelligence to make a contribution to the development—in his case, in the intellectual realm—of the human race.

Alas, too many men throughout history could never say the same. Too many have squandered their creative force and intellectual ability in endlessly seeking to pacify a wife, or gain the five-star approval of a pretty woman. The irony of course is that no woman, deep down, wants her man to be a passive, underachieving lap dog. She wants the lion in him to remain alive. She's just not very good at helping to bring that about, as it's not in her nature. For that, he needs the company of other male lions.

I must stress that, the last two examples notwithstanding, I'm not suggesting that a man's life work may not indeed be centrally based on the role of a devoted family man. To such men, however, I'm not directing these words, but rather to those who will recognize themselves as caught in a life that involves actively repressing or denying their creative force. And nor am I suggesting that men need to be as rigid and cold as Einstein and his list, or as cloistered and monk-like as Kant and his 3 p.m. daily walk. But most men need to understand that their masculine spirit will wither if they fail to be clear and firm about their life work. Of course, that suggests a man knows what his life's great work—his *magnum opus*—is. We'll discuss that in Chapter 11.

Part Three

The Way of the Conscious Warrior

Chapter 7

The Code of the Conscious Warrior

The word 'code' derives from the Latin *codex*, which itself stems from *caudex*, meaning the 'stem of a tree'. The association is interesting, because codes are meant to function as signposts to enable some sort of grounding, much as a tree trunk anchors a tree.

Of course, too often through history such 'codes' have run out of track and overstayed their welcome, operating mainly as vague moral laws confusing to people living in very different times and circumstances compared to when such codes were formulated. That said, the 'code' that follows, consisting of 14 pointers, has been carefully developed over many years of involvement in men's work and is reasonably universal in scope.

As for the question of why we need a code, I suggest that codes provide a framework upon which to base important decisions in life. Oftentimes the moment we find ourselves in presents itself with startling suddenness wherein it may be difficult to find a path through the uncertainties. A worthy code is helpful to fall back on in such times.

The following 14 points comprise what I call 'the Code of the Conscious Warrior'. This Code is followed by a brief outline of some useful archetypes for a man to be familiar with. (Most of these archetypes are established in literature and can be found in various traditions of mythology, alchemy, or Jungian psychology.) It's a given that one could find more than 14 salient points for such an outline. In the interests of some degree of conciseness I've kept it to 14. These points are sufficiently strong and inclusive that I believe they comprise a list that is complete unto itself.

1. Make Your Word Good. Say what you mean and mean what you say. In many wisdom traditions the 'word' is regarded as sacred and all-powerful. Many forms of mysticism, from the highest types of meditation and prayer, to the lower forms of elemental magic and modern teachings on 'manifestation' based on some understanding of the subconscious mind, rely on focused usage of sacred or meaningful words. In the New Testament, John's gospel makes direct reference to the power of the 'Word' in the ultimate spiritual sense. Psychologically, good communication is life is essential for success and well-being. That does not mean that we mechanically 'tell the truth' in all circumstances in life. Some circumstances may require us to be Gurdjieff's 'sly man', a man who can adapt to circumstances and, when necessary, 'do in Rome as the Romans do' (for example, not needlessly upsetting a very young child by telling them Santa is not real or burdening your old and dying grandparent with useless 'honest' information). But as a rule of thumb, truthfulness in life accords with living a life of power and integrity. A man who habitually speaks out of both sides of his mouth is rarely trustworthy. The most recommended mode of communication for men— especially with other men—is straight and direct. Bluntness, without being gratuitously rude, is also masculine and when tinged with goodwill or humor can be very effective. Men do not need to excessively take care of each other's feelings. Direct communication, the vast majority of times, is more helpful for others—and ourselves—than avoidance, triangulation (going through someone else), or sugar-coating. More to the point, make your own word in life count. Do not commit to something unless you are reasonably sure about your decision, but when you do, make your commitment count.

2. Know Thyself. Be mindful. Explore your darker depths. Have an inner-work discipline, some sort of practice of delving into and understanding yourself (meditation, psychotherapy, etc.).

Here again, balance is necessary. While a common problem with men from the earlier generations (born before roughly 1945) was resistance to looking at themselves (it was thought strange, or even unmanly, to undergo psychotherapy), a more common problem for modern men involved in transformational work is over-processing; that is to say, excessive focus on feelings at the expense of taking action in life. So while it is recommended, and even necessary, for any conscious man to cultivate insight into his mind, this needs to be balanced with a proactive attitude toward life. Further, it is recommended to avoid talking excessively about your inner processes, and especially your feelings, with romantic partners—especially during a courtship phase. In general, it's better to share deeper (and certainly darker) feelings with a friend rather than burdening your lover with them. As a romantic relationship matures, deeper emotional intimacy becomes possible and natural, but in the early stages of relationship do not overburden partners with your emotional states.

In addition to psychotherapy, meditation is a very good tool for the conscious warrior. There are many varieties of meditation (see Chapter 9), but the most basic is mindfulness—the practice of being directly aware of whatever it is that you are experiencing in the moment. A conscious warrior generates and sustains energy by not wasting it in excessive and pointless inner dialogue and outer gossip. Meditation trains the mind to become more present and less inclined to drifting off into disconnected fantasies or daydreams.

3. Train Your Body. Practice martial arts, do yoga, or at the least, have a regular exercise regimen. A weak physical body, provided you're not dealing with a particular medical issue, is usually a symptom of laziness and fear of life. A conscious warrior is not a lazy man. He may have off days and brief lazy periods, but he is never ruled by laziness. A trained and healthy body is a superb ally in life. The 'hard' martial arts—karate, tae kwon do, Muay Thai, kick-boxing—are very good for younger men who are aggressive by nature. The 'middling' martial arts—such as *wushu* (kung fu)—are good for most kinds of men. The 'soft' (or inner) martial arts (tai chi, qi gong) are good for middle-aged or older men, or men who are not in rugged condition.

4. Find the Holy Grail, Your True Calling. Discover your highest purpose in life—your work. But not just any work. The task is to find and do the work you are most passionate about. For a man, passionate engagement in work is crucial. In life, your true calling is requirement number 1; everything else is number 2. (You may have more than one true calling in life, but these generally unfold one at a time. Avoid attempting to explore too many 'true callings' at once, or else you may remain a jack of all trades and master of none.)

5. Do Not Fight Down. Be honorable. Do not abuse your powers and strengths by gratuitously dominating lesser men or women. When appropriate, protect those weaker than yourself. Avoid 'keeping score' battles with primary partners (romantic or business). In addition, avoid picking fights with men or women you deem stronger or more advanced than yourself, merely as a way of proving yourself. It's a bad policy that rarely works out. (It only 'works out' when the 'stronger' person is obviously corrupt. But even there, caution is recommended and rash actions are not—it's usually wiser to just turn away and leave.)

6. Gather Courage and Move Forward. In general, face into the fires of life (except when it is clearly wiser to turn away). Do not avoid life. Remember, personal energy basically works via momentum. In order to get up to speed, you have to make efforts, sometimes extraordinary efforts. Once you have the momentum, the 'magic' takes over and things will unfold and opportunities will appear with much less effort. (If they do not, then you have insufficient momentum and more effort is needed!) Courage, and forward direction, are the key antidotes to laziness and fear of life.

7. Hold Space. Avoid being overly reactive. This especially applies to your relationships with romantic partners. Listen and be patient, strong, and resolute, and practice not taking things personally. Space is a crucial element in relationship—it can be understood as the natural counterpart to passionate expression. The latter is needed for closeness and intimacy, but it is space that allows for individual development and the ability of two people to enjoy both connectedness and individuality at the same time. For a conscious warrior, space is important because it is what allows for his deeper connection to the cosmos outside of his own egocentricity. To 'hold space' may sound odd—how does one 'hold' something that is nothing? In this context 'holding space' refers to not just the art of letting go with correct timing, but also a sensitive attuning to the realities of another person. To hold space for another person is to deepen one's understanding of what it means to be selfless. To hold space when spending time in Nature is to deepen one's connection to the cosmos.

8. Be Passionate and Compassionate. Learn to distinguish between the two. They are like fire and water—perfect complements, but if mixed indiscriminately, they amount only to steam (hot air). A man who drowns his passion with excessive compassion is usually ineffectual (too much of a nice guy). Likewise, a man who exercises passion but is weak in compassion becomes too self-centered and arrogant and sooner or later suffers accordingly when his pride gets busted by life. Mastering the balance between passion and compassion is the secret alchemy of true masculinity.

9. Learn, Study, Train. Never rest on your laurels. Study the deepest thinkers from history. Capacity to reason clearly is a masculine trait and works best when supported by the humility and curiosity to learn from those great minds that came before you. To paraphrase Isaac Newton, stand on the shoulders of giants, instead of trying to prematurely become a giant yourself. Learn from older role-model figures. (A 'role model' need not be perfect—some of their flaws may even be obvious to you—but the idea is to learn from them the trade they are good at.)

10. Serve a Noble Cause Greater Than Yourself. You will always be able to find one. When you yourself become that Noble Cause the universe will support you by sending worthy lieutenants or helpers to assist or co-create your project. If it doesn't, it means you are not yet ready. In order to be a great leader, it's first necessary to be a great assistant.

11. Penetrate Life with Your Solar Energy. Be decisive, proactive, take initiatives. Masculine energy can be likened to solar energy—at its best, it radiates like the sun, penetrating the vastness of space with its heat and light, sparking projects, injecting life, fertilizing the ground, and generating productive energy and a chain of creative consequences. A man embodying his solar energy is ready to move beyond the fear of penetrating life while keeping his heart open at the same time.

12. Be in Integrity. Be honorable in your business dealings. In many ways a man's quality and moral fiber is best demonstrated by the way he conducts his business. He may have all the best intentions, values, talents, and charms, but none of that amounts to much if he can't operate in integrity with the world and if he can't balance his budget and pay his bills and debts. Of course, each circumstance is unique. But there is always a high road that can be taken. As with most things, it comes down to attitude.

13. Stay in Relationship. Do not avoid relationships. Stay connected to the important people in your life, and to the world at large. Many men have a natural ability to isolate in their minds and to disconnect from their bodies. In so doing they easily become indifferent to relationships, disconnected from their pain, or they recoil from deeper intimacy. A man must counter these tendencies by making real efforts to extend to the important people in his life.

14. Be a Responsible Son, Parent, Grandparent, Brother, Uncle, Husband, Boyfriend, Grandson, Cousin, Brother-in-Law. Be good to family members and stay in relationship with them if at all possible. You were not born accidentally into your family, and your children were not born accidentally to you—meaning, above all, that your life has *meaning*. In many ways family are your deepest mirrors and among the most significant lessons in your life. And you will never be able to trade them in like a used car or a short-term lover, so get used to them.

Useful Archetypes to Understand

The Fool. The 'fool', as meant here, is the innocent, young man (usually, although he can be older). In many traditional Tarot decks the 'Fool' card is depicted as a young man about to step off a cliff without realizing it. The upside of this is the trust in life, grounded in innocence, that is natural to one who has been loved and believes in their intrinsic worth, even when lacking in worldly experience. The downside is the refusal to grow up, to become responsible, and as is often the case, to forgive one's father.

The Warrior. The warrior archetype is important and central to this book. However, the warrior archetype is a scarred and, in many ways, a dated relic in need of significant overhaul. In short, the warrior needs to become more conscious, both of self, and of other. That said, the historical imprint of the warrior in the collective mind of masculinity should never be abandoned, as his fire, grit, tenacity, and capacity for discipline are cornerstones of masculine quality and effectiveness.

The Shaman-Soul. Psychologically the 'shaman-soul' is a man with thin boundaries, one given to a natural access to the 'liminal' or 'between-worlds' realm. He is an artist and dreamer and visionary by nature, may be sexually conflicted or bisexual (or just highly sexual), and often has scars rooted in early-life traumas (whether physical or emotional). A shaman-soul can be well equipped for the helping professions (such as psychotherapy, related healing modalities, or medicine) and can be capable of marked empathy and compassion for the human condition. Conversely, if unable to escape his personal wounding, he can become mired in self-pity and self-absorption, be ungrounded, entitled, depressed, and ineffectual.

Sly Man. G.I. Gurdjieff, the well-known Greek-Armenian spiritual master, had four categories of spiritual development—what he called the ways of the fakir, monk, yogi, and Sly Man. The way of the Sly Man—what he also called the Fourth Way—is based on the idea of living a spiritual life within the very gritty details of mundane worldly existence. (All the other three ways—fakir, monk, and yogi—require, in Gurdjieff's view, some sort of retreating from the world.) The Sly Man must navigate his way through the complexities of life—for example, running a business, or raising a family (or both)—while at the same time maintaining a spiritual practice of some sort, and using the conditions of his life to grow in consciousness and being. He is called 'sly' because he is not naive (which many less worldly monks, yogis, or shamans commonly are). He is both spiritual and worldly, both pure and street-wise. Many street-wise men are crooked or corrupt; many spiritual men are ethereal and ungrounded. The Sly Man manages to avoid both of these extremes. One of his symbols is the **Black Panther**. He has the alertness and sensitivity of the cat (due to his spiritual practices), and his black coat represents his ability to move through life with stealth—that is, to go about his business in worldly affairs without having to broadcast (or boast) about his developed spirituality. He is an undercover mystic. Even if involved in teaching personal development or spirituality, he does so with humility and with the understanding that he is a vehicle for spiritual strength, not the ego-based source of it.

White Knight. The White Knight, as we mean it here, is a savior and rescuer of women. He is identified with this rescuer-quality, and therefore requires in his life 'damsels in distress'—troubled and dysfunctional women—in order to fulfill his purpose. Sooner or later he burns out, explodes in resentment, or becomes a domesticated lap dog if he does not shed the White Knight quality. (There is of course a business-world version of the White Knight—the one who steps in and rescues a failing company, something that may be entirely appropriate and commendable—but we mean it here in the context of dysfunctional relating patterns.)

Lap Dog. This is a blunt term to describe a man who has become so domesticated by a woman (or man) that he has lost touch with most or all of his Wild Man energy. He is weak and easily controlled, and may feel hopelessly lost in the cult of domesticity. He is often with a strong woman. (Note: not all men with strong women are lap dogs, although many are in danger of becoming so. There are some shining examples, however, of men who are with a strong mate and yet retain their masculine core and maintain a healthy power balance with their partner.)

Beast. The Beast is the inner primal animal that is driven by lust and the desire to conquer. He sees others as objects through which he can achieve some sort of gratification (usually related to sex or power). Part of becoming a Conscious Warrior is to do the 'shadow-work' necessary to take responsibility for one's inner Beast. A man who does not recognize his inner Beast is usually feminized, weak, and lacks passion. Conversely, a man who is dominated by his inner Beast is usually base and stupid, and may be dangerous. The challenge is to work with the inner Beast by honestly recognizing it, consciously embodying it—that is, mindfully feeling its energies and qualities without running from them or being run by them—and thereby utilize the great energy contained in the Beast as a vehicle for your passion in life. The most powerful, alive, and successful men in history all had a strong inner Beast that they befriended and integrated into their life. It is the source of their vitality and passion. One of the symbols of the integrated Beast is the **Green Wolf**. In his healthy aspect he is functional as a loyal 'pack member', being a good team-mate in life, but he is also capable of being a lone wolf, that is, of knowing when and how to seek solitude so as to nurture his creative powers and bring them to successful fruition in the world. The green color symbolizes his connection to both Nature and his own heart. (Needless to say, the darkest version of the Beast can also be found in the symbolism of the wolf—via the werewolf, a strange and tortured beast that is half-human and half-wolf and driven by blind, destructive impulse.)

Green Knight. The Green Knight (deriving from the medieval Grail myths) is one of the most mysterious forces. He is the Trickster, and shows up in your life as a person or circumstance that is particularly trying. He is the great Tester, come to challenge you in some way so as to show your quality (or lack thereof). Castaneda referred to him as the 'worthy enemy'. Anyone who is a thorn in your side, such as a sibling you have a difficult relationship with, or a troublesome ex-lover or ex-spouse (or current), a difficult colleague, friend, parent, or the driver on the road who cuts you off and gives you the finger, can embody the Green Knight for you. The challenge when dealing with the Green Knight is not to explode into reckless and violent reactivity, and nor to cave into meek submissiveness, but rather to meet it from a place of balanced strength—that is, true warriorhood.

Green Lion. In alchemy the Green Lion is a powerful symbol representing vitality and gusto. He is usually shown 'eating' the sun, symbolic of his vital, alive, assertive, passionate, and robust relationship with life. The Green Lion speaks to the idea of energy, and the health that is a function of direct participation in life. When feeling weak our instinct is usually to recoil and rest. Sometimes this is indeed necessary. However, the best policy over the course of the average life is to participate as much as possible. The more we demonstrate energy, the more energy usually comes to us. In the act of 'eating the sun' we become filled with the brilliant energy of the sun—an apt metaphor for the result of claiming, participating, and rising to the challenges of life. There is a direct relationship between participation and health. In general, the more we participate in our life, the healthier we are.

Black Crow. The Black Crow (or Raven) in alchemy symbolizes the initial phase of *nigredo*, or the 'blackening', which represents both the 'cooking' process of life—when difficult circumstances force us to face our ego—and the willingness and accountability needed to deal with it. All men who seek to become true Conscious Warriors must face into their egos first. They must become accountable for who they are, for what kind of personality they have, and stop blaming others or the world (or God) for their challenges in life. The Black Crow represents the beginning of growing up. As a symbol of transformation, it can herald either the coming dawn or the coming nightmare, depending entirely on our attitude and willingness—or lack thereof—to move forward in life.

Red King. An alchemical symbol for the phase of *rubedo* ('reddening'), symbolizing the completion or mastery of the self. As a symbol of masculine psychology, it can be understood as representing the King archetype, which denotes completion. The Red King is the opposite of the dilettante or dabbler, the man who is constantly getting his feet wet but never dives in, let alone masters anything. The Red King is a true master, and as a symbol he beckons men to endure and *never give up* when exploring their passions in life.

Tiger. The main energy embodied by the symbol of the tiger is power. As the strongest of the big cats (surpassing even lions), tigers represent both stealth and raw power. Tigers are also mainly solitary creatures, suggestive of a type of fearlessness and willingness to face into one's essential nature. The Tiger as archetype is relevant for modern men who seek to express the fullness of who they are within the confines of their unique individuality. A man, to be effectual in life, must learn some semblance of teamwork, yes. But he must also learn to trust his inner resources and be willing to explore the depths of his individual talents and capacity for personal responsibility in his life. The Tiger is the supreme bad-ass because he knows who he is and derives great power from this self-knowledge.

The Wildman, Green Man, or Horned God. The Wildman, sometimes known as the Green Man or the Horned God (from the ancient Celtic fertility deity Cernunnos), symbolizes the deep masculine that is well balanced with the feminine energies. Although wild, free, and untamed, he is not afraid of the feminine and has no need to control or subjugate it. He is both masculine and grounded, rational and feeling, lofty and earthy all at once. He represents the best potential ground on which to develop deeper spirituality.

Chapter 8

Shadow Work: Integrating the Beast

The Persona and the Shadow

As touched on in previous sections of this book, the dark side of the male psyche—that is, of the great majority of men—inclines toward a raw primal aggression or, less commonly, a Machiavellian ruthlessness. While it is probably not true that modern men have fewer outlets for primal aggression than our less civilized (or less technological) ancestors, it is doubtless true that modern men have more means by which they can lose touch with this primal core. Accordingly, it is essential I believe for a modern man to have some grasp of shadow-psychology and the ways in which it can help him come to a deeper acceptance of who he is, and of what it means to be male.

Persona is the Latin word for 'mask'. That it is also the root of the English word 'personality' should give some hint at what lies at the basis of the personality, and what we typically understand that word to mean.

In the context of transformational work, the 'Shadow' is a term that was coined by the Swiss psychotherapist C.G. Jung (1875–1961) to describe that part of our nature that is hidden, repressed, and usually unconscious. It is sometimes referred to as our 'dark side'. Freud's version of this he called the 'Id', but the Jungian term is probably more descriptive, and Jung elaborated on it greatly in his work. The Shadow, as per Jungian theory, is comprised largely of the elements of our nature—our repressed feelings and emotions, sexuality, frailties, secret desires, and so on—that we have rejected for various reasons, and as such they have been effectively split off, forming a type of secondary personality that emerges under certain conditions, like stress, anxiety, strong emotions, and anything involving sudden changes. Intoxicants like drugs and alcohol can also bring about the sudden emergence of the Shadow.

There was a period in early life during which we first began experiencing repeated invalidation from our elders. This occurred for us (as toddlers, usually) when total freedom of expression was curtailed in some way. Prior to that we had basically been living in a kind of Garden of Eden where full allowance of expression and our command of the attention of our elders was mostly the case. We lived as miniature gods, our parents fascinated with us and loving, curious and attentive to our every need. (Obviously, this is an ideal and not always the case—in many more painful existences, abandonment, rejection, or abuse is experienced almost from the beginning.)

The general point at which repeated invalidation or disapproval of how we were expressing ourselves was experienced marked the onset of our awareness of *rejection*. We lived through the jarring and painful process of getting the message from our all-powerful caretakers that we were somehow erring, or lacking something, or doing something wrong that was upsetting, annoying, or offending them. It began to seem that we were, quite clearly, no longer completely lovable just for being who and what we are. Something was wrong, we had gone astray—we were flawed and, by extension, *guilty*. (Again, this varies greatly, depending on the general level of maturity and overall inner balance of the parents and/or original caretakers.)

This 'guilt' was not, of course, initially understood by us, but we began to develop what could be called a compromised self-esteem. We began to vaguely sense that there was something wrong with us. And if we were born into a family-system in which generations of self-esteem issues (self-loathing, depression, failure, poverty, mental illness, etc.) were common, it's very likely that we began the process of simply inheriting the residual backlog of psychological issues unresolved by our ancestors.

The Core Wound

As a child we came to realize, by virtue of repeated experiences, that we were capable of incurring disapproval, that limitations on expression were being imposed on us, and more troublesome, that an awareness of our lack of personal power was growing. The intense frustration of the powerlessness, combined with the repeated invalidations from our elders, gave rise to the awareness of emotional, or inner, pain. In Eden there may have been physical pain on occasion, but unbroken awareness of being unconditionally accepted was generally present, for however brief a time. We could pretty much 'get away with' anything, at least in terms of our outer emotional expressions. With invalidation and inner pain, a new element has entered. As the pain is felt more acutely each time (often accompanied by temper tantrums or crying outbursts, which are attempts to discharge the pain), the awareness of the 'core wound' grows. This wound is, in fact, of an order far beyond what we are initially aware of, but the new experiences of rejection and invalidation (as opposed to unconditional, unlimited allowance) make us more aware of it.

The *core wound* is a term sometimes given to describe that tendency we have to believe ourselves unworthy at some deep, hard-to-define level. Everyone experiences the 'core wound' differently. There is a broad range of possibilities in the degree of invalidation and rejection faced by a child growing up. It can range from the entirely appropriate (being told 'no!' when this was what we needed to hear), to levels of extreme abuse, depending on a number of factors, not least of which is the overall maturity of the parents or caretakers. But be that as it may, pain, by its very nature, is *painful*. As we grow up and mature we may learn that to fight against emotional pain (to deny or repress it) solves nothing and in fact ultimately worsens it, but as children our main concern was how not to feel this pain. Thus, we began to look for ways out, for tricks and devices to escape what we were feeling.

Coping with Emotional Pain

The most unpleasant emotion is fear, and specifically, anxiety. The anticipation of emotional pain gives rise to anxiety, and the beginning of lifelong issues connected to fear in general. Fear exists only as a projected thought into the future. When we are in fear, our fear is always about *what is to come next*. As such, we develop skills to cope with fear.

The anxiety, pain, and awareness of the core wound—our core sense of personal unworthiness deriving from repeated invalidations—propels us into a course of action that is largely unavoidable. Fearful of the power of the elders that surround us (parents, older siblings, or other caretakers), and increasingly aware of our own limitations, we slowly begin to develop the ability to be *inauthentic*. That is, our outer personality, our *persona* (mask), begins to develop. This process usually begins between the ages of 2 and 5, roughly paralleling the development of language skill (though the seeds of it are likely planted earlier). The surface personality is originally based on a reaction to pain, and an attempt at disguising, managing, and repressing the anxiety that goes with it. This becomes the habitual face that we show the world. It continues to grow and strengthen through childhood and adolescence, becoming solidified by young adulthood. At that point full identification with it has more or less occurred, with all the associated limitations of that (reactivity, insecurity, fear, etc.). In other words, we have come to believe that we *are* our personality and nothing much more.

As the mask is born, so also is birthed its opposite—the Shadow, or the *hidden* personality. The Shadow becomes a repository for those elements of our nature that are in direct opposition to the surface personality we are developing. The Shadow is the part of us that we have learned to reject, precisely because direct expression of its qualities tends to lead to rejection and pain. Thus, to a large extent the Shadow becomes the polar opposite of our surface personality. For example, if a man is 'nice' and 'passive' in the personality he presents to the world, he is often concealing a more hostile, aggressive inner nature (especially if his outer niceness is exaggerated). Or, conversely, if a man is outwardly rough and hostile in an obvious way, he is often concealing a nature that is timid, sensitive, and sees itself as vulnerable. (These are not, of course, rigid facts; occasionally an outwardly 'warm' person is also 'inwardly warm'. But these seem to be the exceptions. Far more commonly people are capable of polar opposite-type behavior, especially when confronted or pushed to the wall in some fashion.)

A way of imagining this is as the surface personality being just like a mask on our face — with the Shadow or hidden personality being a face on the back of our head, the side of ourselves that others can see or at least sense, but that we are usually blind to. This is something like the dual mask worn by the ancient Roman god named Janus.

Shadow Work

A useful model for doing shadow work is what American philosopher Ken Wilber has dubbed the '3-2-1' process.[1] It is based on the idea that our Shadow elements typically arise in the following 'splitting off' fashion:

1. A painful situation arises in which we cannot cope with our true feelings. An example is a child who is angry at their mother or father. The child soon realizes that to harbor such feelings is too risky because it means that they might lose the love, approval, and protection of that parent. So they gradually disconnect from their true feeling (in this case, anger).

2. Because it is too threatening to feel my anger (because

I might lose the love/approval/protection of Mommy or Daddy), I project my anger outwardly. I begin to 'see' angry people around me. It is not possible that this anger is mine, so it must be these other people who are angry. (A person will commonly project these onto 'monsters' or other scary images, which is one reason why 'scary' movies are culturally popular, providing as they do a screen on which to project shadow-feelings.)

3. Carried on long enough, the original feeling (I'm angry at Mom or Dad) becomes completely dissociated. It is only experienced via outer events. This results in a 'secondary' emotion arising, as a kind of decoy to keep us from facing the primary emotion. For example, a common secondary emotion that arises from the primary emotion of anger is fear, or sadness. A prolonged fear/sadness that is in fact covering up anger can commonly slide into depression.

The process just outlined is a simple 1-2-3 matter—from a personal feeling (anger), to an interpersonal situation ('you are angry, not me', or 'that person in my life is mean and nasty, and I have nothing to do with it'), to a split-off, disconnected state in which a secondary emotion arises (sadness, fear, depression) to cover up the primary, original emotion (anger). In this third stage, we have completely rejected the original emotion (anger) and truly believe it has nothing to do with us.

Shadow work in this case consists of reversing the above process, so that it becomes 3-2-1. This is, in essence, going from 'it', to 'you', to 'I', as follows:

1. Face the issue. (This can be done via writing or talking to an empty chair—imagining a person who has offended you sitting in the chair.) Recognize exactly what it is that is bothering you, and be fully honest about it. At this stage don't worry about taking responsibility for your core feelings—just acknowledge them. Talk or write freely about what is disturbing you. Or talk freely to the imaginary person in the chair. Hold nothing back.

2. Relate to the issue. Get into dialogue with it. Make the issue personal, and speak (to an empty chair, or a person who is supporting you, or via writing) by asking it specific questions— 'What do you want from me? What are you trying to tell me?' etc.

3. Ownership—*become* it. If that which is concerning you is a scary monster (in whatever shape—either a person who you believe has wronged you, or someone gratuitously nasty, or ignoring you, and so on), become that monster yourself. Allow yourself to experience directly the anger, nastiness, dismissiveness, coldness, manipulativeness, etc., within yourself. (Which does *not* mean, of course, acting on it.)

The idea of doing this work is to free up energy that is being drained by constantly repressing elements of your shadow self. In freeing up this energy, you also allow for the possibility of expanding your horizons, both internally (experiencing more authentic compassion for others) and externally (more creative output in your life, simply because more energy has been freed up).

The Authentic Man

Cultivating awareness of both the surface personality and the Shadow takes time, diligence, and commitment, and is done mostly via self-observation and some form of therapeutic work, like the 3-2-1 process just outlined. (Self-observation, or meditation, in and of itself is usually not enough—in fact, it is easy, and common, to simply use meditation as a way to further repress the Shadow elements of our nature.) In time, as our awareness and understanding—and above all, *acceptance*—

of these two aspects of us grows, the ability both have to create suffering in our lives begins to diminish. This is because with the growth in awareness of both *persona* and Shadow comes also the gradual dawning awareness (at first often only in glimpses) of our authentic self. Our awareness of it arises as the conflicting elements of the outer personality and the Shadow are resolved via accomplishing the inner work. This work involves, at heart, our efforts at becoming conscious of all our inner traits and tendencies—to see them with unflinching honesty.

Our authentic self is neither the outer personality nor the Shadow. *It is not some separate 'thing' that we must get to; it is rather who we really are.* It is the integrated harmony of the best of both the Shadow and the outer personality. A man awakening to his best self does not lose the distinct individuality of his outer personality and Shadow. Put simply, he is not just his outer mask (for example, Mr Nice) and nor is he just his hidden, Shadow side (Mr Nasty). Who he *really* is is the best of both—the passion of the dark side, and the ability to adjust to others, to have a moral compass, and to have empathy.

Chapter 9

Clarity of Thought and Meditation

Clarity of thought and the ability to meditate are two prime elements in the life of a conscious warrior. A man who is mentally confused and lacks the ability to contextualize his experiences in life is not a developed man and runs the risk of either being controlled by his baser instincts or drowning in his passions, like a rudderless ship that runs aground because it can't turn off its engine, let alone correctly steer itself. On the other hand, too many men in history have sealed themselves off in their mind, barely able to access feelings at all, and such men can be equally self-destructive or dangerous to others. Men who are 'stuck in their head' often need deeper forms of psychotherapy; this chapter is not addressed to such men, but rather to the typical twenty-first-century male who finds himself frequently awash in confused thinking, hastily buying into fashionable party lines, or overly reactive to larger issues that he's not thinking carefully enough about.

Forms of Unclear Thinking

Magical Thinking and the Post Hoc Fallacy. In this context, 'magical' does not refer to certain legitimate practices of Western esotericism. Magical in this sense refers rather to a type of unclear thinking that is based on an error of logic known as the 'post hoc' fallacy. (The full Latin designation is *post hoc ergo propter hoc*: 'after this, therefore because of this'). This error results from the assumption that if event 'A' comes before event 'B', then event 'A' *must be* the cause of event 'B'. Needless to say many superstitions, some harmless, some merely foolish, and others dangerous, can arise from this type of thinking. Many forms of knee-jerk intolerance, bigotry, prejudices, racism, conspiracy thinking that verges on or drifts into full-blown paranoia, and even religiously motivated wars, are based on magical thinking.

The essence of magical thinking is the association of thoughts based on familiarity, often accompanied by an agenda, coupled with a lack of intellectual curiosity. In older times, prior to the scientific revolution, important truths were ascertained mainly via doctrine and dogma. In other words, something was 'true' if someone of assumed importance had said it was true at some point in the past. This blind adherence to dogma and doctrine results in mechanical thinking, like a robot that has been programmed. A robot has no originality and no ability to question what it is told. (I refer of course to robots as we now know them—perhaps at some point in the future robots will acquire self-determination and the rudiments of consciousness, but we are not there yet.)

A side point here. A robot that operates via mechanical thinking may lack originality and seem to be doing only what it has been told to do, but that does not mean it is less efficient. The most sophisticated chess computers have been, since roughly the year 2000, capable of defeating the world's best human grandmasters. They now routinely beat the top human players. Chess is known to be a game that is devoid of chance or luck; that is, a player's success or lack thereof in a game depends entirely on the clarity of his thought and calculation. (Yes, there is always the luck of your opponent making a bad move, but you still need to find the right moves on your own in order to win.) It might legitimately be asked: how is it possible that chess computers can defeat the best human players if the chess engine lacks any sort of consciousness or ability to think with originality?

The answer doubtless lies in the fact that chess is a game with specific rules and limitations of thought. That is, although you can imagine that your knight has suddenly leaped six squares forward in order to checkmate the enemy king, it cannot actually do this according to the fixed rules of the game. Therefore, your 'original thought' (in this case) is powerless and useless. A chess computer defeats a human because of brute force calculation. It computes every possible move in any given position, and then selects the best one. But it can only do this because of the limitations and rules. The 'best move' calculation is possible only because of the specific rules of the game, making it essentially a sophisticated type of mathematics.

The above is a good metaphor for the average man's relationship with the civilized world. Thinking mechanically— living as others tell you you should live, or seeking merely to fulfill the expectations of your family or peer group, or appeasing authorities and mentors, and so on—can indeed lead to a measure of success on the *material level*. But it will not result in success in the area of clarity of thought and creativity. That is because the 'rules of the game' are very different at these non-material levels.

Confirmation Bias. Confirmation bias is the active searching for information and viewpoints that confirm one's already made-up mind about something. It is sometimes referred to as 'finding the thorn in the rosebush'. There may be a hundred roses and only one thorn, but for one who is convinced that thorns are more real than roses, they will find the thorn. Confirmation bias happens when we interpret events in such a way as to satisfy our pre-existing beliefs about something. A classic mundane example is a believer of Jesus seeing an image of Jesus in a tortilla chip. Many psychic readings work via confirmation bias. The psychic will put out a certain amount of information, often generalized or vague, and the client will selectively interpret the information to confirm desires, hopes, fears, or beliefs. Confirmation bias also shows up in the scientific and academic world, for example in scientific studies that are rated highly by scientists because the studies yield results that confirm their personal positions.

Regression Fallacy. This type of faulty thinking is based on the natural tendency of things to 'regress to the mean (or average)', and then to assume some random cause to be the reason for the change. For example, your sports team wins five games in a row. The more games they win, the greater the odds that sooner or later they will lose a game. If after your sports team wins five in a row and then loses a game you assign cause to that loss due to some arbitrary event that accompanied the loss, then you are likely committing regression fallacy. For example, the team wins five in a row wearing their usual jersey. On the sixth game they wear a different jersey and lose. To believe the loss was caused by the different jersey is regression fallacy.

Strawman. Distorting or exaggerating the viewpoint of someone you have a disagreement with so as to better defeat them. This is a kind of mental manipulation based on fear and dishonesty. Example: In the abortion debate, you are pro-choice, and your friend is pro-life. You then question him or her on why they hate women because they deny them the right to choose. The pro-lifer may not hate women at all, but by painting him or her in this way, you make it harder for them to remain emotionally detached when debating, which increases the chances they will look bad.

Tu quoque. Pronounced 'too-kwo-kwee', the term is Latin for 'you too'. It's the immature tendency to reply to a criticism with a criticism. This sort of knee-jerk response is common with quarreling couples. Example: Her: 'You forgot to take the garbage out.' You: 'Well, what of it? You forgot to put the milk away last night.'

Personal Incredulity. The tendency to dismiss the possibility of something because *we* cannot understand it. Example: Having an enlightenment experience via meditation is not possible, because we cannot imagine ourselves sitting still with a quiet mind for more than five minutes at a time.

Special Pleading. Shifting our positions in order to maintain our beliefs and the view that we are right about something, even in the face of strong evidence that we are probably wrong. Example: We believe that we know a particular person so well that we can predict their behavior. If they behave differently than what we expected, we rationalize it by saying that there must have been special circumstances for them to have acted as they did. The 'normal' person would surely have acted as you know them to be.

Loaded Question. This common ploy is done by posing a question that comes with a presumption. In order for the other person to answer it, they must deal with the presumption, which almost always makes them look bad. Example: You are debating with someone about an economic matter. You then pose a question that includes a reference to the time they filed for bankruptcy a few years ago. The person will likely be flustered and appear less effective debating.

Red Herring. This well-known term derives from hunting. A 'red herring' is a fish with a bad smell that can be used to throw foxhounds or other hunting dogs off the trail of their quarry. In reasoning, a red herring is used to distract someone from the point of their argument. Example: A person acknowledges that usage of assault weapons by criminals is a problem, however adds that people have been violent throughout history. The reference to how people have been throughout history distracts from the issue of assault weapons.

What do all these fine-tuned logical points have to do with development of the masculine spirit? As touched on above, there is a relationship between clarity of thought and masculinity. The reason for the importance of this relationship is because masculine consciousness at its optimum is a natural holder of space, a container that permits the growth of creative forces within it. These 'creative forces' may take the form of feminine consciousness and even specific females in a man's life, but they more often have to do with the man's relationship with his unconscious mind. A man whose thinking is muddled, unclear, and given to lack of critical thought, tends to be a man who lacks the ability to be truly present with others, not to mention to cultivate patience for his own more primal impulses and child-like side.

Clear thinking aids in the ability to provide spacious awareness that is non-defensive and non-judgmental in appropriate ways. Muddled thinking leads to entanglements with others in pointless ways, and to a lack of patience to be truly present with others and with one's own mind.

Meditation and the Warrior

Years ago, in a meditation group I was teaching, I took a group of my students to a movie one night for the purposes of conducting an experiment. The idea was to nudge each other every ten minutes throughout the movie as a means of remembering that we were, indeed, watching a movie.

There were about ten of us, all sitting in one row. The movie was *The Blair Witch Project*, a campy but effective late 1990s supernatural horror flick. The movie had been made on a shoestring budget by two unknown filmmakers, and then promoted via a clever online marketing strategy that sold audiences on the idea that the movie was 'found footage', that is, a secret documentary later discovered that had been made by three young people who had mysteriously disappeared in the Black Hills of Maryland in 1994.

Of course, a little bit of sleuthing soon revealed the obvious, that the film was not a real documentary but was fabricated to make it seem as if it was—a 'mockumentary'. Shot in cheap black-and-white film with a hand-held camera, it was remarkably effective because the three young actors were simply told to go into the woods for a few days and film their natural reactions. Unknown to them, the two directors (Daniel Myrick and Eduardo Sanchez) were stalking them in the woods and making mysterious sounds in the middle of the night to intentionally frighten them. The whole thing worked, resulting in the actors behaving in ways that were indeed consistent with a documentary—that is, they were not following any script, and were not actually acting.

My students were all aware of the plan to go watch this movie and nudge each other every ten minutes. As the movie began playing, we began to do this as pre-planned. It was an interesting exercise, especially with this kind of movie, which had the ability to 'trap' one's attention precisely because of its realistic elements.

About halfway through the movie, one of the men in our group *forgot* the exercise, and when the guy beside him nudged him, he snapped at him in an annoyed fashion and said to him 'Hey, I'm trying to watch the movie!'

We laughed about this later, and it became a good metaphor for the sheer difficulty we humans have with avoiding the tendency to *identify* with what we're experiencing. The man in our group who was pissed off at the guy nudging him to remind him to stay awake wanted, in that moment, to be left alone to experience his identification with his emotional states, and to believe in the reality of the movie he was watching. In many ways, this sums up our capacity to create worlds out of nothing, and to forget who we are. And, moreover, to be angry at anyone seeking to disturb our dreaming.

This anecdote is included in a book for men on conscious warriorhood because for men in particular, the need to be mindful of not identifying with certain emotional states—especially the tendency to personalize things and fail to hold space for others—is very important. A conscious warrior is one who can see ghosts for what they are.

Worth mentioning here is the classic *Star Trek* episode 'Specter of the Gun', first aired in late 1968. It featured Kirk, Spock, McCoy and the rest of the boys being marooned on an alien planet in which they were forced by powerful beings to relive the 1881 Tombstone, Arizona 'Battle of the OK Corral' incident. The *Star Trek* officers were put in the role of the so-called 'cowboys' (the Clanton-McLaury gang), who were fated to lose the famous gunfight with Wyatt, Morgan, and Virgil Earp and Doc Holliday. Spock eventually figured a way out of the whole thing by realizing that the bullets shot at them could only harm them if they truly believed that they were real. Spock knew that the whole thing was a mind-construction, and so could see the bullets for what they really were, ghosts or shadows. He then used his 'mind-meld' Vulcan hypnosis to convince the others of the same. When the Earps and Holliday showed up to kill them, the bullets indeed passed through their bodies without harming them.

The iconic scene of Spock explaining the whole thing predated the *Matrix* movies by 30 years but was essentially describing the same idea, namely, that our minds build a model of reality that conforms to certain *a priori* ideas and sensory input of data. Philosophers have talked about this for centuries, of course, with Kant's writings in the late eighteenth century really going to the heart of the issue, that being that our minds have built-in hardware that predisposes us to see things and experience reality in a certain way.

Meditation, and any efforts at staying awake in life, are the means of escaping from mental constructs that cause us unnecessary suffering.

As touched on in the Introduction, a key element of conscious warriorhood is *divided attention*. Normally in life our attention flows outwardly to the objects around us. G.I. Gurdjieff spoke regularly of the importance of self-remembering (see below), that is, the need to remain aware of self even as we immerse ourselves in the universe around us.

At first glance this may seem an awkward idea to implement— would not attempts to be 'aware of self' when driving a car, for example, be risky if it meant that our awareness of the environment was diminished? Or would awareness of self when seated with our intimate partner mean that we had less attention available for them? After all, is not 'self-awareness' just a more impressive term for 'self-absorption'?

Not so, when we properly understand self-awareness. What is commonly disparaged as self-absorption is more an egocentric, narcissistic fascination with one's own personal drama. Self-awareness is something very different. It is an objective alertness directed inwardly, and it does not impair one's awareness of the outer world. On the contrary, to be aware of one's thoughts, of one's feelings and bodily sensations, is to make one more present in general. In this state we are a better driver on the road, and we are a more engaging and responsive companion to our partner as well. Accidents in life occur more often when we are not paying attention to our psychological and physical states. And inattentiveness to our partner occurs more often when we are unconscious of our own psychophysical states.

All inner work can be reduced to three overarching categories: self-acceptance, empowerment, and self-observation. Engaging the first is the basis of psychotherapy; engaging the second is the basis of all self-expressive forms of work (art, music, ritual/ceremony, martial arts, etc.); engaging the third is the basis of meditation.

Meditation and study are essential aspects on the path of transformation. The essence of meditation is *awareness* and the cultivation of insight. Not awareness *of* anything, but the simple resting in awareness itself. This is called 'consciousness without an object' which if persisted with leads to 'non-dual awareness' (seeing the interconnectedness of all things). For the Western mind, conditioned as it is with intellectual training and the scientific objectification of reality, the notion of 'resting in awareness' may at first seem difficult to grasp, as it may seem too simple and too unconcerned with bearing witness to, or perceiving, anything outside of ourselves. However, if we are concerned with coming to an understanding of our nature, that is, what we really are, then it is going to be vitally important that we develop the ability to see ourselves, and directly experience the ground of our inner being, which is consciousness.

Rene Descartes' famous line, *cogito ergo sum* ('I think therefore I am'), is perhaps the classic summation of the Western rationally oriented worldview that lies at the heart of the rapid advances in science and technology from the seventeenth century and beyond. It also clearly defines the quintessence of a civilization that schools its people in such a way that they become strongly identified with their thinking minds. In such a conditioning, it is only in thought that I can define my identity—I *think*, therefore I *am*. However, if we examine the nature of our thinking processes, we will soon find that when not engaged in a specific discipline that requires our focused attention our thoughts are generally lacking in any cohesive structure that would seem able to truly define our identity. In fact, a simple focusing of attention on our thought process will soon reveal that thought itself is incapable of *directly experiencing* anything, and is most certainly incapable of directly experiencing the nature of our identity (who 'I am'). At the most, thought can describe things, much like a menu can describe a meal or a map can describe an area. Because of this, it is necessary to train the mind to learn to *witness* the movement of thought, something like the movement of clouds through the sky. Doing so enables us to organize our thoughts more efficiently, to utilize their energy creatively, and to recognize that we are not our thoughts at the level of being.

Self-Remembering

Self-remembering, in one form or another, lies at the heart of inner work. It has gone by various names over the centuries within the various spiritual traditions, but it always boils down to the practice of maintaining an elevated state of awareness throughout one's daily life activities. Self-remembering is based on the idea of divided attention. In typical semi-conscious living, our attention flows outwardly, toward the object we perceive. It is a one-way movement of attention, from us, to the object. The less alert, the less conscious we are at the time, the more we are aware of *only* the object, and nothing else. (This is, of course, the basis of being caught up in the external 'glitter' of reality, everything from the dazzle of a charismatic person, to the dazzle of a cause we identify with.) A good example of this occurs in our dreams at night. Typically, our dream state is governed by a lack of self-awareness during the dream. All that is 'real' are the objects (things, people, etc.) of our dream. This is why we do not know that we are dreaming at the time, because there is no substantial self-awareness. Thus, we wake up after and realize that it 'was only a dream'.

In divided attention, what we are endeavoring to do is to 'split' our attention two ways, so to speak. We try to keep our attention on the object of our perception (say, a tree), and, at the same time, we remain aware of ourselves—'I am'. We attempt to remain aware simultaneously of both self and tree. Accomplishing this is an act of self-remembering. In the beginning the practice may seem just intellectual, a forced and artificial mental effort that probably will not be sustained for very long. With consistent practice it becomes easier and more natural and can be done for longer periods of time. Persisted with, we can reach a state where we are naturally remembering ourselves much of the time. As our ability with the method progresses, it becomes less and less a detached mental exercise, and more and more an alive, sensory experience of being *present* in our environment and experiencing the moment more vividly.

To self-remember is to be *present*. Lack of presence is akin to operating in a kind of autopilot state. The main purpose of self-remembering is to begin to learn to experience reality free of mental projections and of the cloud of 'daydreaming' that obscures our ability to truly be here. Self-remembering, persisted with, leads to a quieter mind, a mind that thinks more economically and efficiently and is able to let go and relax when appropriate.

It should be understood that with all meditation methods, including self-remembering, we are not trying to force the mind to be still. Trying to will the mind to be silent usually leads to just repression of thoughts and feelings. Self-remembering is not about repression. It is rather a practice that allows us to be more involved in our life in a real fashion, while being able to see things more clearly and truthfully as well. We can practice while driving, eating, going to the washroom, walking, etc. In the beginning it is good to try this method when not engaged in anything serious, but over time we can do it in increasingly complex situations.

Below follows a broad menu of basic meditation exercises. A good practice can be to try one for one week, the next one for a week, and so on, until you've worked through them all. Each one is complete in itself and could be practiced for months or even years on a daily basis.

Exercise 1: Self-Remembering. Attempt to remember yourself as the one who is having this thought, or the one who is having this feeling, body sensation, etc.—that is, hold the sense of 'I am' whenever possible throughout your daily activities. This does not mean that you can't engage in regular activities or thinking that requires your full attention. It simply means that you remember the sense of 'I am' when having such thoughts, feelings, and so on. In the beginning self-remembering can seem like a tedious mental exercise, in that you have to make a mental effort to remember, 'I am'. But over time this 'I am-ness' becomes less and less a disconnected thought, and more an overall sense of presence, and one that becomes easier to remember.

Exercise 2: Recording Thoughts. Find a ten-minute period of time during which you will be undisturbed. Sit at a table with a notepad, or several sheets of paper, and pen. For ten minutes straight, simply write down every thought that comes into your awareness. It is important to write down *everything*, without censoring at all. Practiced regularly, this simple method will make it clear just how random and apparently unrelated thoughts are, and how fast and how spontaneously they are arising in our mind. (This practice reveals, to some extent, the validity of David Hume's ideas about 'constant conjunctions', and of the way in which so much of what we assume to be cause and effect is really just imagined.) We have simply learned (for the most part) to block and filter out those which seem unrelated to the tasks we are engaged in—or we indulge in such 'unrelated' thoughts, a process we know as 'daydreaming'.

Recording thoughts will also make it clear to us how similar such thoughts are to the nature of our dreams at night. More importantly, the very recording of the thoughts begins to slowly make us more aware of the *field* in which the thoughts are arising—the field of pure awareness.

There are two basic forms of focusing awareness, what we can call 'concentration', and 'attention'. Neither of these is, strictly speaking, true meditation, and yet both are important as preliminary skills to develop prior to tackling the deeper forms of meditation. Concentration is mental focusing in a 'one-pointed' fashion. The mind can be likened a bit to a laser in this regard, in that whatever it concentrates on with unwavering focus will sooner or later yield information, something like a wall being pierced by an information-gathering laser. Or, put another way, as the mind concentrates, thought-associations are stimulated, generally yielding deeper insights into whatever is being concentrated on. The capacity for concentration, like a physical muscle, can be developed with practice. Here is one very well-known and simple technique for sharpening concentration:

Exercise 3: Counting Breaths. At first, attempt this practice for no more than 20 minutes. After a couple of weeks of practice, you can lengthen sessions to 30 minutes, or even one hour. But give yourself some time to work up to longer sessions if you feel inclined to pursue this technique.

Sit down in a comfortable position, either in a straight-back chair, or cross-legged, or semi-lotus if this is comfortable for you. Keep the spine straight but not rigid. Be relaxed, yet alert; calm, but attentive. Take a few deep breaths, and then breathe in a calm, natural fashion. With your eyes closed, locate the inhale/ exhale rhythm of your breathing either in the pit of your belly or at the tip of your nose. Then, breathing at a normal pace, begin to count your breaths. Count only the inhales, and on each exhale, let go and relax. Inhale-one, exhale relax, inhale-two, exhale relax, inhale-three, exhale relax, and so forth. Continue this until there is a break in your attention and you forget which number you were on. As soon as you realize you have lost the thread of attention and have forgotten your count, start over again. Do not cheat; make sure you start over each time you forget. Do not be concerned about how many times you forget. In the beginning you will forget many times and find yourself wandering off into thought-dreams. The important point is to just keep doing it, exercising patience. Persevere until the 20 minutes are up, then make a note of the highest number you reached.

If you persist with this, soon you will be able to retain an unbroken count to very high numbers. This method is a very good tool for sharpening the ability to focus and concentrate. In addition, it affords interesting insights into the nature of consciousness and its ability to 'entangle' us with thoughts, so that we become identified, and lose self-awareness.

Exercise 4: Paying Attention. This method is a simple process of focusing your attention on various parts of your body. As with the previous exercise, sit down and be comfortable. Close your eyes and place your attention on your left foot. Be mindful of the sensations of your left foot. Allow your consciousness to rest as totally as you can on your left foot. After a short time there (about two minutes), move your attention up to the rest of your left leg, scanning from the ankle to the hip. Take about two minutes for this as well. Continue up the left side of the body, allowing about two minutes each for the left side of the pelvis, the left side of your torso, your left arm, left hand, left arm again, left shoulder, left side of neck, and left side of your head. The whole thing should take about 15 minutes to do. Then scan downwards on the right side of your body, starting at the head, and continuing down the neck, right shoulder, arm, and hand, back up the arm again, and down the right side of the torso, pelvis, and right leg, ending at the right foot.

You should take about 30 minutes to scan your whole body. Once done, take five minutes to sit quietly with your attention focused on the totality of your whole body. Simply be aware of it, and any sensations in it. (If at any time you have to scratch, do so with slow, attentive movements. Remain conscious of all movements.)

Exercise 5: Listening to Sounds. This exercise works very well out in Nature, but if you do not have access to a trail where you casually walk or hike, then simply use wherever you find yourself. It is necessary, however, to make sure you will be undisturbed. The exercise is for 20 minutes at first; later you can extend it to 30 or 60 minutes if you feel so inclined.

When walking on a trail through a natural setting (or sitting in your home with whatever sounds are audible), simply focus all your attention on listening to whatever you are hearing. This could be birdsong, wind, the sound of your feet on the ground, your breathing, traffic, people around you, whatever. Just allow all of your attention to dissolve into the sounds. Stay with the sounds. Persisted with, this method is effective for quieting the mind and opening your perception, on more than one level, to a fuller experience of sensory reality. It can lead to a profound sense of connectedness to the world of your sensory experience, as well as to the 'Ground of Being' that, according to the wisdom traditions, both world and consciousness are deriving from.

Exercise 6: Self-Observation. In selected situations throughout a typical day, practice simply observing yourself, without comment or attempt to change anything at all. Just try to catch yourself doing and acting and thinking and feeling and behaving however you may be in any given moment or situation, but don't try to change anything—just bear witness to yourself, be as aware as possible of yourself. This exercise can be a bit difficult in the beginning and as such is best at first to practice in simple, routine situations. These may include when you stop at a red traffic light, standing in line at the bank, interacting with the bank teller, or the waiter in a restaurant, or the grocery clerk, etc. In all these situations, remember whenever you can to simply observe yourself.

Exercise 7: Self-Inquiry. This exercise is best done in a sitting fashion for at least 20 minutes or longer, though it can also be done at any time during the day, as with self-observation and self-remembering.

Self-inquiry is what it suggests: a direct inquiry into the Self. It is the eternal question 'Who am I?' At first it may take the form of a somewhat disconnected intellectual process, attempting to locate the source of yourself among the long lists of self-defining categories that comprise the identity of who you think you are— 'I am a man, woman, parent, doctor, teacher, secretary, clerk, healer, happy person, loving person, sensitive person', etc.—all the way down to more simple self-definitions, like 'I am warmth, love, fear, anger, emptiness, despair', and so on. Eventually, if Self-inquiry is persisted with, the process becomes less and less abstract, as the mind runs out of definitions for itself, and longer spaces of silence appear in-between the answers to the question.

At this point, a deepening is happening in which *insight* in its true sense—'directly seeing within'—is beginning to be aroused, and analytical mind is being relaxed. With persistence, profound breakthroughs are possible with this method, in which the tacit and immediate sense of a deeper and vaster sense of being can arise, often accompanied by glimpses of non-dual consciousness.

Exercise 8: Zen Koan. This method derives from the Buddhist schools of the East, such as in China and Korea, and especially Japan, where it has been widely practiced in the Rinzai Zen lineages. A *koan* is a paradox that cannot be solved by reason (thus, is not a riddle), but can only be penetrated by insight, or a leap to a higher level of understanding. It is very similar to Self-inquiry, and in fact, the question 'Who am I?' is a *koan*.

Traditionally, a practitioner of Zen meditation might work on a given *koan* for many years before breaking through and opening up to a higher level of understanding. This higher level of understanding is poorly approximated by the English word 'intuition', but in fact is best defined by the Japanese word *kensho*, which means 'direct seeing into reality'. Though here again, there is some inaccuracy with the definition, because the breakthrough defined by *kensho* involves a direct understanding and experience of Oneness, which is non-dual, that is, there is no 'seer' who is separate from what is 'seen'.

Choose a rationally insoluble question, such as 'What is the size and weight of love?' or 'Where is the end of the universe?' or 'What is a tree?' or 'What is the sound of one hand clapping?' Then, hold the question within, coming back to it whenever you can, and giving full attention to it. Allow yourself to exhaust all possible intellectual answers, and then continue to inquire into the question. In time, you will notice a shifting inside and the gradual opening of what we may call the 'inner wisdom eye' which apprehends reality in a direct fashion, without images, concepts, or words. This method can be effective for people with strong, active minds.

Exercise 9: Vipassana. Vipassana is an old Buddhist meditation technique believed to originate from the time of the Buddha, and probably even before that. It is very simple and effective, yet requires discipline, commitment, and patience. Begin with 20-minute sessions, and increase up to one hour as you feel ready. Seated comfortably, back straight but not rigid, take a few deep breaths, and relax into yourself. Then, locating the breath in either the pit of the belly, or at the tip of the nose (choose one location or the other, and then stick with it), simply follow your natural in-out breathing rhythm with your awareness. No matter what, keep your awareness on your breath. Simply stay with the breath. At first, you will forget the breath again and again, as you drift off into thought-dreams. That is normal. Try to not get frustrated or self-reproachful; simply keep returning your awareness to the rise and fall of the breath. As you follow the breath, bear witness to whatever is happening, but keep your awareness anchored to the breath. This method is excellent for focusing and grounding, as well as clearing the mind and centering within.

Exercise 10: Witnessing. This is the simplest technique of all, and in some ways, the most challenging. In essence, it involves 'just sitting' and being witness to whatever is happening, or arising, in this moment. In Zen Buddhism they call this *Shikan-Taza*. The meditation can be done sitting with eyes open or closed, and it can also be done while driving, standing in line, or doing anything that requires nothing more than 'autopilot' responses from you. However, in the beginning, you may find it easiest to attempt this in a sitting posture with the eyes closed. In Witnessing, you are resting in your natural state, which is that of pure consciousness, pure awareness. Let your awareness be big, all-embracing, all-encompassing. Let it be natural. And simply rest in it, being purely aware, and nothing else. Let go, and be relaxed and yet alert, sharply watchful, and calmly observant.

Active Meditations

Exercise 11: Deep Breathing. This breathing method consists of 30 minutes of deep breathing, done in three stages, repeated once. It is helpful to do this with some sort of gentle, rhythmic music, though it's not required.

Sitting down comfortably, preferably cross-legged on a comfortable surface, close the eyes and begin to breathe deep, slow breaths. Try to inhale to a maximum, and then relax on the exhale. Have each inhale start in the lower diaphragm, and finish at the top of the chest. Do this slow, deep breathing for five minutes. Then for the next five minutes switch to a somewhat faster pace of breathing, keeping the focus on the inhale, and relaxing on the exhale. After five minutes of this, switch to rapid breathing: short, shallow, panting style. Do this for five minutes as well. Then, repeat the three stages again, for a total of 30 minutes of breathing. Once the 30 minutes are complete, simply sit silently for at least ten minutes. This exercise is especially effective for generating energy and revitalizing.

Exercise 12: Taking Risks. Choose an activity that will challenge you in some way. This activity should be something you have resistance doing, or fear engaging in, and it should involve either a physical challenge, or a challenge in the area of confronting your fears around being judged by others, or being disapproved of by others. Good examples of physically challenging tasks might be climbing up to a high place if you have fear of heights, spending time alone in Nature if you have fear of this, or similarly related activities. For working on fears of disapproval, a good exercise is to apply some sort of creative face paint to your face, and then go out into a public market and walk around, allowing yourself to be seen. Such seemingly absurd activities are actually very effective for drawing attention to unconscious fears that are preventing a greater sense of empowerment in life. The main idea here is to create balance in the personality by pushing ourselves out of our 'comfort zones'.

Self-Realization: Does the Personal Self Actually Exist?

It is a given that by 'Self-realization' the referent is the greater Self, or Ground of Being, not the personal self (ego, personality, etc.). That said, the most obvious, but probably the most commonly missed, of all questions, is simply *who am I*? When universally recognized sages such as Socrates and Ramana Maharshi give supreme weight to this question ('Know thyself' and 'Who am I?'), it suggests something noteworthy (and even Jesus appeared to be addressing the same question when, according to John, he uttered 'I and the Father are one', speaking to an ultimate realization of universal identity).

That said, what these sages seem to be pointing toward is something subtler and more profound than any superficial identification with a greater, higher, or divine self as we would commonly imagine that to be. The Buddha (for one) based his entire teaching on a profound recognition: that the personal self (or ego) does not appear to exist at all when the matter is closely examined via deep and sustained contemplation and meditation. That of course does not mean that 'we' do not exist; rather, it means that our real nature is not at all what we assume it to be, that we are living under the effects of a mental construct and an elaborate illusion. More recent Western philosophers reasoned their way to similar conclusions, most notably Kant and some of the Idealists who followed him, including and up to William James, although few claimed to have direct experience of this alongside their intellectual comprehension. The clearest example was David Hume, who in the eighteenth century wrote:

> ...when I enter most intimately into what I call myself, I always stumble on some particular perception or other, of heat or cold, light or shade, love or hatred, pain or pleasure. I never can catch myself at any time without a perception, and never can observe anything but the perception. When my perceptions are removed for any time, as by sound sleep; so long am I insensible of myself, and may truly be said not to exist.[1]

Hume's conclusion was that perceptions existed, but no self independent of them. Similar conclusions have been reached by contemporary Western philosophers who invoke new and fresh approaches (including neuroscience); two of the more articulate recent examples are Owen Flanagan (b. 1949) and Thomas Metzinger (b. 1958). Flanagan, a neurobiologist and philosopher, is a materialist (or 'naturalist' as he prefers), yet arrives at conclusions remarkably similar to those of certain wisdom traditions that examine the idea of a discrete inner self (and do not find one). In his 1992 work *Consciousness Reconsidered*, in a chapter titled 'The Illusion of the Mind's "I"', he wrote:

> We are egoless...the main idea is that the self emerges as experience accrues, and it is constructed as the organism

actively engages the external world...in this sense the ego is an after-the-fact construction, not a before-the-fact condition for the possibility of experience...the posit of the mind's 'I' is unnecessary.[2]

Metzinger, a German philosopher, published a difficult book in 2003 called *Being No One: The Self-Model Theory of Subjectivity*, and then wrote a more layman-friendly version of it called *The Ego Tunnel: The Science of the Mind and the Myth of the Self* (2009). He drew from neuroscience, robotics, and experiments with virtual reality, but his central point is simple: we do not have, never had, a 'self'. It is the various functions of our brain that generate the conditions leading to our subjective construction of the self. This 'inner self' is little more than an imagined homunculus, a 'little person' dwelling within, that we assume to be at the command seat of our consciousness, picking and choosing what thoughts to generate each moment, and appearing to exercising a free will with assumed autonomy. Metzinger wrote:

No such things as 'selves' exist in the world...We are Ego Machines, but we do not have selves. We cannot leave the Ego Tunnel, because there is nobody who could leave. The Ego and its Tunnel are representational phenomena: they are just one of many possible ways in which conscious beings can model reality...the Ego is merely a complex physical event — an activation pattern in your central nervous system.[3]

Both Flanagan and Metzinger agree that the 'self' is essentially a representation, a process of mental phenomena brought about by a number of factors, but lacking an intrinsic nature. This is very close to what the Buddha taught (though without the comprehensive psycho-spiritual instruction that the Buddha provided to support the realization of no-self; and without the systems of development offered by the Western esoteric tradition that seek to ground the *representation* of self within the context of something much greater).

Analytical Meditation

Owing to the challenges of healthy ego-formation and the central illusion that the ego generates (separation), the wisdom traditions are clear that the ego or sense of personal isolation ultimately lies at the source of human suffering. This is due to the premise that ego is all about limitation. The Sanskrit term for ego is *ahamkara* (literally, 'I-maker'). It is regarded as basic to survival, but seen as getting in the way of higher truths precisely because it thinks in terms of personal ownership only—'my ideas, my-self, my feelings', etc. It has difficulty in understanding what is *not* I. That in turn sets up and reinforces a false division between self and universe, and leads to a deep-seated mistrust in what appears to lie 'outside' of self. Analytical meditation is a method to see directly into the emptiness of the ego-self.

Exercise 13: Analytical Meditation. We can try a thought-experiment of 'analytical meditation', as follows. Does the body exist—independent of it being solely a conceptual entity?[4] And if so, can we locate it? Let us examine the matter. The body consists of arms, legs, organs, and so on. It is a construction of various parts. But each part is not the body. We cannot say that the arm is the body, or the eye is the body. Clearly that would be nonsense.

Can a grouping of non-body parts make a body in anything other than a conceptual sense? Practically speaking, ten chairs together do not make a table. Four legs and a table top together may make a table, but 'table' exists only as a conceptual label. Seen clearly, the table is really the legs and the top. Similarly, the body does not truly exist other than as a *conceptual entity*. It is purely a concept, a label. And this is the same wherever we look, and is true for whatever we look at. What is a hand? A grouping of fingers, skin, etc., none of which is a hand. Therefore, there is no hand in any absolute sense—there is only the *concept* of a hand, a pure abstraction existing only in the mind. The same applies for all so-called objectively existing things. Wherever we look, we see only the externalization of our *ideas*, all the way down to subatomic particles and empty space.

So, if nothing exists inherently in objective reality, beyond it being an externalized concept, then what about if we look within? Clearly our 'I' is not consistent, as it can be related to many things—thoughts, moods, feelings, memories, and so on. 'I' is a composite of many different mental and even physiological states. Because it would be unsound to refer to one state as 'me'—I am anger, I am fear, I am this memory (but not that one), etc.—then the same thing can be concluded, that being that this 'I' has no real inherent existence as something specifically and separately definable. 'I' is not a discrete thing, isolated from everything else.

If this is so, what is left over? In some traditions it is called 'luminous emptiness', in others 'cosmic Mind', a kind of continuous whole in which there is no *truly real* division between what we experience as 'me' and the universe. That may be called 'absolute reality'. Then there are conventional realities to be recognized, such as the reality of 'I feel hungry, tired', etc. In the investigation of absolute reality, conventional reality is not ignored or denied.

Three Additional Pointers

1. Avoid Unnecessary Talk. A classic way to squander energy is via unnecessary talk—'babbling'. Pay attention to your speech and notice when you talk mainly to control anxiety, or to manipulate others, etc. Learn to listen and hold space (especially with women). Avoiding unnecessary talk does not mean that you become nothing but a silent monk or a Clint Eastwood high-

plains drifter; it means you bring mindfulness into your speech as well, and speak more from your center, rather than from mechanical patterns. To quote the great German poet Goethe:
Enough words have been exchanged;
now at last let me see some deeds!

An important tendency for men to be mindful of is **boasting**. A thing I have observed time and again with certain men when they join a men's group is the tendency to speak of their accomplishments or better qualities before anything else. Sometimes they appear very reluctant to be even marginally vulnerable and will avoid, for many meetings, any communication about the weaker areas of their lives. One is left scratching one's head about why they have joined the group in the first place, since it appears that they've come to instruct the group or impress the men with their knowledge or experiences. Many such men do not last long in a worthy men's group, as other men detect their boasting and become tired of it, or they themselves soon realize that they are not really capable of being emotionally honest with other men.

It has been argued by some that the primary motivating factor of a man is competition. When I first was introduced to this idea I was reluctant to embrace it, as I'd known at least some men who did not seem to be run by this. But over the years as I was exposed to greater and greater numbers of men via my involvement in men's groups, I began to see the reality of it.

It's here where the inner work becomes very subtle and even tricky, because while identifying one's tendencies to boast (or bullshit) is important, we are not involved in the business of stamping out all competitive tendencies. To do so would be unrealistic and lean too perilously toward feminization. The primary motivating factor of most women is relationship (connecting, and all the dramas that surround that). Men need to connect too. But a man also needs a sword of some sort, some edge to wield in life in order to fulfill, express, and enjoy his masculine energy. The key qualifier is 'healthy'. A man needs to find ways to embrace his competitive spirit in a healthy-minded fashion.

2. Identification. A main cause of suffering in life is taking things too personally, which stems from identification. Remember always that you are *not what you do*. If you are a cook for a profession, that does not mean you are *nothing but* a cook (or scientist, or artist, or musician, or doctor, lawyer, accountant, between jobs, etc.). First and foremost, you are a conscious being. Second, you are a man. Third, you have an occupation (and talents). *But you are not your occupation or your talents.* You are something much more. Remembering this aids in avoiding the nasty emotions that can arise from taking things too personally in life.

3. Boldness. The following quotation—usually attributed to Goethe, but in fact, except for the concluding three sentences, written by the Scottish mountaineer W.H. Murray (1913–96)— sums up an essential masculine quality as well as any book can:

> Until one is committed, there is hesitancy, the chance to draw back. Concerning all acts of initiative (and creation), there is one elementary truth, the ignorance of which kills countless ideas and splendid plans: that the moment one definitely commits oneself, then Providence moves too. All sorts of things occur to help one that would never otherwise have occurred. A whole stream of events issues from the decision, raising in one's favor all manner of unforeseen incidents and meetings and material assistance, which no man could have dreamed would have come his way. I learned a deep respect for one of Goethe's couplets: 'Whatever you can do, or dream you can do, begin it. Boldness has genius, power, and magic in it. Begin it now.'

Chapter 10

Guidelines for Intimate Relationship

The following is a short list of pointers helpful for navigating the challenging waters of intimate relationship. The list is short by design. In general, it's not necessary—or arguably, even good—for men to spend excessive amounts of time processing their feelings around intimate relationships. However, some brief guidelines are in order, so that a conscious warrior does not lose all or most of his life-energy endlessly struggling with the thickets and thorns of intimate love. As the Indian mystic Osho once said: 'A woman is not a problem to be solved. A woman is a mystery to be loved.' Therefore, ask yourself only if you love your significant other *enough*. If the answer is truly yes, then give up trying to 'solve' her, figure her out, or fix her. You won't be able to anyway. Rather, become grounded in who you are by exercising the confidence that grows from accomplishing your goals in life. In that way you can be the best man you can be, and at the same time, be the best partner for your mate.

1. Give Your Energy

Be sincere and total with your partner. Don't be stingy with your energy. Demonstrate abundance by exercising generosity of spirit with her. You can do this in so many ways, even if you lack the material resources.

2. Learn to Listen with Curiosity

Most women will have a greater need to talk about themselves than you will about yourself, and most women will have a need to describe their subjective life to you, the complex inner world of their feelings and emotions. Sometimes your partner may appear chaotic to you, or at least compared to most men. She may also appear hopelessly self-absorbed. Be patient with this. As she feels more and more safe with you, she will relax and reward you for your patience and willingness to bear witness, without judgment, to who she is. And if you are talking about yourself more than her, if you are the one lost in endlessly processing feelings with her, then develop some quality relationships with men so that you can take your darker feelings to them instead.

3. Don't Take Things Personally

This is arguably the most important interpersonal lesson to learn in life. In the world of relationship, more suffering is caused by taking things personally than by anything else. To personalize issues, to insert your reality into your partner's reality when it's unwarranted or inappropriate, is to reinforce the fragility of your ego. Diminish useless self-importance by practicing not taking things personally. Remember, the vast majority of the time when you think something that is troubling your partner is about you, it isn't. And even when it *is* about you, you can make everything easier by *not reacting*. When emotionally charged, take one conscious deep breath and delay reacting, even if just for a few seconds. In general, when personally offended and angry about something, wait 24 hours before responding. (Excepting those rare cases when present-time action is required, such as in serious boundaries issues, or when the welfare of someone close to you is threatened.)

4. Be Playful

Lighten up. See the humor in things, notice the absurdity of life, develop a sense for the ridiculous. Smile and wink more. Understand what it means to have a twinkle in your eye. Frame issues with humor when possible. Making a woman laugh is far more effective than trying to fix her and far more powerful than angrily invalidating her.

5. Be Spontaneous and Avoid Routines

Don't be robotic with your partner. Be creative; surprise her in small ways. By doing so, you demonstrate that she's important to you. Women are very sensitive to this. Don't treat them like one of your buds. Guys usually enjoy routines with each other, but this doesn't work so well with women. Be spontaneous when you can.

6. Stay in the Beginning

'Stay in the beginning' is one of the great secrets of Tantra and forms of conscious relating. The other Eastern expression that speaks to this is 'Zen Mind, Beginner's Mind'. What makes intimate relationship magical in the early romance phase is the way everything is fresh, alive, unknown and unexpected, like visiting a mysterious land for the first time, like being very young again. This state of mind can be practiced—it involves letting go of positions in your mind. Avoid making your mind up about her. Enjoy the unknowable mystery that she is, but more to the point, practice the aliveness that comes from being willing to see her as new every time.

7. Bring Consciousness to Your Fingertips

The meaning here is literal and straightforward. When touching her, do so with awareness in the tips of your fingers. Be precise and present in your touch. Mindfully contact her body with the furthest extensions of your physicality, the fingers of your hands, and in specific, the fingertips. This is both actual and metaphor.

8. Move Slowly

Contact your partner's being from the centre of your own, and in particular, from the centre of your mindful presence. Do not rush—physically, emotionally, intellectually. Build up toward things. This all applies physically too, of course.

9. Have a Man-Cave

Men need a centre within the greater confines of their home. If living alone, keep your place in order. If living with your mate, try to establish that room or at least area of your home that is yours to do your work or exercise some creativity. If moving in together, avoid, if you can, moving into her home. Her natural tendency to domesticate, to permeate the home with her presence, will make it difficult for you to ever feel grounded in your masculine core. Instead, try to find a home together where you both have a fresh start. It's also generally workable if she moves into your home, provided you have enough space to accommodate her. This setup works better than the reverse as she will more naturally make herself at home than you would if clumsily moving into her place.

10. Have Good Men in Your Life

You cannot do well in life in intimate relationship if you do not also have quality brothers in your life—men who can be there for you, men who can challenge you when need be, men who have your back when need be, men who you care enough about to reciprocate all that. So many times, conflict issues in intimate relationship can be made much easier or even solved altogether when a man has quality male friends to share consciousness with. The main reason for this is that women are not well equipped to hold space for men, to listen to them process their feelings—unless they are willing to move more into a mother or big sister role. Even if they are willing or able to do this, the erotic charge in the relationship will usually decline, sometimes to an unrecoverable extent.

Chapter 11

Magnum Opus, the Mature Masculine, and the Art of Decisiveness

Genius is 1 percent inspiration, 99 percent perspiration.
—Edison

Solar Power

What is the purpose of a man's life? It is to accomplish his Great Work, his *magnum opus*. A poignant example of this—perhaps the most famous in the Western world—is the death of Jesus on the cross. Of course, the life of Jesus was not documented in one book—there are three synoptic gospels (Mark, Matthew, and Luke) and four canonical gospels when John is added, along with several other apocryphal ones, and they do say different things. I've always been impressed by the conclusion of Jesus' life as described in John's gospel. In John 19:30 he is recorded as having said 'It is accomplished' (from the Greek word *tetelestai*). Immediately after he utters these words, he 'gives up the ghost'.

Jesus' life is the stuff of legend; historically there is a great deal of uncertainty around most of the details of his story. As presented in the gospels Jesus clearly had a mission, one he was driven to accomplish, and although his journey was far from typical it is still marked with a number of extraordinary signposts that exemplify the creation and completion of a *magnum opus*.

Jesus' last words in John's gospel are sometimes translated as 'It is finished'. This is also significant, insofar as a key element of what I call the 'mature masculine' is the ability to complete things, and thereby gain the confidence that accompanies such accomplishment. To accomplish something is indeed to 'finish' it, even if it remains imperfect. The distinction is important. Accomplishing or finishing something is not about making it

221

absolutely perfect. It is about having the endurance to see things through. Only in completing things can we approach mastery, and mastery is the essence of the mature king. But mastery is not about perfection, for the simple reason that life is a continuous process, not a static object.

When Leonardo Da Vinci was in the last decade of his life he continued to fiddle with the *Mona Lisa*, even carrying it around with him as he relocated his residence several times in his final years. Over many years he poured a tremendous amount of energy into the painting (part of the reason for its hypnotic power — it is literally filled with Leonardo's brilliant energy). It was not painted in one night. It was a magnum opus, a life's Great Work, and it clearly reflects that. But was the painting perfect? As far as Leonardo was concerned — and who should know better? — it was not. Perfection is an idea that suggests sterility, and creative power, like life, is never sterile.

Jesus on the cross is regarded, by religious convention, as a symbol having to do with sacrifice and the salvation and ultimate redemption of the common person. But I think it's much more than that (however cosmic 'that' may be). 'It is accomplished', or 'It is finished', is the triumphant cry of a man who did what he had to do — not in the mechanical, foolish manner of a man doing something destructive or pointless, but in the manner of a man whose life was full of aspiration and oriented completely toward a great cause in which he played a key part. A man who completes his Great Work is not a solitary note, even if he is playing solo; he is an instrument in an orchestra and his music is essential to the greater piece.

What stops a man from recognizing his role in cosmic life? What blocks are in his way? A number of them have been touched on in the course of this book, but a few bear looking at more closely. Of course, most of this is based on cultural context — a warrior in the army of Genghis Khan or in service of one of the Japanese shoguns faced very different 'cosmic lessons' than the average materially privileged Western man sitting in front of his computer. Modern men face challenges unique in history, some of which are connected to over-stimulus and a weakened attention span. In the final analysis, however, these are not impressive excuses. All men must pass beyond the prince stage into true warriorhood, in the sense of growing beyond childish dependencies, entitlement, or brooding resentment in order to get truly and properly untracked.

A man needs to locate his Holy Grail in life, but the Holy Grail is not a woman (with apologies to Dan Brown). It is his deep calling, his reason for being, and it is all about *work*. A man does not inhabit his masculinity until he cultivates a true work ethic. That is to say, he must leave nothing behind when he goes out on the field. If a man's life is not governed and led by passion—and I speak here of passion that is free of exclusively self-serving agendas—then he meanders and eventually questions his purpose. Such a man is ineffectual in most areas of life.

This is a crucial point to consider, because without such direction a man is not inhabiting his masculine polarity. Despite modern technology men still hold within them the long history of cultural conditioning that requires them to live as hunters and adventurers (and even, dare I say it, conquerors). When modern men become too soft, too passive, too lost in the sheer triviality of social networking and online surfing, they lose what edge they had—or worse, they occasionally explode in acts of resentful intensity in which their underlying frustration (or, more lethally, their rage) is triggered with deadly consequences.

As Bly repeatedly pointed out, men weak in their masculine core usually lack healthy relationships with older men. Twice annually I run weekend seminars for men. These workshops largely consist of processes that the men enact together. In one of them the older men in the workshop—men over 50—are asked to sit up front together, preferably wearing sunglasses. All the younger men are then invited, one at a time, to sit in front of them and speak spontaneously, from their gut. Often what emerges is plenty of anger, sometimes hate, and occasionally a plea for money. Only rarely will a younger man sit up front and voice appreciation (or, as one rare man once did, ask forgiveness for his 'bratty', entitled brothers).

Younger men frequently don't like older guys, and the more ambitious younger men often dream of bringing down the king (or the plant foreman). It's not usually the personality of the older man that is at issue; it's what he represents. He represents power and control (as well as material strength). He and his ilk run most of the world (how many political or business leaders are under 50? Some, but not many. The youngest US presidents to assume office over the past century have been Bill Clinton at 46 and Barack Obama at 47). Accordingly, younger men frequently get mired in extraordinary frustration, compounded by both the testosterone coursing through their system and the simple reality that time moves very slowly when younger. To be told 'You'll understand when you're older' means nothing to the young, and usually only incites more contempt for the older person who utters those forgettable words. The younger guy wants it now, and finds it difficult to wait for tomorrow. He has a 'need for speed'. Even if he's intellectually oriented or introverted, his tendency toward bombast or arrogance will surface via his views about the stupidity of older people.

Maturity and Solar Wisdom: What Was It Really All About?

David Letterman (b. 1947), the iconic late-night talk show host and comedian who hosted two long-term American TV shows (*Late Night* on NBC and *The Late Show* on CBS) from 1982 to 2015, during which he conducted thousands of interviews with thousands of guests, made some remarkably sage-like comments when interviewed six months after his retirement:

When you're doing it for so long, and for each day...you believe that what you are doing is of great importance and it is affecting mankind wall-to-wall. And then when you get out of it you realize, oh, well, that wasn't true at all. It was just silliness. And when that occurred to me, I felt so much better and I realized, geez, I don't think I care that much about television anymore. I feel foolish for having been misguided by my own ego for so many years...my wife will say 'Well, look at what you've accomplished.' And I'll say, 'Well, what have I accomplished?' And she says, 'Well, look. You've employed a lot of people for a long time...' So I always laugh and think, okay, I've put a lot of people to work. And that's usually the end of the conversation.[1]

Letterman began his career as a rather edgy interviewer. He could be funny and charming enough if he liked his guest but he could be acerbic, sarcastic, and merciless if he didn't. I didn't particularly enjoy watching him in his earlier years (the 1980s, when he followed Johnny Carson's *Tonight Show* on NBC). However, after open heart surgery, the 9-11 attacks in his city, and the birth of his son in 2003, Letterman mellowed into a far more likeable character. By the time he was in his sixties (2008 and beyond) he was showing some of the maturity that marks what I call 'solar wisdom'. This is the kind of wisdom that understands one's craft and performs it with excellence, but is not especially attached to outcomes or how it is being perceived by others. While solar power is engaged when a man finds his path and embraces it with passion, solar wisdom blossoms when a man performs his highest function in a way that is less and less personally involved. He may still be doing many things, but he's less and less attached to the need to prove himself via his work. He is removed personally—meaning his work is less egocentric—even if his work flourishes (or is perhaps picked up by others).

Letterman specialized in self-deprecation, but he was no slouch. As of now he's the longest serving late-night talk show host in American history, unlikely to be surpassed anytime soon. Prime aspects of 'king energy' are mastery and completion, and Letterman accomplished both in his long career. By the end he had mellowed nicely in his craft and was an effortless interviewer, despite the standard surface act of self-parody.

It's arguable that 'solar wisdom' is not possible for a man under 50, or even under 60, as it requires a certain level of life experience before one can ripen into such a state, and that's probably true to some degree. However, I think it's possible for younger men to achieve a very similar level of wisdom, especially if they have not avoided life, relationships, and engaging their passions. A man of 35 who has lived a full and thoughtful life can surpass in wisdom a man of 50 who has let much of life pass him by.

There is a direct relationship between engaging life fully and personal attachment. The more we engage life, the less attached we tend to be on the level of egocentric needs for recognition. The less we engage life, the more we tend to be sensitive to how the world perceives us, the more egocentric, and the more fragile.

Engaging life fully is not about how much stuff we do, or how many places or things we see, or how many people we sleep with. It's about the quality of our presence, what we bring to the table, how we show up in whatever it is we're doing. Living a life of passion and balance, work and play, creativity and contemplation, celebration and intimacy, leads to freedom and true wisdom. This is a wisdom that doesn't worry about its immortal status in the scheme of things, because it recognizes that the deeper values are impersonal.

Alas, such recognition is not really possible if we haven't first investigated the personal. This is why we have to live *as if what we do makes a difference*. At the end of the day, we may come to see—as Letterman did—that it was all 'just silliness'. But before then it's a better policy to live life as if it's important and what we do is an important contribution to it. Such an approach keeps us from copping out or playing small. We're part of a game and the idea is to play it, and play it fully. When the day comes to stand on the sidelines and wistfully chuckle at all the players on the field grinding it out, we'll know it.

Below are some exercises for training the will so that we can accomplish things in life—and in so doing, play the game of life fully. An ideal conscious warrior has a very focused will and personality. Some seem to have this quality naturally, but it can also be developed.

Conscious Discipline and the Art of Decisiveness

Conscious Discipline: If chronic 'laziness' (a widespread and common condition) can be generally defined as resistance to life, and in particular, the fear of self-expression and of experiencing success, then 'discipline' can be viewed as the antidote to such fears. It is important here to understand that we are not referring to 'discipline' as the word is commonly understood. We are referring rather to *conscious* discipline. Discipline is qualified here because typical discipline is often only routinely, half-heartedly, grudgingly or mechanically undertaken as part of a general program to advance in life based on how we have been told we *should* advance, such as through a typical career, with the approval of key family, peer, and societal members around us. This sort of discipline—'mechanical discipline'—is usually enforced on us from the outside, and while it has its merits in early life, it is ultimately limited in terms of its ability to help us locate our highest calling. Mechanical discipline is a developmental stage in the process of learning conscious discipline.

Once we have begun to balance and deconstruct elements of our personality via self-acceptance and self-observation, we begin to access our underlying essence and to develop it in such a fashion that we gain glimpses into our higher Self and our highest calling in life. It is then usually a matter of acquiring and practicing discipline of some sort in order to bring about the conditions and circumstances that will help this chosen life-path to best unfold.

The root of the word 'discipline' is the same as that for 'disciple', the Latin *discipulus*, which means 'learner'. To cultivate conscious discipline is to be a true learner, one who is capable of growing by absorbing the teachings, wisdom, and understanding necessary to advance on their life path. Without such discipline it is very difficult, if not impossible, to truly learn, let alone advance and accomplish. An untrained mind can accomplish little.

In facing the need for discipline, we are inevitably confronted by our own resistance to it, which is largely based on the resistance to maturing.

For the first decade of our life things were mostly done for us, and in many cases, things 'magically' appeared in our life with minimal awareness on our part, such as meals, shelter, attention, advice, etc. An essential part of the maturation process is learning some degree of self-reliance, which grows in direct proportion to our willingness to practice conscious discipline. As this discipline develops, we are forced to confront our fears around self-expression, personal power, and ultimately, responsibility. This is because conscious discipline, when practiced over an extended period of time with consistency, ultimately leads to proficiency, excellence, or mastery of some sort, which often translates into success. Such success (at whatever perceived level) almost always involves a degree of responsibility. All of this will activate our core fears around living and expressing the vastness and greatness of our pure potentiality, which is the main cause behind the resistance to conscious discipline. It is, in the end, connected to the fears of truly 'showing up' in life, of being 'big', and the perceived responsibility and freedom that accompanies such a stance.

Practicing Conscious Discipline: Once you have located inwardly a passion you wish to actualize, and what your dream would be around fulfilling this passion, set yourself the task that for five days out of every week you will always do at least *one thing* that is geared toward *bringing about* that dream. The very nature of 'dream' implies a future potential, but conscious discipline always addresses the here and now in a very practical manner. At the end of each of the five days, mentally review what you have accomplished during that day. Acknowledge efforts made (regardless of the nature of the results), and if there were no efforts made, honestly inquire into the reasons behind your inactivity. Practice this for one month. Eventually, it will become part of the natural flow of your life, where conscious discipline is undertaken much as basic life activities are, such as eating, washing, speaking, sleeping, and so on. When this discipline begins to be *enjoyed*, then it is a sure sign that success is beginning to manifest or will soon follow. By 'success' is meant in this context the expression of what excites and fulfills you in life in such a way that you feel supported by life in what you are doing.

Decision-Making: The most crucial aspect of acquiring conscious discipline is the ability to make decisions—to be decisive. The words 'decision' and 'decisive' both derive from the Latin *decidere*, which means to 'cut off'. The meaning is important to understand. Enacting a decision, being decisive, involves 'cutting off' indecision, or the inertia or immobility of the mind.

It is in decision-making that the personal will is developed and strengthened, much as a physical muscle is by repeated use. Of course, such a 'muscle' can be strengthened and then simply used for wrong or unhealthy reasons. In the context of psychological and spiritual growth, the development of personal power must be wedded to discriminating intelligence in order for this power to be utilized in a proper way that does not result in negativity rebounding.

Ultimately, in the further stages of inner awakening, the whole notion of personal will is seen in a very different light, being more part of the fabric and flow of the greater Reality, in which there is understood to be less and less a sense of a separate 'doer' who is apparently making all these decisions. However, prior to acquiring the insight to begin to understand this bigger, non-dualistic picture, it is necessary to learn to exercise our *personal* will and power. If such exercising is done properly, it gradually leads to the dawning awareness that our own higher will is already connected to a greater reality, or life path, that is our highest calling (and is, from the ultimate perspective, one with it). However, as Lao Tzu once wrote in the *Tao Te Ching*, 'The journey of a thousand miles begins with a single step.' In time, we begin to see that this 'first step' is as important as any other step.

The Decision Exercise: In this exercise we begin with very simple tasks, which may be completely mundane and even unrelated to anything outwardly productive. That is because what we are here learning is how to *consistently* perform certain actions; indeed, it is such consistency that lies at the heart of all productive decision-making capacity.[2]

Choose a simple, mundane activity, such as cleaning your bathroom sink faucet, or mirror, or sweeping the kitchen floor, or standing on a stool in the corner of your room. The activity chosen should be unimportant. The idea is to do it efficiently — and at the *same time* every day. This latter is crucial to the success of the exercise. That is because in doing it at the same designated time every day we begin to train ourselves to believe that we are truly and fully capable of *accomplishment*. As this is believed at deeper and deeper levels of the mind, such capacity for accomplishment can then be exercised toward greater and greater ventures in life. The power behind this exercise, in spite of its simplicity, should not be underestimated. Its power lies precisely in its consistency—much like Aesop's fable of the tortoise and the hare: the tortoise gets to the finish line first because he does not stop moving forward. In the end, it is *consistency* that creates results, not speed.

Once you have chosen your activity—for example, wiping the kitchen sink faucet for ten minutes—then make an agreement with yourself that you will do this activity every day for seven straight days, at the *exact same time* each day. That time could be 3:00 a.m., or 9:47 a.m., or 11:06 p.m.—it does not matter; what matters is that you do not waver any day from the appointed time. If it is 9:47 a.m., then the faucet must be wiped—with attentive excellence—every day at precisely 9:47 a.m., for ten minutes. In addition to this, each morning as soon as you awaken, take a moment to visualize yourself wiping the faucet at 9:47 a.m. And, at the end of each day, before falling asleep, take a minute to mentally review and visualize having wiped the faucet that day at 9:47 a.m. The visualizing is important, even if your capacity to do so is limited.

The key here is *persistence*. If you are successful at doing all this for seven straight days, you will feel results. The manner in which such results manifest is different for each person, but the most common feelings are those of a sharper sense of decisiveness, more positive, uplifting energy, more wakefulness and increased vividness of perception. Eventually the exercise can be applied to more complex and challenging tasks, but in the beginning it is very important to choose something unimportant and simple that you are sure you will not fail at, so as not to incur the risk of failure and subsequent self-doubt and abandoning of the practice. The key to much in life is confidence. Confidence arises from the conviction that you can complete tasks, and complete them efficiently. As Gurdjieff once said, 'If you can do one thing well, you can do *anything* well.'

Chapter 12

The Shaman

Earlier in this book I mentioned Native Indian sweat lodges. I participated in my first 'sweat' on a hot August day in 1992. I'd organized it for my men's team at the time (we were called the 'Cro-mags'; the logo of our team T-shirt featured a giant mag wheel being ridden by a caveman). I had contacted my Metis friend Phil to conduct the lodge. Phil was part Cree Indian, part French Canadian, but was raised in Western Canada and spoke in a flat Canadian English accent with that slight Native lilt. He was in his early forties at the time. Although he had been immersed in Native spirituality for many years, I was surprised to find out that he'd not yet led a formal sweat lodge. He took my request of him to lead this for my men's team as some sort of sign that he was ready. He consulted with his tribal elders and they gave him the green light to go ahead.

Phil was co-owner of a local bookstore that specialized in Native and Celtic spirituality. I took my men's team (about seven guys) to meet him at the bookstore. Although Phil was only about 5 ft. 6 or so, he was stocky and moved about with a certain stealthy confidence. Combined with his braided black hair and classic Native features, decked out in some beads and buckskin, he cut an impressive figure. Some of the guys on my men's team were clearly impressed; one or two were even nervous to shake his hand, fearing perhaps that he might cast some spell or deem them unworthy of warriorhood.

Phil was friendly and down to earth, however, and soon put everyone at ease. We chatted a bit and then he had to go attend to a customer. Someone wanted to buy some beads.

A few days later I rounded up the rest of the Cro-mags and we drove an hour out of town to the designated sweat lodge site. It was prepared when we arrived. Phil's assistant, known

in local sweat lodge circles as the 'fireman', was busy prepping
the lodge and the fire that would heat the volcanic rocks. Water
would be poured onto these rocks in the lodge, creating the hot
steam that was basic to the experience. This, combined with the
pitch black (all flaps of the lodge were pulled down, blocking all
outside light), along with the rounds of songs and prayers, made
for a full-on experience. There was nothing half-baked about an
authentic, traditional Native sweat lodge. The ceremony, which
lasted several hours, was concluded with a feast, a potluck
dinner featuring salmon, corn on the cob and bannock bread.

Over the years I took many groups of people, men and
women, into sweat lodges facilitated by Phil. I grew to respect
his skill as a facilitator. During one sweat lodge, in the depths of
the darkness, extreme heat, and fervent prayer with 30 men and
women crammed in, he loudly boomed that the 'spirits' were
bestowing a name on me. I eagerly awaited what I hoped would
be some fierce, brave, or exotic-sounding name. 'Your name', he
announced with a flourish, clearly struggling with the heat—he
sounded like he'd just finished a marathon race—'is to be "Just
a Man"'.

The lodge fell silent. I felt a passing moment of deflation, but
that was soon countered with the thought of how cool it was to
be named in a sweat lodge ceremony at all. At the end of the day,
during the potluck feast, I approached him. He was munching
on some corn on the cob. 'Just a Man,' I ventured. 'Interesting
name...what is the Cree word for it?' He frowned. 'Hmm,' he
replied, 'not sure. I was only given "Just a Man". I'll get back to
you on that.'

He never did, because I doubt there is such a term in Cree. It
was a uniquely English name for a uniquely Western ego. I got
the message. For much of my life I'd not felt like 'just a man',
but tended to alternate between the polarities of 'better than'
and 'less than' others. Shamanic, or spiritual wisdom, lies in
the recognition of not just the uniformity of things, but more

importantly the interdependence of living beings within the web of life. A shadow aspect of male 'magician-type' ego is to seek and glorify in the specialness of being different, and to resist the recognition of interdependence with the rest of life.

Years later I was participating in another sweat lodge in a different part of town. This one was led by an enormous Salish Native man named Reuben George. Turns out he was the grandson of Chief Dan George, the Hollywood Indian made famous by his iconic role in the 1970 film *Little Big Man* with Dustin Hoffman. 'My heart soars like a hawk to see you again' was the line immortalized by Chief Dan. As it came to pass, Reuben bailed out after the first round of the sweat lodge, turning the remaining three rounds over to his assistant. The assistant had a resting-scowl face. I think he had doubts about me and my group. He proceeded to cook us severely for the rounds he ran. The heat was so intense that several guys dropped out before the final round.

I was one of the men who escaped the blazing heat after only three rounds. 'What the hell,' I said to myself. 'I'm just a man.'

* * *

The shaman—also commonly referred to as the magician— is a unique masculine archetype and in a book on 'conscious warriorhood' warrants a chapter of his own. Shamans could be both feared and respected and often had complex relationships with tribal chiefs. A good example is that of the Mongol shaman Kokochu and his legend, as recounted in *The Secret History of the Mongols* (an extraordinary document written sometime in the thirteenth century after the death of Genghis Khan, and subsequently surviving down the centuries in Chinese translations).[1] The shaman, renowned for his power, was suspected of seeking to challenge the rule of the great Horse Lord himself. As historian David Morgan wrote:

We are presented with the picture of a very nervous Genghis who did not feel secure until the shaman had been safely done away with; and even then, a supernatural story was concocted to explain the disappearance of the body as divine judgment on him.[2]

The masculinity of a tribal shaman was sometimes less obvious and at times eclipsed by what might seem to be more of an androgynous quality. Female shamans, also known as medicine women, wise women, sorceresses, witches, etc., have of course been common throughout history. The male shaman has, however, often held a position of unique power within his culture or tribe and is particularly interesting for his contrasts with the warrior or king. Perhaps the most famous Western pairing in this regard is the mythic King Arthur and Merlin.

What follows is an outline discussion of shamanism, followed by capsule biographies of three famed Amerindian shamans.

Shamanism

The word 'shaman' derives from the Tungusic tribes of Siberia (*saman*). The term 'shamanism' was originally used by Western anthropologists to describe the priests of the indigenous spiritual practices of Mongolia and Turkey, as well as Siberia. Over time it came to be popularly used to describe the 'spirit doctors' of older cultures around the world (in Africa, the Americas, Oceania, Australasia, and so on).

There are clear and undeniable commonalities between shamanism and the practices of magic and sorcery, and in many cases these terms are interchangeable. For example, most of the magical practices of the ancient world (Sumeria, Babylonia, Egypt, Greece, Rome, and so on) were concerned with gaining personal advantages via the usage of certain techniques. These techniques were usually connected to the idea of forming a contract (of sorts) with a spirit-being of some kind; or in other cases, they involved more of what we would call in present times 'psychic powers' or 'psychological techniques', that is, working with thought, emotion, and intention, in such a fashion so as to cause some desired change in one's life.

The practice of using shamanic or magical techniques to gain advantages in one's life is categorized in modern times, by many popular writers, as 'low' or 'elemental' magic. However, undeniably many if not most of these practices used by ancients were not exactly noble in intention. They belonged to the realm of what is now usually categorized as 'black' magic. It should be stressed, however, that in older times the distinctions between 'white' and 'black' kinds of magic were not clear or even considered that important; in that regard, older magic practices may be thought of as various shades of gray. (Needless to say, these terms, 'black', 'white', 'gray', are modern contrivances.)

For example, common magical practices in ancient Rome involved the usage of 'curses', and 'binding curses', where an intention was expressed to cause a restriction of some sort—and this usually involved restricting another person in some fashion. 'Talismans' (symbols to attract positive influence) and 'amulets' (protective symbols) were common, and the average street magician was all about helping his clients to gain power of some sort in their worlds. The basic psychology behind this has changed little over the millennia. We have other sorts of 'magicians' now to help us with our common lot in life—lawyers, doctors, psychotherapists, priests, accountants. Although the general moral standard may have advanced, there are still plenty of 'gray magicians' from within our professional ranks, not to mention those of the darker forms.

Core Shamanism

The idea of 'core shamanism' was conceived by anthropologist Michael Harner to define some of the fundamental intentions and practices of shamanism found worldwide, underlying the different cultural accretions and symbolic forms. (The term 'neo-shamanism' refers more to a mélange of practices drawn from shamanism and other traditions, with its practitioners being prone to romanticizing the ideal of the shaman, often overlooking some of the darker and grittier elements of the indigenous cultures and traditions associated with shamanism.) The practical work of core shamanism can be outlined as follows:

1. Life Assessment. Entering the path begins with a proper assessment of our life. We demonstrate our readiness by signaling our willingness to straighten out our outer life. While not mandatory for *inner* shamanic practices or experiences, it is a given that one's inner work will be more effective if one's outer life is reasonably balanced. To paraphrase Gurdjieff, if we are weak in our life, chances are we will be weak in the inner work. This point is very useful to counter any tendencies to use shamanic or other forms of esoteric work as an escape from worldly responsibilities or relationships. That does not mean, of course, that our outer life should be some shining example of impeccability in order to begin shamanic work. It is a given that people entering the esoteric path are looking for certain answers or solutions to their life. However, as a rule of thumb our inner work will go only so far if our outer life is not proceeding apace. Being accomplished at journeying on the inner planes means little if we can't pay our cellphone bill.

2. Inner Work (Visioning). The essence of the Inner Work of shamanism is utilizing methods for inducing altered states of consciousness. While there are many possibilities here—solitary retreats in Nature, fasting, prayer/meditation, or entheogenic usage being some well-known ones—the most common and traditional is employing 'sonic driving' (rhythmic drumming or rattling) at a rate of between 4 and 7 Hz. What happens when one is exposed to such monotonous and rhythmic sound is called 'brainwave entrainment', the term given to describe the result of brainwaves falling into synch with an external stimulus. This stimulus could be a sound (as in traditional drumming or rattling) or a rhythmic pulse of lights, as in various light-emitting machines designed to mimic Alpha or Theta wave frequency. A key component of various 'synchronizer machines' has been to induce a state where the brainwaves of the left and right hemisphere are synchronized, which allegedly results in more consistently positive states of mind. While some of this has been marketing hype by companies selling such devices, there is in fact a body of evidence from scientific studies showing that various forms of artificially induced brainwave entrainment can have beneficial effects, such as relieving migraines, helping with attention deficit disorders, and so on. There are also potential risks, especially to those prone to seizures.[3]

The Theta waves (and low Alpha waves) associated with this state produce the conditions in the brain that are ripe for shifts in consciousness in which imagery is more vivid and spontaneous. Traditionally this is called 'having a vision'. It differs from mere imagination (or daydreaming) in that it has a sudden, unexpected quality to it, much in common with typical sleeping dreams.

The way the brain responds to the sonic drive of a rhythmic beat has been theorized as follows: the sound of the instrument causes the brain to focus on it to the exclusion of other stimuli in the environment. Eventually the brain lets go of exclusive focus on the main sound (the drumming or rattling) as well, while at the same time remaining aware of it in a semi-conscious fashion (something like how we ignore the sounds of a refrigerator or a ticking clock, even as we semi-consciously know they are there). This leads to a state where the brain is only marginally aware of its outer environment (including its own body), freeing up consciousness to attend more closely to the subjective states that are always there, but usually masked by our preoccupation with outer stimuli from our body or our environment. (This is essentially the same principle underlying our dreaming life when we sleep; the deep relaxation of the body and disconnection from external stimuli allows the brain to unfold an alternate reality that our consciousness becomes absorbed in.)

It should be added here that entering the shamanic trance state and its altered consciousness does not mean that we have no more autonomy or that our individuality is dissolved. However, it *does* mean that things are fundamentally different. Time, space—and most importantly, self—are all altered in varying ways, and accordingly, so is our experience. Another good parallel is the lucid dream (a dream where we realize, to whatever degree, that we are dreaming). In a lucid dream everything is fundamentally different from our waking life, and yet at the same time we retain a sense of individuality. It is only upon waking that we realize more clearly these differences of space, time, and self.

Having a subjective experience or vision, however subtle or profound, is one thing; utilizing its revelations in one's life is entirely another. Many people throughout history have delved into strange and otherworldly subjective experiences, but far fewer have applied them usefully to their outer lives. The essence of shamanic work may be defined as *practical magic*. The main objectives are healing, gaining useful information, and direct guidance for one's life (or the life of another). What distinguishes this from more conventional spiritual guidance is the commitment to learning to access the deeper realms of one's mind via one's own efforts. It is a means by which the practitioner can achieve his or her own insights.

3. Outer Work (Tracking). The Outer Work of core shamanism— defined here under the category of 'Tracking'—is based mainly on the practice of self-remembering. There are many facets of self-remembering. Key words associated with it are *mindfulness*, *presence*, and *impeccability*. These three together comprise Tracking, which in this sense refers to a mindful and alert approach to life based on sincerity of intent. The idea is to track not just the details of our outer life, but also our own mind. To 'track' one's ego is to remain mindful of its manifestations, and especially, its shadow components. When we fail to track our shadow, we get lazy, and our shadow shows up *as* other people in our life, often in ways that are unpleasant for us. Equally so when we fail to track our outer life, things get messy as our unaccountability eventually adds up and we are footed with an oversized 'bill'.

A. *Mindfulness*. To be mindful is to notice what is going on, both around us, and within us. Mindfulness is commonly associated with sitting meditation practices, but it also refers to 'active meditation', which is being alert to both our environment and our inner responses to it.

B. *Presence*. 'Presence' in this context is about engaging in one thing at a time with full attention to what we are doing. Of course, some situations in life require us to multitask. But as a rule of thumb the clarity of our life reflects our ability to truly engage in what we are doing. If eating, to eat with full awareness of the food. When talking with someone, to listen attentively to them and to speak mindfully. When working at whatever task we are doing, to do so attentively. For men, this can be especially important, owing to our marked ability to disconnect from our bodies and live mainly in our heads.

C. *Impeccability*. The word 'impeccable' derives from the Latin *impeccabilis*, the literal meaning of which is, interestingly, 'not liable to sin'. To understand the point of this we must understand the real meaning of the word 'sin'. Although it is typically associated with minor and major moral transgressions, it can more usefully be understood as a rupture between the relationship of the individual self and its higher potential. In this sense, to 'sin' is to stray from one's higher purpose in life, and from one's true potentiality—in a sense, to *waste time*. To be impeccable, or to strive for impeccability, is to make use of our precious time on earth to, quite literally, *do our best* at whatever we are engaged in. Poetically this has sometimes been referred to as 'following a path with heart'. To follow a path with heart is to live passionately and with a higher purpose always in mind. The higher purpose is important, because it's possible to engage passionately in all sorts of trivial or dead-end pursuits.

A key word that is helpful to invoke here is *legacy*. When we try to imagine what the end of our life will look like, what our years on earth amounted to, we are trying to conceive of our legacy. The legacy referred to here is not the typical egocentric notion, the immortalizing of our name no matter what the costs or deeds involved. We are not concerned with constructing monuments to the ego. Legacy as it's meant here is the recognition that we exercised sincerity of intent throughout our life, that we truly gave it our best shot. If we did, the exact heights of our success are less important.

There is a passage from the New Testament that speaks to this: 'What is the price of two sparrows—one copper coin? But not a single sparrow can fall to the ground without your Father knowing it' (Matthew 10:29, NLT). The idea is that the spiritual source of existence—whether we think of it as God, the soul, our higher mind, the life-force, the universe, etc.—registers everything, even the sparrow's fall. So too should we realize that our life is not a dress rehearsal; every moment is *live action*. The key is to make every action count, which is the key behind living an impeccable life. It's not about being perfect, but rather about the attitude we bring to bear on the smallest details of our life: sincerity of intent.

Shamanic practice is based on the essential point that we have a transpersonal, or transcendental, wisdom within us that can be accessed. Learning to do so, however, is never an overnight process. It requires a passionate commitment and willingness to endure through frustration, boredom, and doubts about the efficacy and even the point of engaging such work. After all, it is always easier to consult some apparent outer source of wisdom about the direction, or even the purpose, of one's life. To really engage the inner work of communing with the realm of spirit and what exactly that implies is a path that will test us, but the result cannot be quantified in value.

Shamanic Cartography

The essence of shamanism may be said to be a working relationship with what esoteric traditions call the 'subtle planes' of existence. These inner worlds can be understood in several ways. Modern psychoanalysis, as rooted in the Freudian worldview, tends to minimize the significance of mystical experiences of any sort, explaining them away as regressive fantasies connected to the 'oceanic' feeling of oneness with the mother. In this view the 'inner worlds' are merely aspects of the subconscious mind, and any form of interacting with them ultimately serves the strengthening of the personal self. Jungian theory (via the work of psychotherapist C.G. Jung) sought to add more dimensions to the psychoanalytic interpretation of mystical experience. In this connection key Jungian ideas are those of the collective unconscious, archetypes, and synchronicity. The collective unconscious was deemed by Jung to be a vast repository of symbols, mythic patterns, and archetypes that we can tap into (accidentally or intentionally) and draw from. This domain should be understood as something we abide in, rather than it being within us.

We can intentionally interact with the collective unconscious — what in a shamanistic sense is understood as 'inner journeying' —

by using what Jung called 'active imagination' (the modern term is 'guided meditation', although 'guided' does not mean, in this sense, that someone else is determining your experience). Synchronicity holds the key to understanding the interdependence between inner world and outer world, and why it is possible to bring about outer world changes via inner world activities. For Jung, the purpose of such inner work is always to bring about integration, or wholeness, for it is this which the self naturally strives for.

Shamanic theory in general—like Western esoteric doctrine with its roots in Plato and older traditions—offers a tripartite view of reality: a physical world, a subtle (or archetypal) world, and a purely spiritual world. In shamanic theory, the middle domain—the subtle world—is itself broken down into sublevels, most commonly recognized as, again, three: the Lower World, the Middle World, and the Upper World. Below is a brief outline of these three levels, and corresponding ideas found in Western esoterica.

1. Lower World. This is the domain of totem spirits or power animals. Something of this idea can be found in the Western traditions of the magician's or witch's 'familiar' (a spirit in the form of an animal that accompanied them). The famed fifteenth-to sixteenth-century German scholar and sorcerer Cornelius Agrippa, author of the highly influential *Three Books of Occult Philosophy* (1533), was rumored to be accompanied everywhere by a mysterious black dog, and witches were often reputed to be accompanied by cats or other 'sinister' animals. But apart from these limited and theatrical examples it seems as if the Western esoteric tradition has either forgotten, given scant interest to, or never fully discovered and explored the idea of the totem or power animal. Psychologically, the Lower World may be said to roughly parallel the subconscious mind.

2. Middle World. This is the realm where the dead go to (what the Tibetan tradition calls the *bardo*, and what the Christian tradition calls 'purgatory'). The realm itself contains sub-dimensions, some of which are thought to house vast records. In the lower levels of the Middle World is found what Western esoterica calls the 'lower astral', or what some traditions refer to as the 'hell realms'. Here we find entities caught in negative experiences, the realm of lost ghosts, demonic spirits, those working off negative karma, and so forth. It corresponds with many of the hellish realms described in religion (Judeo-Christianity, Islam, Buddhism, etc.) and literature (Dante's *Inferno*) or art (part of Michelangelo's Sistine Chapel frescos, or certain of the paintings of Hieronymus Bosch). Psychologically, it corresponds to the ego or personality.

3. Upper World. In this realm are found the benevolent spiritual guides, traditionally known as deities, gods, goddesses, and so on. Western esoterica calls this the 'higher astral', or sometimes the 'mental' or 'causal planes' or the 'fifth dimension'; in religion it is represented by the various heaven or paradise worlds. Western Freudian-type psychoanalysis had no real parallel for this idea (other than the 'super-ego', which represents ethical and moral codes), but transpersonal psychology recognizes it as the transpersonal or higher self.

Dark Shamanism (Assault Sorcery)

It is part of the modern popular concern with the nobler aspects of native cultures (along with shame of the darker aspects of Euro-American colonialism) that contributes toward a romanticizing of these cultures and their histories. As recounted earlier in this book and amply documented by such distinguished war historians as John Keegan, some of the most extreme brutalities and cruelties of any cultures worldwide have been perpetuated by some Central and North American Indian peoples. Many of these brutal rites—including torture and ritual sacrifices—were pre-Columbian, and so cannot be simply blamed on the arrival of the Europeans.

The darker nature of certain indigenous cultural practices was not limited to warfare or religious rituals. It is also found in shamanic practice. The 'core shamanism' or 'neo-shamanism' promoted by late twentieth-century New Age thinking has tended to ignore—or on occasion be blissfully unaware of—the darker elements of shamanism found in virtually all worldwide indigenous cultures. Dark shamanism (the Western esoteric parallel term would be 'black magic')—sometimes called 'assault sorcery' by anthropologists—has been documented worldwide.[4]

A prime function of the shaman has always been as a healer—a doctor of the body, the mind, and spirit. In the West, these categories have become sharply divided along distinct lines: medical doctor (for the body), psychiatrist or psychologist (for the mind), and priest (for the soul). The traditional shaman tended to encompass all three domains, reflecting the fact that indigenous shamanic cultures lacked a worldview that differentiated clearly between levels of reality. Alongside all this, the traditions of shamanism and magic have been rife with deception, in some cases, intentional, in other cases, relating to liminal states of mind confused with corporeal reality.

As mentioned above, in older Western cultures, especially the Greco-Roman and those of the Fertile Crescent, it was not so easy to distinguish between 'white' and 'black' magic. Most magic in general involved employing secret means to gain personal advantages in one's life. Magic was not especially concerned with the matter of spiritual development (that was found in the Mystery Traditions). Older shamanic traditions are not so different. For example, Eliade cites a Russian scholar who reported that some Siberian shamans (the Yakut) have been fully involved in the invocation of both 'high' and 'low' spirits. This dovetails closely with the tradition of the Mediterranean or European magician (from antiquity, through medieval, Renaissance, and modern times) who dealt with everything from angels to demons and all those between.

The main distinction in shamanic cultures has been between the shaman and the 'sacrificing priest'. Except in certain rare cases, sacrifices (of animals, and in more extreme cases, people) have been carried out by a tribal priest, not the tribal shaman. That may, via our modern filters, render the shaman in a much more admirable light, but the fact remains that darker forms of shamanism, including aggressive assault sorcery (with its main intent being the harming or killing of enemies), has been practiced by shamans worldwide throughout history. If in that sense only, shamanism and its traditional practitioners have reflected the ambiguities of the human condition.

Central and Northern Asian cultures frequently have both what are called 'white' and 'black' shamans who deal with higher and lower spirits respectively. The highest gods are usually understood to be relatively passive and disinterested, with supplication to them proving useless in all but the most grandly important of matters. The lower spirits are, however, understood to be interactive with humans and to be sufficiently identified with them as to have interest in their affairs. Calling on them, communicating with them, summoning them, sometimes even sacrificing to them, is thought to yield results since they have some vested interest in the affairs of humans. Many of these 'lower' spirits are associated with the Underworld (in contrast with the 'higher' spirits of the Sky), although it would not be accurate to assume that these Underworld spirits are all of ill nature. Many of them were 'demoted' via the practice of history being written by conquerors. The gods of the defeated culture simply become the demons of the victorious culture—an amusing example of the subjective nature of religious mythologies.

Many traditional shamans are understood to travel both to the higher worlds and their elevated spirits, and to the lower worlds and their lower spirits. Interestingly, when one examines the so-called qualities of these lower spirits (whether from shamanic or Western 'goetic' sources), one is left with the disquieting view that they are remarkably like humans—capable of all sorts of acts, from the good to the evil, but in general manifesting a concern with personal agendas. It is the very rare human who truly rises above concerns with personal agenda. The lower spirits tend to exhibit this trait, thus making their relationship with humans one of strange familiarity.

Brief Bios of Three Notable Shamans

What follows are brief outlines of the lives of three famed American Indian men: Sitting Bull, Crazy Horse, and Black Elk. The first two were warrior-chiefs and shamans who lived and died in the nineteenth century. The third, Black Elk, though he did see some battle as a young man, was more purely a shaman (who, in later years, converted to Catholicism). These men certainly had their differences: Sitting Bull was most renowned for being a tribal chief but he was also a warrior and shaman; Crazy Horse was a fierce warrior who led and inspired via legendary courage and demonstration, and was also very much a shaman; Black Elk, younger than the first two, lived a long life that spanned the latter half of the nineteenth and the first half of the twentieth centuries. He was the Sioux medicine man who was the voice behind the classic 1932 book *Black Elk Speaks* by renowned journalist John Neihardt.

It could be argued that Sitting Bull and Crazy Horse are not ideal representations of the shaman-figure owing to the complex and multifaceted roles they played, and that someone such as Wovoka (1856–1932), the Paiute spiritual leader, would be a better example—he being one of the key figures behind the 1889 Ghost Dance movement that was meant as a religious and political counterforce to US land incursions and the demise of the Native Indian way of life. I focus here on Sitting Bull and

Crazy Horse not just because of their fame, but because they represented an especially potent form of masculinity that involved the unification of many inner archetypes—the warrior and shaman being the two most relevant. Black Elk is added as he represented a key transmission of a body of knowledge and a record of a way of life that was in danger of being lost entirely.

Impressive shamanic figures from numerous cultures across the planet abound throughout history. And nor is the shaman the uncommon and rare figure anymore that he is sometimes still thought to be. A recent gathering in Mongolia of some 400 indigenous shamans, documented by Kevin Turner in his excellent 2016 work *Sky Shamans of Mongolia*, illustrates that point. The three men chosen here, though all members of the Sioux Indian nation and all from one part of the world, are looked at for reason of familiarity for Western readers, not to represent diversity.

Sitting Bull

Sitting Bull (1831–90), although ultimately a flawed human, was, in many ways, the quintessential 'conscious warrior'.[5] He was a famed Hunkpapa Lakota tribal leader, warrior, and shaman whose name in popular culture became synonymous with the American Indians' last attempts to hold off the onslaught of the white man and his gradual invasion of their homeland. His personal greatness lies in the unusual balance he manifested of tribal chief, warrior, and mystic (holy man) rolled into one.

Born in present-day Montana (some sources say present-day South Dakota), his childhood name was Jumping Badger. At 14 he accompanied his father and some other Lakota warriors on a raiding party against an enemy tribe, during which he displayed remarkable bravery. He was subsequently named Tatanka Iyotake (literally, 'Buffalo Bull Sitting Down', abbreviated to Sitting Bull—a technically inaccurate translation, as the Lakota name implies being in the *act* of sitting, while the English translation implies already sitting. The name is also sometimes translated as 'bull who is intractable or stubborn' —consistent with the act of sitting down). An interesting feature of the early tale of his adolescent bravery is how it was followed by a community feast thrown by his father, to acknowledge the young Sitting Bull. This feast included a ceremony of initiation into manhood, during which Sitting Bull was gifted with various warrior accoutrements (including a horse and shield). The tale of his bonding with his father and formal initiation into manhood is a classic example of what is so often lacking in the modern Western world.

Sitting Bull acquired fame in the late nineteenth century mainly for his reputation as the leader who 'defeated Custer', notably at the famed Battle of the Little Bighorn in June of 1876, in which almost two thousand Indian warriors overran a few hundred US soldiers. Known popularly as 'Custer's Last Stand', it was, ironically, neither a true last stand nor a battle in which Sitting Bull directly participated. According to the meticulous forensic work of historian and archaeologist Richard Fox, the actual battle was more of a rout in which Custer's battalion, overwhelmed by a vastly superior number of Sioux and Cheyenne fighters, fell quickly into disarray and soon collapsed.[6] Sitting Bull was, however, a unifying figure within his own culture, if controversial and seen in greatly varying lights, and he was one of the main tribal leaders of the Plains Indians during the time of the famed Custer battle, even if he did not see action in the battle. He was present during the fighting; but as a 45-year-old tribal chief at the time, with years of brave field action behind him, he allowed the younger warriors to engage the Little Bighorn battle.

In 1868 a shaky peace treaty had been negotiated between the Sioux and the US government, but by the mid-1870s it was collapsing as prospectors, finding gold in the Sioux territories (mainly the Black Hills), began their inevitable incursions. The government essentially ditched the treaty and declared war on all tribes that interfered with prospectors. (The more sanitized version is that the US government wanted all Sioux tribes to move to the reservations, regarding all who refused this new edict as 'hostiles'.) The Plains Indian tribes, led by Sitting Bull, mostly resisted the government decree to move to the reservations, fighting for a decade before ultimately losing in the face of the sheer numerical and technological superiority of the US army.

Sitting Bull's father, Returns Again, was a noted warrior. Sitting Bull, as a child, seemed to show a lack of natural warrior ability and was dubbed 'Slow' (prior to receiving his name Jumping Badger). This is noteworthy because shamans historically have not been inclined toward warrior qualities. Sitting Bull was unusual in that he appeared to have all three dimensions within him: warrior, shaman, and tribal leader. The warrior was not obvious in his childhood disposition, but became more so in his adolescence.

By his early thirties Sitting Bull was made leader of a Sioux organization called the Strong Heart Society. Shortly after this, in the mid-1860s, he was actively involved in direct combat with American soldiers. The culture he lived in did not honor cowardly men, so it's a given that Sitting Bull showed bravery in battle, alongside the natural charisma and force of character he had. The combination of these accomplishments and qualities resulted in his being made supreme Lakota Chief in 1868. (The title has been disputed, it should be mentioned, by some historians who suggest that the Plains Indian tribes were not sufficiently organized, and their hierarchies not sufficiently coherent, to allow for a supreme leader. At the height of his power Sitting Bull did, however, command the allegiance of most major Plains Indian tribes. In this regard, he was similar to Genghis Khan in his ability to bring together stubborn nomadic groups.)

Sitting Bull and his unified warrior tribes won several key battles, culminating in the Little Bighorn victory over Custer.

The loss angered the US government, which then vastly increased its military presence in the area. Sitting Bull, having the wisdom to realize defeat was inevitable, took some of his people to Canada (to the present-day province of Saskatchewan) where they remained for several years. The move was notable, and something that revealed the shaman, or holy man, in his character. A simple warrior would be inclined to stay and fight, interpreting 'honor' more in the light of a never-surrender pride. A wise man understands when to back away, especially if he's responsible for the lives of many people.

Sitting Bull returned to the USA in 1881, where he was promptly thrown into prison. He was let out a few years later, at which time he joined Buffalo Bill Cody's traveling show, becoming a sort of actor and entertainer (for which he was well paid). Predictably this undignified arrangement did not last. Sitting Bull then retired to a simple life, remaining true to his Indian spirituality by rejecting Christianity. When the Ghost Dance revival—a political and spiritual group ceremony designed to bring about an end to the white man's dominance— began in 1889, Sitting Bull joined it, a decision that ended up costing him his life. When Indian agent police tried to serve an arrest warrant in 1890 (fearing his influence on the Ghost Dance movement) Sitting Bull resisted, and in the ensuing chaos when a scuffle broke out between officers and several of Sitting Bull's supporters, he was shot and killed. He was around 59 years old.

For most of his adult years Sitting Bull was no peaceful or passive holy man. He was a fighter and a leader of fighters, engaging in guerilla warfare against US forts and organized battalions of soldiers. (His closest modern-day parallel might be Nelson Mandela, who in his early years was also a guerilla fighter before growing into a peaceful statesman.) Guerilla warfare involves smaller forces using all sorts of irregular tactics to inflict damage on larger armies (small skirmishes, hit-and-run tactics, sabotage, etc.). During these years Sitting Bull functioned largely as a resistance fighter.

Between 1866 and 1868 the Oglala Sioux leader Red Cloud fought the only successful Indian war ever waged against the US army, based mainly on periodic attacks on American forts. In 1868 the Americans agreed to a treaty with Red Cloud, the terms of which were rejected by Sitting Bull, who continued his guerilla warfare. It was around this time that the more hawkish Sitting Bull was apparently chosen as supreme chief of the Sioux over the more diplomatic Red Cloud, although the actuality of his power over all Sioux was not consistently recognized by all the tribes.

In Indian lore Sitting Bull's legend includes his reputation, during his most rebellious times, as having 'strong medicine'. According to his nephew, White Bull, he had extraordinary spiritual power and was considered to be a *Wichasha Wakan* (literally, 'man of spirit', or 'holy man'). That he was also tribal chief marks him as unusual (a modern Western equivalent would be a four-star general who is also a respected priest and medical doctor rolled into one). His personal impressiveness was well described by his contemporary General Miles ('Bear Coat' to the Sioux), who wrote that Sitting Bull was a 'man of powerful physique, with a large, broad head, strong features, and few words, which were uttered with great deliberation; a man evidently of decision and positive convictions'.[7] These qualities as described by the American general are quintessentially masculine, which, when wedded to a spiritual sensitivity, makes for a remarkable man altogether.

His status as a shaman or holy man involved his undertaking certain extreme austerities, such as prolonged fasting and self-punishment (inflicting small wounds to his arms) during Sun Dance rituals. It was during one of these rituals that he had a powerful vision that involved hundreds of US soldiers falling dead into a Sioux encampment. The vision was taken as a prophecy that the Plains Indians would ultimately triumph and emboldened many Sioux and Cheyenne warriors to rally to Sitting Bull's cause. This vision did in fact play out (in the iconic Little Bighorn battle) but failed in the long run.

The reason for the failure—as interpreted by Sitting Bull—was highly interesting and instructive. He said that part of his vision included the message that the Indians should not desecrate the bodies of the dead white soldiers at Little Bighorn, nor should they steal their belongings. The Indians did not heed this advice, and in fact mutilated many of the bodies and confiscated many of the belongings. According to Sitting Bull this was bad, as it was a metaphor for the Indian desiring and coveting the things and ways of the white man—the very thing that would be a key part of the future downfall of the Indian. This would indeed be borne out as correct prophecy in certain ways.

Crazy Horse

Crazy Horse (circa 1840–77) is a more enigmatic figure than Sitting Bull, but no less compelling. Part of his mystique is that no legitimate surviving photograph of him has been found. (There is a photo allegedly taken in 1877, the year of his death, that some have claimed is of him. Most historians believe the photo is not of Crazy Horse. For the curious it can be googled online. I count myself among the disbelievers.)

Crazy Horse was born sometime around 1840, possibly a year or two earlier, in present-day South Dakota. The name 'Crazy Horse' in Lakota is *Tasunka Witko*, which has not been accurately translated into English. 'Crazy Horse' seems to suggest that the man is like a horse that is crazy, when in fact the direct translation is 'His Horse Is Crazy'. How he got the name is significant and relevant to a book on the masculine spirit. The most accepted legend is that Crazy Horse, at around 15 years of age—when his name was 'His Horse in Sight'—participated in a war raid on an Arapahoe band. His brave performance (he brought back two scalps) earned the approval and pride of his father.

The story is virtually identical to what happened to the young Sitting Bull, even down to the respective ages of the two young men. Sioux culture, as with many aboriginal cultures, celebrated the attainments of its young men via initiation, ceremony, and feasting. The male elders of the culture celebrated the young men and boys who demonstrated bravery. The bravery of a young man in the Modern Western world is usually limited to what he can do in a computer game, or at best, in a controlled sparring match in a boxing or martial arts gym. The bravery required by young Native Indian warriors—going into life-or-death combat armed with arrows, clubs, and knives at the age of 14 or 15—is so far from the world of modern young men as to be difficult to conceive of. (Of course, that does not apply to many parts of the world, or even to urban ghettos in the industrialized West, where young men have their own version of 'going into battle armed with clubs and knives'. But this book is aimed mainly for early twenty-first-century Western men growing up in a technological era raised by working fathers who were not particularly involved in their upbringing, or at the least, were unable to provide the initiatory confirmation so needed by young men.)

As mentioned, the name 'Crazy Horse' was not a silly or light-hearted reference to a horse acting crazy. It rather referred to a young brave whose horse was animated by spiritual power, likely from the mythical thunder beings, all suggestive of a young man backed by spiritual forces and destined for great things.[8]

Crazy Horse's shamanic qualities were revealed in a series of visions he had when he was a boy of around 14 years. These inner experiences were brought about in part by the infamous 'Grattan Massacre', an event in August of 1854 in which a group of hundreds of Sioux warriors killed 30 US soldiers. The event was triggered when a cow from a Mormon caravan wandered into a Sioux camp. The Indians proceeded to butcher and eat the cow. The Mormon owner of the cow then demanded retribution (according to Indian lore, he was offered three horses as compensation, worth far more than the cow itself, but declined the offer). When US soldiers were sent to investigate and arrest the cow thieves, for some reason they shot and killed the Lakota Sioux chief. The Sioux then retaliated by surrounding the army detachment and killing all 30 of them.

The rather absurd event of the cow, coupled with the arrogance of the army detachment, became a prime factor that led to the First Sioux Indian War. Young Crazy Horse was a witness to the Grattan Massacre. Shortly after, he went on a vision quest, a solitary retreat in which a warrior sought to pierce the veil between this world and the next, in so doing gaining valuable spiritual guidance. Crazy Horse received a number of vivid visions, several of which seemed to be prophecies about his future as a great warrior, and the means by which he could become an invincible one.

Throughout the late 1850s and 1860s Crazy Horse was an active part of the military conflict with the US army, the origins of which lay in the ambitions of the USA to expand its territory, particularly to mine the gold in the Black Hills. Crazy Horse was known as uncommonly strong and resolute, and this was not just related to his legendary ability to avoid being struck down in combat. He was also renowned for refusing to permit photos to be taken of him or to ever sign any document. In general, he displayed a remarkably pure spirit (and arguably, prideful stubbornness), in part because of his steadfast resistance to being assimilated by a foreign culture and its ambitions. He lacked the political acumen of a Nelson Mandela, a Mahatma Gandhi, or even a Sitting Bull, but he had an even fiercer drive and unwillingness to bend to would-be overlords.

Crazy Horse was an integral part of Custer's defeat at the famed Battle of the Little Bighorn. Unlike Sitting Bull who was present but on the sidelines in the actual battle, Crazy Horse was in the thick of the fighting, and according to available reports of firsthand witnesses he fought with great bravery, seemingly fearless in the face of death (an attitude very similar to the highest military ideals of the samurai in particular). He was the archetypal aggressive combatant with supreme confidence who had no qualms about riding close to the enemy and being shot at. (This idea was rendered, with black humor, by the character 'Colonel Kilgore' played by Robert Duvall in Coppola's 1979 Vietnam War drama *Apocalypse Now*. Kilgore routinely struts into the middle of enemy fire, full of bravado as bombs burst around him, narrowly missing, while he never so much as flinches. The narrator remarks about the 'weird light' around Kilgore, and how 'you just knew he would never get so much as a scratch'.)

The US army adopted a 'scorched earth' policy following Custer's defeat, bringing to bear their far vaster military resources against the remaining Plains warriors. Crazy Horse, predictably, fought on long after Sitting Bull had fled to Canada with his band of followers. His last battle was in early 1877 in Montana, which was followed by a winter of virtual starvation for him and his people. In May of 1877 Crazy Horse formally surrendered near Fort Robinson in Nebraska. Several months later, while residing in a nearby village, he was stabbed with a bayonet by one of the guards and later died of his wounds. He was in his late thirties.

Black Elk

Black Elk (*Hehaka Sapa*) was a generation younger than Sitting Bull and Crazy Horse. He was probably born in 1863 in present-day Wyoming. (Plains Indians counted time in moons and seasons and thus exact birthdates typically relied on family memories and other inferences.) He was the seventh of nine children. Black Elk was the nephew of Crazy Horse's father, making him a cousin to Crazy Horse. Like Crazy Horse he was an Oglala Sioux, and a hereditary shaman. His father, grandfather, and great-grandfather had all been shamans, also named Black Elk.

Sioux shamans were categorized in different ways. A *zuya wakan* was a war prophet, and a *wapiya* was a healer of mind and body. The latter was further divided into the *pejuta-wicasa*, those who worked with plant medicines, and the *wicasa wakan*, those whose wisdom and faculties of extrasensory perception were cultivated via direct inner experience. Both Black Elk and Sitting Bull were recognized to be of this latter type.[9]

From a very young age Black Elk received visions and what modern terminology would call psychic experiences or exposure to paranormal phenomena. Young Sioux boys typically entered manhood by engaging in a purification rite known as a vision quest, but in Black Elk's case these visions visited him spontaneously many years prior to his puberty, one of the traditional signs of a potentially powerful future medicine man.

Black Elk was a 'bear shaman', as were his ancestors, recognized to be custodians of a powerful totemic energy. 'Bear medicine' among the Sioux was commonly associated with medical healing and the transmission of healing methods and knowledge of herbs and cures. How such information and energy was imparted to the bear shaman was typically via trance work, or psychological shape-shifting, where the shaman was in effect ceremonially 'possessed' by the spirit of the bear totem. This method of inner alignment with a totem spirit is common within shamanic traditions worldwide. The Romanian anthropologist Mircea Eliade outlined many examples in his landmark 1951 work *Shamanism: Archaic Techniques of Ecstasy*.

At 9 years of age Black Elk received a particularly extensive and powerful vision that involved meeting six 'Grandfathers'. Each of these Grandfathers appeared as spiritual guides to Black Elk, offering information and reinforcement important to his future special role in the welfare of his people in the face of their coming troubled times. Arguably this 'special role' played out as prophesied in the talks he gave to author John Neihardt in 1930 that resulted in the famed book *Black Elk Speaks*, a work ultimately destined to be studied on college campuses and read by hundreds of thousands of people in the century to come.

Black Elk was present at the Battle of the Little Bighorn in 1876 as a 13-year-old boy. According to his memoirs as recounted to Neihardt, he recorded a kill. In the heat of battle when an American soldier lay dying on the battlefield, Black Elk was instructed by one of the Sioux warriors to dismount his horse and scalp the soldier. Because his knife was dull he had difficulty doing the deed, so he shot the soldier in the head and then scalped him. He said that looking back at his actions on the battlefield that day he felt no remorse, due to the subjugation of his people by the white man.

Following the success of Little Bighorn, the American army gradually overran the remaining Plains Indian bands, leading to Sitting Bull's escape to Canada and Crazy Horse's surrender and murder thereafter. In 1878 Black Elk followed Sitting Bull into Canada. During this time, he had strong visions but was not ready to talk about them, much less act on them. In his later teen years, he was encouraged by the shaman Black Road to honor his visions. He did this via a ceremonial re-enactment referred to as a 'horse dance', after which he received confirmation from tribal elders to be a young medicine man.

In 1881 Black Elk returned to his Oglala people on the Pine Ridge reservation in South Dakota, feeling the importance of assuming his higher calling as a holy man for his people. Between 1883 and 1886 he worked directly with people in a healing capacity, functioning as a tribal doctor and priest. He experienced some success initially, but over time he despaired at the assimilation of his people and the loss of their cultural identity.

In 1886 Black Elk joined Buffalo Bill Cody's Wild West Show, believing that he should learn something of the white man's ways, and seeking a respite from the despair of the reservations. (The pay was marginal; he received $25 a month, about two-thirds the average pay for a white person in those days.) He saw several large American cities via this traveling show, including New York and Chicago. At that time those cities already boasted populations of around 2 million and 1 million respectively. One can only imagine how bewildering and overwhelming such an experience must have been for a young Sioux Indian who had never known a gathering of more than a few thousand before, and in a simple natural setting at that. Not unpredictably, Black Elk did not like the experience with the show and felt saddened and unhappy at what he saw, in particular with what he perceived as the white man's disconnection from the power of Nature.

After separating from Buffalo Bill's show, Black Elk became involved in another stage show and traveled extensively throughout Europe. In Paris he formed an intimate relationship with a young French woman named Charlotte, with whom it was rumored that he had a child. At that time he fell ill and Charlotte nursed him back to health. During his illness he had visions, which involved him seeing his people back on the reservation in South Dakota, their plight, and how much they needed him. When he recovered, he returned to his homeland.

Not long after his return he found out about the burgeoning Ghost Dance phenomena that had been initiated in present-day Nevada by the Paiute shaman Wovoka. The Ghost Dance revival movement had begun in 1889, the same year Black Elk returned from Europe. The Ghost Dance was a circle dance designed to induce trance states and psychological powers that were best epitomized by the so-called Ghost Shirt, a garment believed to be invincible against the power of bullets. The whole enterprise was meant as a giant catalyst to revive the morale and spirit of a broken people, and as such it played into the designs of those Indians interested in a potential future rebellion and even revolution against the white man. Equally as such, it was regarded by the American government as a dangerous insurgent force to be stamped out. All of this culminated in the disastrous conflict at Wounded Knee in 1890, when close to 200 people—most of them Sioux Indians and most of them women and children—were massacred. Black Elk was present at Wounded Knee but survived the event.

Encouraged by his subjective visions as well as practical advice from elders, Black Elk forsook more martial and rebellious ways and devoted himself to marrying, raising children, and his career as a medicine man. Around the year 1900, in his late thirties, he converted to Catholicism as part of a general decision to embrace white culture and integrate his spiritual wisdom into it, rather than remaining in reaction to it. This decision marked him as very different from icons of rebellion such as Crazy Horse and Sitting Bull, and even the more diplomatic chief Red Cloud. Black Elk was a true traveler and it was his destiny to journey through different cultures and understand them from the inside.

Black Elk lived as a Catholic for the remaining 50 years of his life. In 1930 he met John Neihardt, who over many months conducted the famous interviews that resulted in the book *Black Elk Speaks*. Black Elk left behind a number of descendants when he died in 1950 in his late eighties. His life and legacy were honored by many, including notable figures such as the Swiss psychologist C.G. Jung and the famed scholar Frithjof Schuon. His legacy was unique for the times and cultures that it spanned, and for the eloquence of his words as documented in *Black Elk Speaks*.

Chapter 13

Last Battle of the Conscious Warrior: Mastering the Mind (Enlightenment)

It may be questioned what a topic like spiritual enlightenment is doing in a book for men on 'conscious warriorhood', but in fact not only is it relevant, it is the culmination of all the efforts of the true warrior. The ultimate struggle is not against corporeal enemies; it is with the very complexities of one's mind. However, the conscious warrior is not, strictly speaking, one who aggressively conquers his mind. He is one who deeply understands the nature of his mind, and in so doing overcomes its illusions, resulting in a profound inner freedom.

The East, and in particular India, has always held a position of historical significance in relation to the idea of spiritual enlightenment. In addition to India, sophisticated and elegant systems designed to guide a sincere seeker to enlightenment evolved over the centuries in such places as Southeast Asia, Tibet, China, Japan, and Korea. The West has a rich history of esoteric teachings but has generally been less concerned with the idea of enlightenment than it has been with a close relationship with the divine. Enlightenment as a state of 'oneness' with existence is classically Eastern, even if some Western mystics did seem to be referring to it as well in some of their writings (good examples are Meister Eckhart and Jacob Boehme, as well as some of the Sufi and Kabbalistic mystics).

The importance of the masculine component in teachings on enlightenment was probably best summarized by the modern Western Advaita teacher James Swartz, who in his book *How to Attain Enlightenment* (2009) remarked that 'a masculine temperament' was a necessary qualification for enlightenment, adding:

This quality is not gender related in so far as men can suffer from its absence and women can be blessed with it. It is a take-charge, seize-the-day attitude, the power to appreciate what has to be done and to do it without dithering. It does not conflict with the feminine quality of acceptance and surrender, nor with the wisdom to appreciate the futility of struggling in the face of subconscious tendencies that cannot be easily dissolved by inquiry. In large part, spiritual growth depends on how quickly the inquirer sizes up subjective and objective problems and lays them to rest. Without this quality, the seeker will allow a resistant ego to have its own way when it is not in the best interests of inquiry. It is the willingness to show a bit of tough love and resolutely stick to the inquiry. Life is short and every day that you do not move forward is a lost opportunity.[1]

Two outstanding examples of spiritually enlightened men—both from the twentieth century and both from India—were Ramana Maharshi (1879–1950) and Nisargadatta Maharaj (1897–1981).[2] Like most young seekers of the 1970s–80s, I too had my requisite copy of Nisargadatta Maharaj's famed book *I Am That*. Admittedly, I struggled with it. It seemed to contrast poorly with the wonderful lucidity and simplicity of Ramana's works (especially as presented with commentary by Arthur Osborne, who must have been one of the finest chroniclers of the life of an awakened sage ever, as well as a true prose master).

Nisargadatta did not teach the lazy man's way to enlightenment. He was a fierce teacher, a kind of embodiment of the masculine deity Shiva, and had much more in common with the old Chinese and Japanese Rinzai Zen masters and the path of 'sudden awakening'. The fact that he himself had attained Self-realization in a relatively short time (under three years of intensive meditation practice) no doubt shaped his teaching style. There are many stories of his passionate approach, his bluntness and ruthlessness, and his seeming lack of patience with lazy students or seekers who were merely 'spiritual tourists' come to see the latest guru. All of this is clear enough in surviving videos of some of his talks and interactions with students. One can see from these videos, mostly recorded when Nisargadatta was already in his eighties, his fiery nature, as well as his obvious passion. His manner was diametrically opposite to Ramana Maharshi's serenity.

Nisargadatta's student Maurice Frydman, a Polish Jew who had once lived at Mahatma Gandhi's ashram, recorded a series of Nisargadatta's talks, translated them from Marathi (Nisargadatta spoke no English), and published them in 1973 as the book *I Am That*. As mentioned, this book went on to achieve classic status, having a strong influence on many young Western seekers, especially during the 1970s and 1980s (and continues to do so). The main quality of the book is the direct forcefulness of Nisargadatta's presence, and the uncompromising clarity of his answers to questions put to him. A number of seekers over the years would report that they'd had profound openings and even direct awakening experiences merely by reading the book. More than one seeker claimed that the book itself was a legitimate spiritual transmission.

On the jacket of *I Am That* is the line, 'The real does not die, the unreal never lived'. We can contrast that with a well-known line from the mystical text *A Course in Miracles*: 'What is real cannot be threatened, what is unreal does not exist'. This is one of the classic refrains of Advaita-based teachings, and it was the central point that Nisargadatta drove home over and over again in 30 years of teaching. When his guru had said to him, 'You are not what you take yourself to be', he was preparing Nisargadatta for that essential realization, which ultimately became his main teaching tool. That is the ultimate pointer toward higher truth, and the time-honored rallying cry of genuine mystics and Self-realized sages everywhere. It is what shakes a seeker, or a potential seeker, out of the conventional slumber of typical life, where we (remarkably) come to take for granted mediocrity, that we should somehow be satisfied with what has been put in front of us and what we have supposedly accomplished. Truth-seekers throughout history have had to work against the grain of convention, and frequently against an unspoken taboo not to challenge these conventions, foremost of which seems to be the consensual agreement that you are what you take yourself to be. It may be confidently said that no movement toward Reality can occur until we first begin to challenge that assumption. I am not what I take myself to be is the beginning of awakening, the first glimmer of light upon a murky inner landscape.

Similar to Ramana, Nisargadatta did not exclusively teach Self-remembering or Self-inquiry, both of which are part of the path of *jnana yoga* (realization of truth via mental discipline and penetrating insight). If he felt that a seeker's temperament warranted it, he would advise them to follow a path of devotion (*bhakti yoga*). Regardless of the choice made to follow whichever path, Nisargadatta taught (paradoxically) that at the ultimate level there is no such thing as 'free will' or a 'doer'. He said that the mind and body, created as they have been by endless preceding causal factors, are largely mechanical. The mind has the ability to create the illusion of being a 'doer' or a 'chooser', but in fact it is 'doing' and 'choosing' based purely on past causes. The true Self actually does nothing, being merely a silent witness to all that is arising in the field of consciousness.

Accordingly, there is 'doing' but there is no 'doer'. There is walking, but no walker. There is reading, eating, and sleeping, but no reader, eater, or sleeper, and so forth. To see directly into the illusion of the wilful doer is the same as seeing into the illusion of the false self, the separate personality. There is always only functioning occurring, but no actual 'entity' behind the scenes pulling levers to make things happen. Because there is no actual doer, the questions of 'bondage' and 'liberation' are rendered meaningless. For who is there to be in bondage? And who is there to achieve liberation? The whole idea of enlightenment, or any sort of 'spiritual path', is rendered meaningless once we grasp the essential truth, that there is no discrete entity that is 'me' to attain any such thing—and nor is there any discrete entity that is 'me' to suffer miserably. We suffer only because we are caught in a deep illusion in which we appear to exist as distinct entities.

All these ideas have become well known among sincere Western seekers since the late twentieth century, especially those who have studied some Advaita (or Buddhism). And all of them are easy to misunderstand and misuse. The idea of there being 'no doer' is extremely susceptible to a confused interpretation and to being hijacked by the ego. It needs to always be borne in mind that when men like Ramana or Nisargadatta speak of there being no real personality, or no actual doer, they are speaking from the perspective of one who has put enormous effort into coming to that realization. Ramana may have awakened in one 30-minute burst of intense focus and longing for truth, but he subsequently spent many years sitting in solitary meditation, sometimes in dark and miserable vaults, almost starving his body, perfecting his clarity and wisdom. Nisargadatta spent nearly three years meditating for many hours—'all my available time' was how he put it—without fail, making stupendous concentrative efforts. And so, while these sages ultimately saw into the illusion of the personal self and free will, they only got to that place of clarity by making profound effort—and an effort that was, above all, full of a burning passion for truth. No less is required of us for the same realization. There is no free pass to awakening. To merely 'know' that there is no separate self, or wilful doer, and yet to not attempt to directly realize this—to summon no effort or burning passion to truly see and know this—is worse than useless, because we run the risk of dreaming that we are awake.

We may in (absolute) truth already be enlightened, but we still need to do something about it—and by 'doing something about it', I'm speaking ultimately of cultivating passion. Nisargadatta's extraordinary energy was, in my eyes, a demonstration of his aliveness and passion for truth.

Hyper-Masculine Spiritual Ambition and the Dark Night of the Soul

Several years ago I was attending a talk by a teacher from the Karma Kargyu school of the Tibetan Buddhist tradition, and he was commenting on the Buddhist ideas of 'space' and, in particular, 'emptiness'. The word 'emptiness' is a somewhat inadequate translation of the Sanskrit term *shunyata*, which refers to the formlessness of ultimate reality, and to the understanding that nothing possesses discrete, intrinsic existence (or put more simply, nothing is truly separate from everything else).

At one point in his talk the teacher made an interesting remark. He commented on how the direct realization of emptiness often results in the arousal of fear from within the mind. I call this an 'interesting' observation not because I think it is surprising, but rather because I've found that it is so rarely mentioned or discussed in general.

I had the fortune to begin my path of spiritual seeking at a young age. This was partly brought on by a disturbing recreational drug experience I passed through in my early adolescence, the difficult aftermath of which eventually compelled me to search for the deeper meanings of life. In my early twenties I underwent lengthy periods of sustained spiritual practice. On one occasion, when I was around 24, I undertook a three-week-long solitary Vipassana meditation retreat. During this retreat, which I was able to sustain with a daily practice of many hours of meditation and periods of fasting, I found myself entering progressively into deeper stages of practice. The whole thing culminated, near the end of the three weeks, with a type of 'inner explosion' in which I underwent a *satori* (the Zen term for a 'sudden awakening').

The main feature of this sudden awakening was a profound and direct realization that the 'I' or personal self is 'empty', non-existent beyond the level of conceptual appearance. In one sudden deepening of awareness and understanding, I saw that the 'I' is a mental construct, a type of ongoing daydream, with no real substance. In the realization of that 'emptiness' were found qualities best defined by terms such as vastness, aliveness, and enormous vitality. (These terms are really just pointers to an experiential reality that is beyond concept.)

Moments after this awakening I found myself sitting in my kitchen, marveling at the aliveness of a red dishcloth in front of me. I still vividly remember what happened next: a wave of pulsating energy rose up my spine until it reached the area of my heart. There, it suddenly stopped, as if meeting a barrier of some sort that it could not move beyond.

Suddenly a thought arose in the mind, which went something like 'This is too much for me, I can't handle it.' In that moment my world turned upside down. Within seconds I found myself moving from a blissful state of aliveness to a sheer panic attack. My heart began racing and I suddenly found myself terrified about something, although there was no way to define what that something was.

Try as I might I could not control the fear, or let go of it, or move it through me in any way. My whole body-mind was engulfed in this fear, which included both sheer panic and an impending sense of doom. It seemed as if my heart might pound out of my chest, which of course amplified the fear-thoughts, compounding the whole matter.

This state of abject terror subsided somewhat after a few hours, only to leave me in a deeply disturbed, dissociated state. I felt numb and cut off from reality, disconnected from everything. For several nights I could not sleep. Whenever I would close my eyes a dull yellowish glow was shining like a lamp 'inside' my head, making sleep impossible. Exhausted, I finally fell asleep after three or four nights. The dreams I had were violently primitive to a shocking degree.

The inner storm eventually passed. After a week or so, still somewhat ill at ease, I felt well enough to venture out. I met up with a fellow spiritual seeker, a man who had been 'on the path' for several decades. He told me about a similar experience he once went through that left him 'on fire' for three years. This was strangely comforting to hear, reinforcing my belief that I had not in fact nearly gone insane. Rather, I'd passed through something very much like what the sixteenth-century Christian mystic St John of the Cross had called the 'dark night of the soul', a necessary purification, imbued with suffering, for any who sincerely seek absolute inner truth.

About five years after this experience I was doing a month-long meditation retreat in a mountain cabin, when the panic arose again, only this second time to a milder degree. I began to understand that much of this was about psychological purification, a type of catharsis of the unconscious, but that what was ultimately going on was that I was working through the ego's fear of emptiness, the fear of its own death.

There are some memorable accounts of this process of encountering deep fear in the face of the realization of the emptiness of the personal self, within the literature of some twentieth-century seekers. Two vividly described accounts can be found in Gopi Krishna's *Kundalini: The Evolutionary Energy in Man* (1967) and Suzanne Segal's *Collision with the Infinite* (1997). Both these writers described prolonged horrific states that they passed through that were terrifying and recurring. Another good work is Robert A. Masters' *Darkness Shining Wild* (2005), telling the story of a therapist and spiritual teacher with a large following who suffers a six-month-long 'bad trip' after overdosing on a powerful psychotropic, including his often-fruitless struggles to overcome the inner horrors with meditation and therapy.

Masters' ordeal was brought about by a drug, but Gopi Krishna's and Suzanne Segal's were entirely triggered by meditation practice, as was my own. Either way, the fear encountered is the result of the ego-self's attempt to maintain its existence in the face of the overwhelming realization that it does not actually exist as a discrete entity. It is something like standing in front of a mirror and watching one's body slowly disappear before one's very eyes.

Over the years I've always been puzzled by the relative scarcity of descriptions of this process in print. That seems to be reflected by the fact that very few meditators or seekers I've talked to over the years are familiar with the experience. I think of that as being a good thing, of course. To live through this type of experience is truly hellish, and one can only be relieved for the sake of others if they are spared it.

There have been some specialized writings that have addressed the matter, most noteworthy being the excellent work of Stanislav Grof, via his anthology *Spiritual Emergency* (1989) and *The Stormy Search for the Self* (1992, co-written with his wife Christina). In these works, Grof and other writers explore the matter of difficult and even terrifying states encountered by one committed to an awakening process. But by and large this is a field of research that is not generally familiar to the average seeker.

I have, naturally, questioned deeply over the years what could bring about such difficult experiences. Some suggest it is related to spiritual zeal and over-extending oneself without proper guidance (Gopi Krishna's angle). Others suggest it is connected to significant psychological wounds (such as repressed memories of abuse or early life trauma, including the birth-trauma), or even to medical conditions (all of these were speculated on in Segal's case). My own view includes all of these possibilities, along with the idea that any sort of spiritual practice that is undertaken with a view to escaping this world, as opposed to waking up within it, is susceptible to inner disturbances.

Right motivation for beginning an inner search is always important, because if we are 'using' the work for any other purpose than self-understanding, then we are going to get burned sooner or later. That is because the process of awakening is inherently deconstructive. Elements of the ego-mind get 'taken apart', so to speak, and illusions, delusions, and all sorts of lies get exposed. This is why the Tibetan master Chogyam Trungpa once issued the warning: 'Better not start on the spiritual path. But if you start, you had better finish.'

Some Western esoteric teachings (such as those drawing from the Jewish mystical teachings of the Kabbalah) are well familiar with the challenges of authentic awakening, referring to a type of 'abyss' that a seeker must pass through in which the ego-mind is stripped away, leaving one utterly naked psychologically. That is a good metaphor for deep awakening, because it indicates just how much is at stake in the process. There is a tendency to underestimate the strength and tenacity of the ego-mind. But if we take teachings such as *The Tibetan Book of the Dead*, for example, seriously, then the tenacity of the ego-mind to survive is such that its impulses and habits pull us back into incarnation again and again. (Pull 'what' back into incarnation? Exactly, and that is the Zen koan to trump all Zen koans.)

In my own case, it was in part via the words of the great Advaitin sage Ramana Maharshi that I began to understand more fully what was going on with the whole process of encountering deep fear in the face of the intention to awaken to one's true nature. It was really the second of his 'Forty Verses on Reality' that summed up the whole matter for me:

Those who have an infinite fear of death take refuge in the Feet of the supreme Lord Who is without birth and death. Can the thought of death occur to those who have destroyed their 'I' and 'mine' and have become immortal?

The implication is that our deepest fears derive from our identification with separate form, and in particular, with the body. The 'I' is perpetuated by identification with form (body, of whatever sort).

Anyone who has ever had the odd sleep-state experience of being 'stuck between worlds', caught in a dream world, knowing one is caught, and feeling unable (or, commonly, paralyzed) to get back into one's body, has a good idea of how deep our attachment to form penetrates into the unconscious mind. The late twentieth-century well-known Tibetan master Thubten Yeshe once 'returned' from a near-death experience (he had a heart condition, and eventually passed on at age 49). Upon his return, he remarked on how difficult it had been to remain clear and conscious in the 'inner realms' while his bodily life hung in the balance. Even he, a highly trained lama and meditation master, found the material of his unconscious mind that he was encountering very difficult to deal with.

What seems to happen as the barrier between conscious self and unconscious mind dissolves—the experience of which both deep meditation and impending death tends to provoke—is that we face the deeper reality of our ego-mind, and the full power of its attachments and delusional thoughts. This is why Trungpa said it was better not to start on the spiritual path unless we're committed to going the whole way, because once faced with the deeper reality of our ego-system, the temptation to retreat (in whatever fashion) can be very strong.

According to the theory of most Eastern wisdom traditions, it is attachment to form—an attachment that is itself arising from a deep fear of formlessness—that compels us to re-associate with another human form (body). This need not be taken literally; it is a valid and powerful idea as metaphor alone. We are literally repeating our erroneous and delusional viewpoints over and over throughout a typical life, continuously re-inventing the wheel, going over old ground that we have walked many times before, thinking that now, finally, we are really getting it right, and so forth. Most lives are deeply repetitive, much like being born over and over in a kind of mindless fashion. (Anyone who has been in multiple love-relationships—in current times a relatively common thing—can attest to this with a little bit of hindsight. The same patterns repeat, just with different outer forms.)

The deep fear of embracing formless consciousness is there because from the ego's perspective, it is deeply unknown. The ego knows form; indeed, it perpetuates form, and a powerful attachment to it. The irony of course lies in the reality that pure consciousness is our actual nature, the one thing we truly do know—the one thing that we truly are. But the trick of the ego-mind is to convince us that we do not know consciousness-without-form, and that moreover, it is dangerous and deeply threatening.

When Ramana says, 'Can the thought of death occur to those who have destroyed their "I" and "mine" and have become immortal?' he is not providing any 'medicine' to heal our fears by investigating them, catharting them, embracing them, etc. He is proposing something far more radical and direct. He is telling us to stop pruning the bush and instead go to the root of the matter, the very conceptual structure of the 'I' itself. He is saying that all fears stem from the primal position assumed by the egocentric psyche, that of being a separate self.

But how do we 'go to the root' of this matter? There are basically two approaches, apparently distinct, but working well in tandem. They are the meditation methods of 'resting' (or 'witnessing') and 'inquiry' (or, as it is sometimes called, 'analytical meditation').

In the Tibetan tradition, the term for 'resting meditation' is *shamatha*, and it literally means 'getting used to', or 'becoming familiar with'. In this practice we put our attention on the out-breath, and simply witness the arising of this moment, and all movement of thought within the mind. We let go, yet remain sharply present and alert, not focusing the mind on any particular thing. In so doing, we 'become familiar' with the nature of resting awareness. The second approach, inquiry, involves an active usage of our mind as a type of 'probe'. We use the mind to actively search for the 'I' — within the body, within the mind, anywhere we imagine we can look.

Inquiry shows us, directly, that we cannot truly find this 'I', no matter how long and how intensely we search for it.

Now you may be wondering, how exactly does this approach to uncovering the ego-mind's fundamental delusion handle the problem of the fear that can be aroused in the face of this realization? Are we not simply back where we started, at the top of this chapter, when I reported the deep terrors encountered in the face of deconstructing this core delusion?

We are, and that is why we're left with the essential issue underlying all of this. It is motivation. We need to have the correct motivation for engaging the awakening process. This correct motivation can be characterized broadly as a mature longing for ultimate truth, helped along by an open and deep curiosity.

The problem with the 'awakening nightmare' of my early twenties was that although I had the open and deep curiosity, my longing for ultimate truth, though there, was not yet mature. That meant I was not purely seeking ultimate truth; I was more properly engaged in a deep desire to escape the pain of my present-time existence.

We awaken through our existence, not away from it. Awakening is not a dissociative process. The first part of Ramana's passage above, 'Those who have an infinite fear of death take refuge in the Feet of the supreme Lord Who is without birth and death...' speaks to the 'function', if you will, of the fear of death. It serves to compel us to seek the deathless — our timeless essence.

Ramana, of course, was himself famously driven by his sudden fear of death to seek his deathless true Self, which he did in one revolutionary burst of pure intention. He himself was gripped by deep fear just prior to his Realization, and though just 16 years old at the time, was imbued with uncommon 'inner maturity' and readiness to surrender totally to what unfolded within him. (Years of refining his understanding lay ahead, but the ego's existence as a supposed discrete entity basically evaporated for him at that moment.)

Spiritual Bypassing and Icarus

The term given at the top of this chapter—'hyper-masculine ambition'—relates to the issue of spiritual bypassing, in the following way: When men tap into the power of their testosterone-driven ambition, this can easily result in a kind of over-reach. The ultimate symbol of this over-reach from mythology is probably Icarus, he who infamously flew too close to the sun. Icarus's wings had been fashioned from feathers and wax. The heat of the sun melted the wax, and Icarus plunged into the ocean and drowned.

The 'hidden' part of the Icarus myth, one usually overlooked or rarely mentioned, is that Icarus's wings had in fact been made for him by his father, Daedalus. Prior to flying, Daedalus had warned his son against flying too high, driven by the stilted self-confidence that derives from excessive pride. Alas, Icarus did not listen.

The message in that myth in many ways encompasses a large part of the theme of this book. A conscious warrior is one who ultimately learns from his mistakes—or at the least, he avoids mistakes that result in the extreme consequence that Icarus faced.

All young men, especially those equipped with drive and ambition, will go astray at some point, even if only in marginal ways. But such 'going astray', such wanderlust that breaks with convention, need not come in such a reckless fashion that the young man spends years or even his whole life in a state of regret, having burned bridges beyond repair — or worse, burning his wings and crashing to his doom. It's possible to learn and engage the valuable quality of temperance at a young age.

It's also a reality that each generation faces its own unique challenges that cannot always be properly understood by previous generations. It's always fallen to younger men to find their way through the wastelands of their times, even as these 'wastelands' seem rich with possibilities among their pitfalls and dangers. These young men do well to listen to the worthy older warriors in their tribe, yes, but they also must find and exercise the courage to be accountable and awake, and sometime, just sometimes, to take real risks — risks which may indeed involve them 'breaking' from stale tradition that has outlived its purpose. The conscious, courageous warrior may be one of the last best hopes for humanity.

Notes

Introduction

1. Lawrence H. Keeley, *War Before Civilization: The Myth of the Peaceful Savage* (New York: Oxford University Press, 1996), p. 37.
2. www.turkanabasin.org/2016/01/evidence-of-a-prehistoric-massacre-extends-the-history-of-warfare (accessed April 6, 2018)

Chapter 1

1. Edward Read Barton, ed., *Mythopoetic Perspectives of Men's Healing Work: An Anthology for Therapists and Others* (Connecticut: Bergin and Garvey, 2000), p. 3.
2. For the noted pro-feminist writer John Rowan's objections to these ideas (which were first formulated by Holly Sweet), see Barton, *Mythopoetic Perspectives of Men's Healing Work*, pp. 239–40.
3. Ibid, p. 4.
4. Michael A. Messner, *The Politics of Masculinities: Men in Movements* (Oxford: Altamira Press, 2000), pp. 18–19. Essentialism has its roots in ancient Greece, where it was argued that underlying 'forms' (Plato) or 'substance' (Aristotle) lead to making a physical thing what it is. In philosophy, essentialism is all about the primacy of essence, the unalterable 'thingness' that makes something what it is. The opposing view in philosophy is existentialism, which argues that 'being' is primary, and how being manifests moment by moment. Both abstract arguments can be defended intellectually, and both are relevant to gender studies. A basic position of psychotherapy is that a person must come to some degree of self-acceptance to heal and grow on inner and outer levels. Essentialism—*I am a man,*

I have masculine traits, etc.—is obviously addressed there. But the existential viewpoint, *I am a man only insofar as I manifest manliness day by day in my life*, is equally valid. It could be said that an essentialist viewpoint aids initially in self-acceptance, while an existential position aids in accountability.

5. Michael S. Kimmel, *The Politics of Manhood* (Philadelphia: Temple University Press, 1995), p. 301.
6. Kay Leigh Hagan, ed., *Women Respond to the Men's Movement: A Feminist Collection* (New York: HarperCollins, 1992), pp. 27–8.
7. Sylvia Walby, *Theorizing Patriarchy* (Cambridge: Polity Press), 1997.
8. Starhawk, 'A Men's Movement I Can Trust', in Hagen, ed., *Women Respond to the Men's Movement*, pp. 27–38.

Chapter 2

1. Robert Bly, *Iron John: A Book About Men* (Boston: Da Capo Press, 2004), p. 100.
2. See the 2006 study in the *Journal of Clinical Endocrinology and Metabolism* at www.endocrine.org/news-room/press-release-archives/2006/testosterone_lvls_in_men_decline.
3. Alexander Lowen, *Depression and the Body: The Biological Basis of Faith and Reality* (New York: Penguin Books, 1972), p. 151.
4. See www.psychologytoday.com/us/blog/all-about-sex/201 611/dueling-statistics-how-much-the-internet-is-porn (accessed March 2, 2018).
5. See www.psychologytoday.com/blog/the-sexual-continu um/201307/new-brain-study-questions-existence-sexual-addiction (accessed October 10, 2017).
6. See www.nbcnews.com/think/opinion/sexual-harassment-deluge-progress-feminists-must-beware-backlash-ncna820896 (accessed November 20, 2017).

Chapter 3

1. Antony Cummings, *Samurai and Ninja: The Real Story Behind the Japanese Warrior Myth that Shatters the Bushido Mystique* (Tuttle Publishing, 2015), p. 7.
2. See, for example, John Keegan, *A History of Warfare* (Toronto: Vintage Canada, 1993).
3. Thomas Keightley, *Secret Societies of the Middle Ages: The Assassins, the Templars, and the Secret Tribunals of Westphalia* (York Beach, ME: Red Wheel/Weiser, 2005), p. 171. Originally published in 1837 anonymously, and later in 1846 by M.A. Nattali, London.
4. James Wasserman, *The Templars and the Assassins: The Militia of Heaven* (Rochester, VT: Inner Traditions, 2001), p. 155.
5. Malcolm Barber, *The Trial of the Templars* (Cambridge: Cambridge University Press, 1980), p. 5.
6. H. de Curzon, ed., *La Regle du Temple* (Paris, 1886), pp. 11–70.
7. Peter Partner, *The Murdered Magicians: The Templars and Their Myth* (Oxford: Oxford University Press, 1982), p. 4.
8. www.the-orb.net/encyclop/religion/monastic/bernard.html (accessed March 20, 2014).
9. Partner, *The Murdered Magicians*, pp. 48–9.
10. David Morgan, *The Mongols* (Oxford: Blackwell, 1986), pp. 37–9.
11. Ibid., pp. 62–3.
12. Ibid., p. 51.
13. Ibid., p. 88.
14. Ibid., p. 93.
15. Keegan, *A History of Warfare*, p. 207.

Chapter 4

1. Barry Allen, *Striking Beauty: A Philosophical Look at the Asian Martial Arts* (New York: Columbia University Press, 2015), p. 3.

2. Keegan, *A History of Warfare* (pp. 40–1).

3. Inazo Nitobe, *Bushido: The Soul of Japan* (Kodansha International, revised edition, 1905, reprinted in 2002), pp. 34–5.

4. Paul Elliot, *Warrior Cults: A History of Magical, Mystical, and Murderous Organizations* (London: Blandford Books, 1998), pp. 133–4.

Chapter 5

1. The main source I consult here is John Keegan's *A History of Warfare* (Vintage, 1993). Keegan (1934–2012) was acknowledged by many peers as the dean of military historians of the late twentieth century.

2. www.claimscon.org/study (accessed April 16, 2018).

3. www.ohio.edu/orgs/glass/vol/1/14.htm (accessed May 18, 2015).

4. See T.R. Fehrenbach, *Comanches: The History of a People* (New York: Anchor Books, 2003).

5. For a good complete treatment of the kamikaze, see Raymond Lamont-Brown, *Kamikaze: Japan's Suicide Samurai* (London: Rigel Publications, 1997).

6. Steve Zaloga, *Kamikaze: Japanese Special Attack Weapons, 1944–5* (Oxford: Osprey Publishing, 2011), p. 12.

7. Adam Lankford, *The Myth of Martyrdom: What Really Drives Suicide Bombers, Rampage Shooters, and Other Self-Destructive Killers* (New York: Palgrave Macmillan, 2013), p. 61.

8. James Hollis, *Under Saturn's Shadow: The Wounding and Healing of Men* (Toronto: Inner City Books, 1994), p. 11.

9. Lea Terhune, *Karmapa: The Politics of Reincarnation* (Boston: Wisdom Publications, 2004), pp. 195–6.

10. I have written at length about him in my earlier work, *The Three Dangerous Magi* (Winchester: O-Books, 2010).

11. For a good account of the problems between Ouspensky and Gurdjieff, see William Patrick Patterson, *Struggle of the*

Magicians: Why Ouspensky Left Gurdjieff (Fairfax, CA: Arete Communications, 1997).

Chapter 6

1. Jeffrey K. Mann, *When Buddhists Attack: The Curious Relationship between Zen and the Martial Arts* (Tokyo: Tuttle Publishing, 2012), pp. 126–7.
2. Penor Rinpoche's written statement about Seagal can be read online at www.palyul.org/docs/statement.html (accessed April 8, 2017).
3. Mike Tyson on Oprah Winfrey show, October 12, 2009.
4. www.kqed.org/science/11450 (accessed March 25, 2018).
5. Fritz Peters, *Boyhood with Gurdjieff* (Fairfax, CA: Arete Communications, 2006), pp. 136–7.
6. Layton, 114.
7. Walter Isaacson, *Einstein: His Life and Universe* (New York: Simon and Schuster, 2007), pp. 185–6.

Chapter 8

1. Wilber, with his characteristically comprehensive approach, covers this theory thoroughly in his *Integral Spirituality* (Boston and London: Integral Books, 2006), pp. 119–41.

Chapter 9

1. David Hume, *A Treatise of Human Nature* (1739).
2. Owen Flanagan, *Consciousness Reconsidered* (Cambridge: The MIT Press, 1992), pp. 177–82.
3. Thomas Metzinger, *The Ego Tunnel: The Science of the Mind and the Myth of the Self* (New York: Basic Books, 2009), pp. 8, 208.
4. This meditation is from the Tibetan Buddhist tradition. See Geshe Kelsang Gyatso, *Mahamudra Tantra: The Supreme Heart Jewel Nectar, an Introduction to Meditation on Tantra* (Glen Spey, NY: Tharpa Publications, 2005), pp. 130–9.

Chapter 11

1. www.whitefishreview.org/archives/2015/12/david-letterman-interview (accessed December 15, 2016).

2. For a fuller discussion of the decision exercise see Roberto Assagioli, *The Act of Will* (Baltimore: Penguin Books, 1974).

Chapter 12

1. *The Secret History of the Mongols*, translated by F.W. Cleaves (Cambridge, MA: Harvard University Press, 1982).

2. Morgan, *The Mongols*, p. 43.

3. www.brainworksneurotherapy.com/what-brainwave-entrainment (accessed November 15, 2016).

4. An excellent source, thoroughly researched and contributed to by a number of scholars, is the anthology *In Darkness and Secrecy: The Anthropology of Assault Sorcery and Witchcraft in Amazonia*, edited by Neil L. Whitehead and Robin Wright (Durham, NC: Duke University Press, 2004).

5. Three reliable sources for well-researched information on Sitting Bull are Robert M. Utley, *The Lance and the Shield: The Life and Times of Sitting Bull* (New York: Ballantine Books, 1993); Bill Yenne, *Sitting Bull* (Yardley, PA: Westholme, 2008); and Ernie Lapointe, *Sitting Bull: His Life and Legacy* (Layton, UT: Gibbs Smith, 2009). The first two are accounts written by reliable historians; the third is a short work authored by one of Sitting Bull's great-grandsons.

6. See Richard Allen Fox, *Archaeology, History, and Custer's Last Battle* (Norman, OK: University of Oklahoma Press, 1993).

7. Joe Jackson, *Black Elk: The Life of an American Visionary* (New York: Picador, 2016), p. 138.

8. Thomas Powers, *The Killing of Crazy Horse* (New York: Vintage Books, 2011), p. 8.

9. Jackson, *Black Elk: The Life of an American Visionary*, p. 25.

Chapter 13

1. James Swartz, *How to Attain Enlightenment: The Vision of Nonduality* (Boulder, CO: Sentient Publications, 2009), p. 79.
2. I have written separate chapters on both men in my 2012 publication *Rude Awakening: Perils, Pitfalls, and Hard Truths of the Spiritual Path* (Winchester: Changemakers Books).

Suggested Reading

The list below contains, needless to say, a wide spectrum of views concerning men and masculine psychology and spirituality. Concerning the works listed, suffice to say I agree with, and just plain like, some of them more than others—and some of them are merely old favorites of mine involving a masculine 'hero's quest' for truth—but all of them are valuable and insightful and worth reading.

The Art of War, by Sun Tzu

In Search of the Miraculous: Fragments of an Unknown Teaching (1949), by P.D. Ouspensky

Meetings with Remarkable Men (1963), by G.I. Gudjieff

Journey to Ixtlan (1972), by Carlos Castaneda

He: Understanding Masculine Psychology (1974), by Robert Johnson

The Horned God: Feminism and Men as Wounding and Healing (1987), by John Rowan

Iron John: A Book About Men (1990), by Robert Bly

Fire in the Belly (1991), by Sam Keen

The Code of the Warrior (1991), by Rick Fields

Absent Fathers, Lost Sons (1991), by Guy Corneau

King, Warrior, Magician, Lover (1992), by Robert Moore and Douglas Gillette

Women Respond to the Men's Movement (1992), edited by Kay Leigh Hagan

The Trickster, Magician, and Grieving Man (1993), by Glen Mavis

The Myth of Male Power: Why Men Are the Disposable Sex (1993), by Warren Farrell

Under Saturn's Shadow: The Wounding and Healing of Men (1994), by James Hollis

The Politics of Manhood: Profeminist Men Respond to the Mythopoetic Men's Movement (1995), edited by Michael S. Kimmel

The Way of the Superior Man (1997), by David Deida
Mythopoetic Perspectives of Men's Healing Work: An Anthology for Therapists and Others (2000), edited by Edward Read Barton
Facing the Dragon: Confronting Personal and Spiritual Grandiosity (2003), by Robert Moore
No More Mr. Nice Guy (2003), by Robert Glover
How to Attain Enlightenment: The Vision of Non-Duality (2009), and *The Essence of Enlightenment: Vedanta, the Science of Consciousness* (2014), both by James Swartz
The Way of Men (2012), by Jack Donovan
The Rational Male (2013) and *The Rational Male: Preventative Medicine* (2015), both by Rollo Tomassi
Men on Strike: Why Men Are Boycotting Marriage, Fatherhood, and the American Dream, and Why It Matters (2013), by Helen Smith
To Be a Man (2014), by Robert Masters
Waking Up (2014), by Sam Harris
12 Rules for Life (2017), by Jordan Peterson

Acknowledgments

Thanks to my publisher Tim Ward, who gave extensive feedback on this book. To be fair to Tim, he didn't share all the viewpoints expressed herein, but his dedication to the project was evident via his pointed questions and criticisms, and he provided helpful input to some key areas of the book. Thanks also to John Hunt for his efforts to spread worthy ideas around the planet, to Mollie Barker for her careful proofing of the text, and to the rest of the production team at Changemakers Books. Finally, my thanks to the men of the Samurai Brotherhood, the men's community I launched in Vancouver years ago, whose members continue to provide me hope for the future of humanity.

About the Author

P.T. Mistlberger was born in Montreal in 1959 and was educated at John Abbott College and Concordia University. He is the author of four previous books (*A Natural Awakening, The Three Dangerous Magi, Rude Awakening,* and *The Inner Light*). Since 1987 he has worked as a transpersonal therapist and transformational seminar leader, and has taught in numerous major cities around the world. He has been involved in participating in and facilitating men's groups since the early 1990s and is the founder of the Samurai Brotherhood, a community for men (www. samuraibrotherhood.com). He resides in Vancouver, British Columbia.

CHANGEMAKERS
BOOKS

TRANSFORMATION

Transform your life, transform your world - Changemakers
Books publishes for individuals committed to transforming their
lives and transforming the world. Our readers seek to become
positive, powerful agents of change. Changemakers Books
inform, inspire, and provide practical wisdom and skills to
empower us to write the next chapter of humanity's future.
If you have enjoyed this book, why not tell other readers by
posting a review on your preferred book site.

Recent bestsellers from Changemakers Books are:

Integration
The Power of Being Co-Active in Work and Life
Ann Betz, Karen Kimsey-House
Integration examines how we came to be polarized in our dealing
with self and other, and what we can do to move from an either/
or state to a more effective and fulfilling way of being.
Paperback: 978-1-78279-865-1 ebook: 978-1-78279-866-8

Bleating Hearts
The Hidden World of Animal Suffering
Mark Hawthorne
An investigation of how animals are exploited for
entertainment, apparel, research, military weapons, sport, art,
religion, food, and more.
Paperback: 978-1-78099-851-0 ebook: 978-1-78099-850-3

Lead Yourself First!
Indispensable Lessons in Business and in Life
Michelle Ray
Are you ready to become the leader of your own life? Apply
simple, powerful strategies to take charge of yourself, your
career, your destiny.
Paperback: 978-1-78279-703-6 ebook: 978-1-78279-702-9

Burnout to Brilliance
Strategies for Sustainable Success
Jayne Morris
Routinely running on reserves? This book helps you transform
your life from burnout to brilliance with strategies for sustainable
success.
Paperback: 978-1-78279-439-4 ebook: 978-1-78279-438-7

Goddess Calling
Inspirational Messages & Meditations of Sacred Feminine
Liberation Thealogy
Rev. Dr. Karen Tate
A book of messages and meditations using Goddess archetypes
and mythologies, aimed at educating and inspiring those with
the desire to incorporate a feminine face of God into their
spirituality.
Paperback: 978-1-78279-442-4 ebook: 978-1-78279-441-7

The Master Communicator's Handbook
Teresa Erickson, Tim Ward
Discover how to have the most communicative impact in this
guide by professional communicators with over 30 years of
experience advising leaders of global organizations.
Paperback: 978-1-78535-153-2 ebook: 978-1-78535-154-9

Meditation in the Wild
Buddhism's Origin in the Heart of Nature
Charles S. Fisher Ph.D.
A history of Raw Nature as the Buddha's first teacher, inspiring
some followers to retreat there in search of truth.
Paperback: 978-1-78099-692-9 ebook: 978-1-78099-691-2

Ripening Time
Inside Stories for Aging with Grace
Sherry Ruth Anderson
Ripening Time gives us an indispensable guidebook for growing
into the deep places of wisdom as we age.
Paperback: 978-1-78099-963-0 ebook: 978-1-78099-962-3

Striking at the Roots
A Practical Guide to Animal Activism
Mark Hawthorne
A manual for successful animal activism from an author with
first-hand experience speaking out on behalf of animals.
Paperback: 978-1-84694-091-0 ebook: 978-1-84694-653-0

Readers of ebooks can buy or view any of these bestsellers by
clicking on the live link in the title. Most titles are published
in paperback and as an ebook. Paperbacks are available in
traditional bookshops. Both print and ebook formats are available
online.

Find more titles and sign up to our readers' newsletter at
http://www.johnhuntpublishing.com/transformation
Follow us on Facebook at
https://www.facebook.com/Changemakersbooks